*By the hard work of others, we are led
to the most beautiful things that have been dragged
out of darkness and into the light.
Everyone is invited to experience the light
of every age and every people.
So, let us walk hand in hand with those from every age.
Let us turn from this brief and transient time
and offer our minds and hearts to the past,
which is long and eternal.*

—Seneca, *On the Shortness of Life*

THE CLASSICS CAVE

Sugar Land

THE CLASSICS CAVE

the earliest light for a brighter life

www.theclassicscave.com

ARE YOU looking for the best books ever? Or new ways to read and benefit from them? To practice what you've read? To learn and grow a little? Let the Cave be your guide!

THE CLASSICS CAVE (the Cave) is an educational* organization centered on the classics of Greek and Roman antiquity, with an emphasis on the best of ancient Greek literature.

OUR MISSION is to shine the light of the past into the present for a brighter life today.

OUR GOAL is practice—the application of ancient wisdom and ways to our contemporary lives.

WE publish books, develop and provide online content, organize and do outreach, and produce and distribute a variety of print and other media intended to entertain and educate, inspire, encourage, and cultivate.

VISIT THE CAVE online (www.theclassicscave.com) to support our mission and to access a growing catalog of engaging books and other beneficial content designed for individuals, educators, groups, and all others interested in benefiting from ancient literature.

SUPPORT THE CAVE by telling others about our work and by leaving a positive review online. You may also wish to buy a book or join The BAGL Club or the AAGS (to adopt an ancient Greek). Or sponsor the BAGL. Or partner with us by giving a donation. Thanks!

With GRATITUDE, we thank our readers, members, sponsors, donors, and all participants in Cave content—you who make the work and outreach of the Cave possible. Without you, the Cave would not exist!

*For the Cave, **education** is that happy transition from ignorance to knowledge; from foolishness to wisdom; and from mediocrity or vice to excellence or virtue, culminating in good habits and character.

In Praise & Recognition of the Cynics

"Authorities usually describe Greek Cynicism as a philosophy in which the object was virtue; it has also been said to be "following nature," and the Cynics have been called primitivists, i.e., imitators of the Golden Race of Hesiod. . . . Although the Cynics repudiated learning, they claimed to possess wisdom; for, did they not know the road to happiness?"

—Farrand Sayre, *Greek Cynics*

"In the modern world no one voluntarily lives, as did the Cynics, at subsistence level. . . . The Cynics were missionaries, and their message was that life could be lived on any terms the age could impose . . . the Cynics represented a standard with which we are unfamiliar—that of the minimum."

—Donald R. Dudley, *A History of Cynicism*

"In fact a minimum of life, an unfettering from all coarser forms of sensuality, an independence in the midst of all marks of outward disfavor, together with the pride in being able to live in the midst of all this disfavor: a little cynicism perhaps, a little of the "tub of [the Cynic] Diogenes," a good deal of whimsical happiness, whimsical gaiety, much calm, light, subtle folly, hidden enthusiasm—all this produced in the end a great spiritual strengthening, a growing joy and exuberance of health."

—Friedrich Nietzsche, *Human, All too Human*

"Cynicism is a kind of philosophy. It is not the worst sort of philosophy, either, nor the least honored, but a match for the most excellent."—Julian, the Roman emperor, *Oration 6*

"The Cynics hold that the goal of life is to live according to virtue. . . . Some have said that Cynicism is a shortcut upon the path of virtue."

—Anonymous, reported by Diogenes Laertius, *Lives*

"Time makes even bronze grow old. But your glory, Diogenes, will endure through every age. You alone revealed to mortal men the teaching that self-sufficient living is a way of life that is not burdensome."

—Inscription written on a statue dedicated to one of Cynicism's founders, Diogenes of Sinope

"I also admire the disdain that Diogenes [the Cynic] had without exception for every human good. He declared himself wealthier than the Great King [of Persia] since he needed less for living."

—St. Basil the Great, Christian bishop of Caesarea
How to Benefit from Reading Greek Literature

"Alexander, Gaius Caesar, Pompey—what are these to Diogenes [the Cynic], Heraclitus, and Socrates? These penetrated into the true nature of things—into all causes, and all subjects."

—Marcus Aurelius, Roman emperor, *Meditations*

"There are few natures, whether of body or soul, that are able to pass over from an inferior life to one of unmixed good—though such a nature did belong to [the Cynics] Diogenes [of Sinope and] Crates [of Thebes] . . . and people like that. . . . It was when they were reduced to poverty that they genuinely pursued philosophy. It was then they began to live a truly human life according to nature, demonstrating the true wealth found in the simple life."

—Simplicius, *Commentary on Epictetus' Handbook*

"But what is Caesar to a Cynic? Or a proconsul? Or any other but for Zeus who sent the Cynic to serve him . . . the Cynic is the father of all men . . . so well does he care for all . . . as a father, as a brother, and as the minister of the father of all, the minister of Zeus."

—Epictetus, *Discourses*

"The Stoics say that the wise man will play the Cynic since the Cynic philosophy and way of life is a shortcut to virtue."

—Apollodorus, *Ethics*

THE BEST OF
THE CYNICS

THE BEST OF
THE CYNICS

The Lives, Writings & Teachings
of the Ancient Cynics

The Best Parts in Translation
with
a Narrative Summary of the Rest

selected, introduced, and edited by
The Classics Cave

CAVE BEST OF SERIES
the best of the classics for today

THE CLASSICS CAVE
Sugar Land

The Best of the Cynics:
The Lives, Writings & Teachings of the Ancient Cynics

ISBN 978-1-943915-32-3

Published in the United States by
The Classics Cave
P.O. Box 19038
Sugar Land, TX 77496
contact@theclassicscave.com
www.theclassicscave.com

The Classics Cave (the Cave) is an educational organization centered on the classics of Greek and Roman antiquity, with an emphasis on the best of ancient Greek literature. Our mission is to shine the light of the past into the present for a brighter life today. Our goal is practice—the application of ancient wisdom and ways to our contemporary lives. We publish books, develop and provide online content, organize and do outreach, and produce and distribute a variety of print and other media intended to entertain and educate, inspire, encourage, and cultivate.

Visit the Cave online (www.theclassicscave.com) to support our mission and to access a growing catalog of engaging books and other beneficial content designed for individuals, educators, groups, and all others interested in benefiting from ancient literature.

For the one entering this great work . . .
Pause for a moment before its door.

Such is the holy gift the Muses give to human beings.
—Hesiod, *Theogony*

CONTENTS

PART 3
Points of Wisdom & Ways of Practice from the Cynics

OTHER MATTERS OF INTEREST
Related to the Cynics

CAVE BEST OF SERIES
INTRODUCTION
the best of the classics for today

H AVE YOU EVER considered how many excellent works of ancient Greek and Latin literature there are to read? Think of all the significant works of poetry and prose—of all the epics, tragedies, comedies, histories, philosophies, orations, biographies, and more!

The problem, of course, is in the approach. How should you read them all? It is The Classics Cave's goal to offer a possible solution—and so the Cave Best of Series, which presents the best of an author, title, or group of authors.

Take the author, title, or group you have in hand. Of the available versions of the work, the Cave Best of Series version is unique for a few reasons. One, it is much shorter than most renditions of the work—oftentimes the number of pages totals anywhere from one-third to one-half of other versions.* Consequently, if you are pressed for time or do not know how many hours you would like to invest in reading the work, then the Cave Best of Series version may be for you.

That is not to say you will not get the whole work—the whole story or discourse or whatever the work centers on. Rather, you will get it in two forms—another unique feature of the Cave Best of Series presentation of a work. Whereas most versions offer either the whole or parts of a work (without any significant explanation of what happens in between each part), the Cave Best of Series version gives you the best or most significant parts in translation, along with a narrative summary of the rest that will tell you exactly what is going on in between. This means you will get the full content, feel, and experience of the work without missing out on anything essential.

And that's important. Unlike study guide versions that offer summary outlines alone, you will have extensive passages and narrative summaries of the whole work that will allow you to judge for yourself what is happening, what characters are central, what themes are significant, what the arguments are and whether they succeed or not, and the like—all depending on the work itself.

This is what the Cave Best of Series offers: the whole work in translated and narrative summary form, making for a relatively quick read that will let you come to terms with the work by yourself.

Not only that but there is also an information-packed introduction that is meant to draw the reader into and answer the most significant questions about the author and the work. Why should we care about *this* author and *this* work? What are the essential facts we should know? What are the work's most important ideas and themes? There is always a full exploration of these points that references the work itself as well as any pertinent scholarship.

Toward the end, there is a section presenting a "Plan of Life" (or something similar), "Points of Wisdom," and "Ways of Practice" related to the author. The latter "Ways" consist of workbook or journal-like prompts and exercises intended to motivate the reader to feel, think, and act in beneficial ways according to the author's "Points of Wisdom" (just as ancient readers or auditors would).

Finally, there is a unique section called, "Other Matters of Interest Related to [the Author]." It offers additional information about the author, whether a summary of the work, a cast of characters found therein, maps, a glossary of relevant Greek terms, suggestions for further reading, and so on.

In the end, when you read the work as presented in the Cave Best of Series, you will be entertained, educated, and, we at The Classics Cave hope, motivated to practice—to act in an intentional, specific manner toward a better life. With this in mind, welcome to the . . .

Cave Best of Series
the best of the classics for today

---

* Even so, whole, or mostly whole, works are sometimes included in the Cave Best of Series if the work is particularly short.

INTRODUCTION

The Cynics are the most characteristically Greek expression of that view of the World as Vanity Fair, and the consequent rejection of all current values, and the desire to revert to a life based on the minimum of demands.
—Donald R. Dudley, *A History of Cynicism*

L UIS E. NAVIA WRITES that "the word cynic generally conveys negative ideas in modern languages."[1] It's true. Crack open a dictionary and you may well find something along these lines defining the *cynic* or *cynical*: "A person who believes all people are motivated by selfishness." Or: "A person whose outlook is scornfully and often habitually negative." Or: "Negative or pessimistic, as from world-weariness."

You may recall when you were young, say in your teens, feeling cynical—something you somberly and with a great deal of sincerity reported to a friend late at night. "I'm so cynical." The inevitable response, accompanied with a sigh: "Yeah, me too."

But little did you and your friend know! If only you had been familiar with another dictionary definition, then you may not have seen yourself as cynical at all—at least not in the ancient sense. Or possibly you would have embraced the term with gusto. The *other* definition? "A member of an ancient Greek philosophical school who believed virtue to be the only good and practice of self-control to be the only way of achieving virtue."[2]

It's strange, really, that one word can have such divergent meanings. Isn't selfishness bad?—and pessimism and a habitual negativity? And isn't virtue something good, as well as self-control? We may naturally ask, then, how did the idea of cynicism go from something presumably good to something presumably bad?

To answer the question very briefly, we must look to the ancient critique of certain Cynics that was offered during the Roman Empire, if not earlier. According to Lucian of Samosata (second century AD), for example, there were many Cynics who preached Cynicism without actually living it, negatively criticizing people and their way of life without practicing a life of virtue. As such, went the critique, they were hypocrites, frauds (one may think of certain modern, even cynical, politicians, ministers, or gurus).

So it was by the eighteenth century that Edmund Burke labeled Jean-Jacques Rousseau a "cynic" as one who advocated certain ideals but failed to live up to them. According to David Mazella, Rousseau's "French and British detractors used his writings to assemble a public image remarkably close to the features of what would come to be known as the modern cynic: atheistic disbelief, habitual distrust of others, shameless indifference to conventional morality, and a hypocritical gap between word and deed."[3]

There are more twists and turns to the story. But to conclude our brief tour, at best the modern understanding of the term "cynic" takes into consideration only half of what Cynicism first was—the negative, the brash, the eye-brow raised, irony-tinged, self-focused half. If so, then what about the other half? What about the good of Cynicism that was admired for nearly a millennium from its founding around 400 BC to its decline toward the end of the classical world some eight hundred years later? And why should we care to know?

WHY SHOULD WE CARE ABOUT THE CYNICS?

The Cynics and their way of life influenced the Greek and Roman worlds for centuries, from the rise and development of Cynicism around the end of the fifth and beginning of the fourth centuries BC to its demise sometime toward the fall of the western half of the Roman Empire in the late fifth century AD. This is the first reason why we should care about the Cynics—for their long-term influence.

Although the impact of Cynicism ebbed and flowed over time, there were always individual Cynics roaming from city to city that made a strong impression on the population. Antisthenes and Diogenes were the first, followed by many others over the next eight hundred years. So far as we know, Sallustius of Emesa, who was born around 430 AD and likely lived into the early years of the sixth century, was the final one. At least he is the last name we possess in the historical record.[4]

For the eight centuries in between the earliest and latest Cynics, the average person would have encountered Cynicism through its representatives who lived and begged and taught in the open air. There they would be in the typical Cynic outfit, walking along the road, or standing in the marketplace, or sitting by a temple taking care of their own business, or talking with others, preaching even, criticizing society and urging everyone to wake up in order to live freer, more authentic and self-sufficient lives. As for the better off, they absorbed Cynicism through education. As Raffaella Cribiore explains in her work on ancient Greek and Roman education, the "Sayings of [the Cynic] Diogenes dominated education at all levels."[5]

The truth is that Cynicism had nothing truly original to offer, not in terms of basic philosophical ideas anyway. There was no startling theory regarding how we humans come to know things or about the nature of reality. In fact, Cynicism mostly shunned such questions. What it *did* have to offer, though, and this to a fevered degree, was a way of life, a practice. It was this offering—that of moral training, of intense practice toward a better way of life in accord with nature— that was its greatest influence on those alive and those to come.

The Cynics lived a radical life, and in doing so they served as moral exemplars for others. Later Stoics referred to the Cynic way of life as a "shortcut to virtue."[6] Plato is supposed to have said of the Cynic Diogenes of Sinope that he was a "Socrates gone mad."[7] If so, then Diogenes was in step with the example of Socrates found in the now mostly lost Socratic dialogues of Antisthenes, a Socrates who "was undoubtedly ascetic, a 'man with a mission.'"[8] Over time Diogenes himself was held up as a moral exemplar to others. In his classic history of Cynicism, Cambridge don Donald R. Dudley explains that "for the Cynics and Stoics Diogenes became a second Heracles, the ideal *sophos* [wise man] who could be used to emphasize any worthy moral or exemplify any desirable characteristic."[9] Diogenes' student Crates of Thebes was another moral exemplar.

But more. According to the ancient biographer Diogenes Laertius, and confirmed by the Roman emperor Julian, Crates "was the originator of the noble doctrines of Zeno," the founder of Stoicism.[10] In this way, Cynicism influenced moral philosophy and its practice as it developed during the Hellenistic period and beyond. In the case of Stoicism, Cynicism, as the "shortcut to virtue," was the ground out of which the great tree of Stoicism grew. Dudley judges that "the Cynic element, present in Stoicism from its foundation, was maintained [for a very long time] . . . indeed the noblest conception of Cynicism ever formulated was to come from the Stoic Epictetus."[11] And whatever Stoicism eventually touched, for instance, the Neoplatonism of Plotinus, Cynicism also touched in some vicarious way—however challenging to detect with precision.[12] We can even see its influence, though in a far different and roundabout manner, on the hedonist Cyrenaic school and its offshoots in terms of a shared "contempt for accepted values."[13]

The latter contempt, colorfully expressed in the Cynic penchant for outspoken criticism, points to another way in which this radical philosophy influenced Greek and Roman culture. Over time certain Cynics developed two new forms of discourse or writing. One was the diatribe, a literary genre that frankly "treats of ordinary human problems in a common-sense spirit."[14] In his work on Greek rhetoric, the ancient writer Hermogenes of Tarsus says that the "diatribe is a moral exposition of some brief topic."[15] Dudley describes it as a dialogue that dispenses with one of the speakers.[16] In this sense, it is more a speaking *at* than a speaking *with*. Nothing is so much being searched for as it is demonstrated by means of "allegory, anecdote, . . . quotation, [and] its appeals to an imaginary adversary," among other devices.[17] The other genre was the satire. More specifically it was the Menippean satire that zeroed in on certain ideals and practices in order to lampoon them. "In the writings of Menippus, the Cynic spirit of mockery of human values was all-pervading."[18] As a form of seriocomic writing (in Greek, Strabo called such writing *spoudogeloios*, a blend of the serious and the amusing), the satire came to have a unique place in Roman literature, influencing such writers as Lucian of Samosata, who wrote a number of satires, as well as about certain Cynics and aspects of Cynicism. It is doubtlessly for this Cynic genre that Friedrich Nietzsche much later labelled the Cynics "the humorists of antiquity."[19]

In another form of criticism, beginning, we might say, with Diogenes himself and his disdain for Alexander the Great—at least the stories that were told about his disdain, Cynicism played a role in the "philosophic opposition" to several Roman emperors that occurred in the latter half of the first century AD.[20] This form of criticism was closely tied to Cynic frankness of speech and outspokenness (*parrhēsia*). Without going into details, such opposition resulted a few times in the expulsion of Cynic and Stoic philosophers from Rome. We also know from Dio Chrysostom that Cynic preaching was responsible for stirring up frequent riots among the people of Alexandria.

As the centuries passed, the Cynics and their radical approach to and ideas about living continued to influence other people and other ways of life in the ever-changing Greek and Roman worlds. One instance is the Judaism of Philo of Alexandria (first century AD). Much of his writing hints at strong ties to Cynic and Stoic writing, including the diatribe. So, concludes Dudley, "the Cynic ingredients of the older Stoicism reappear in [Philo's] ethics, as do the standard themes and figures of the popular preaching which was common to Stoic and Cynic alike."[21]

Otherwise, there was the Cynic influence on Christian theology and practice. As for the former, there is St. Basil of Caesarea's letter to the monk Ourbikios (Urbicius) about self-control, which was, as we'll see, a typical Cynic theme. Not only does Basil praise self-control as any street-preaching Cynic would do, but in a manner that seems to echo St. John's declaration that God is the Word (*logos*) or that God is love (*agapē*), he goes on to suggest that God himself "seems to be self-control (*enkrateia*) . . ." Why? Basil explains that God seems to be *enkrateia* because God "desires nothing . . . being without need, he is wholly satisfied."[22] As for practice, the historian of philosophy Frederick Copleston remarks that "we find evidence of a Christianized Cynicism . . . in the person of Maximus of Alexandria," who, Dudley suggests, "may well have combined the Cynic garb and the Christian faith."[23] According to an oration of Gregory of Nazianzus

(Nazianzen), Maximus is "one who follows our [Christian] faith in an alien garb . . . [He] is a Cynic not through shamelessness but through freedom of speech, not through gluttony but through the simplicity of his daily life."[24]

This same Christian Cynicism, or the influence of Cynicism on Christianity, may be observed relative to early Christian monasticism and ascetic practice—though, as Dudley admits, the tie is "hard to trace."[25] Still, the impact was enough for one recent writer to conclude that "there is general agreement that [Cynicism] helped shape the direction of Christian asceticism."[26] This same Cynic-inspired practice, doubtlessly based on the example and sayings of Christ himself (whom some have compared to a wandering Cynic preacher), eventually inspired later Christian practice during the Middle Ages. Scholars cite likely ties to Irish eremitism, the Albigensians and Cathars, and such mendicant orders as the Dominicans and the Franciscans.

The Cynic influence did not end with the waning of the Middle Ages and the advent of the modern world. Rather, as the classics scholar R. Bracht Branham concludes, "the afterlife of Cynicism . . . [was] the liveliest and most varied of the ancient philosophical sects."[27] Its impact extended to European philosophy, politics, and literature. We see it in the works of Desiderius Erasmus, Michel de Montaigne, Jean Jacques Rousseau, Denis Diderot, Friedrich Nietzsche, Michel Foucault, and Mikhail Bakhtin; we see it in the theories of political and social anarchism; we see it in the revival of Menippean satire during the Renaissance, and in its influence, according to "the heterodox argument of Mikhail Bakhtin" on the "genealogy of the modern novel."[28] Of course, as we have already observed, we may also see ancient Cynicism's influence on the modern phenomenon of cynicism, which has led to the largely negative use of the word today.

Given Cynicism's enduring influence, we may also note the strong reactions that it elicited in the form of praise or blame. This is the second reason why we should care about the Cynics. Whether to acclaim them and their way of life or to condemn them, people felt strongly about them for nearly a millennium. Cynicism was something that demanded a response.

On the praise side of the ledger, the Stoic philosopher Epictetus held that "the ideal Cynic was the highest type of philosopher."[29] The Roman emperor Julian judged Cynicism to be "a match for the most excellent" of philosophies, particularly admiring the example of Diogenes of Sinope.[30] "Some," we are told by Diogenes Laertius, "have said that Cynicism is a shortcut upon the path of virtue," the path that was itself considered the highest and therefore best road to happiness for most ancient philosophers—no small thing.[31] To give a few more examples, the Roman geographer Strabo acknowledged the Greek colony of Sinope for "produc[ing] excellent men," among whom was the Cynic philosopher Diogenes.[32] Pliny the Elder included the same Diogenes in a short list of "the masters of philosophy."[33] If we were to include all the others in the ancient world who valued Cynicism in one way or another, or who admired individual Cynics, we would have to add Zeno of Citium, Apollodorus of Seleucia, Seneca, Dio Chrysostom, Marcus Aurelius, Apuleius, St. Basil the Great, St. Gregory of Nazianzus, and the Neoplatonist commentator Simplicius, among others.

The negative side of the ledger begins with Plato's suggestion that Diogenes was a "Socrates gone mad."[34] Even if the statement is apocryphal, it nevertheless points to the general reproach that Cynicism was extreme. Dudley explains that many Romans "would have regarded Cynicism as offensive vulgarity."[35] Cicero is a good example of this sentiment. "The Cynic philosophy," he declared, "should be wholly rejected. It is hostile to a proper sense of shame."[36] The much later Christian rhetorician Lactantius echoed Cicero's sentiments in suggesting that the Cynics "took away all sense of shame."[37] Similarly, St. Augustine of Hippo berated the Cynics for overlooking "the modest instincts of men" by declaring it was okay to have sex in public—though, he speculated, it is likely that no Cynic ever actually went through with the act. Regardless, he asserted that if any Cynic tried to copulate in public in his day, "they would be spat upon, not to say stoned, by the mob."[38] Others criticized the Cynic practice of begging as a kind of dependent freeloading. "They say they are self-sufficient, but in fact . . . they need the rich for food and cooks to satisfy their gluttony." Tatian, the Christian philosopher who condemned them in this manner, suggested that, for the Cynics, philosophy was "the art of getting money."[39] Lactantius similarly accused the Cynics of wishing to beg for food rather than working honestly for it, an act that, if universalized, would lead to the economic collapse of any polity, he judged. "If everyone imitated the wisdom of these [Cynics], how would states exist?"[40] For one ancient voice, Cynic begging and frugality contradicted the gifts of nature provided by God: "If this sort of contentment is to pass for wisdom, God must have been all wrong in making sheep woolly, filling grapes with wine, and providing all our infinite variety of oil, honey, and the rest."[41] Then there were all the fake Cynics. A whole chorus of critics denounced these—even some who praised the more ideal form of Cynicism, writers such as Lucian of Samosata, Martial, Petronius, Seneca, Epictetus (at times), and Dio Chrysostom (also at times), among others.[42]

Despite all the criticism, and despite all the fakes who did in fact make a bad name for the philosophy and way of life, Cynicism did have, as we have seen, a tremendous influence on the world of the ancient Greeks and Romans, an influence that has continued into our own era. Accordingly, we might ask what we may presently learn from ancient Cynicism. This is the third reason we should care about the Cynics—for what they are able to teach us today.

If we care to, we may learn from the Cynics what may be called the *modification of desire* or *desire reduction*. Stating "desire reduction" in positive terms, we may learn simplicity from them, the art of simple living. Looking at their viewpoint from one angle, we see that the Cynics realized that if happiness is the satisfaction of desire (an idea going back at least to Homer), then the best way to be satisfied is to drastically reduce desire. The Cynic Diogenes of Sinope "used to say that it was characteristic of the gods to need nothing, and that, consequently, when a man desires very little or nothing at all, he is like the gods."[43] He was like Socrates in this way of thinking. Describing a very Cynic Socrates, or the Socrates after whom the Cynics modelled themselves, Diogenes Laertius observes that he "was a man of great independence or self-sufficiency"—the attribute of *autarkeia* that was extremely important to the Cynics. Citing a number of examples, he goes on to relate that "often, when Socrates looked at all the goods for sale in the marketplace, he would say to himself, 'How many things I neither want nor need!'"[44]

Such "desire reduction" would go a long way in curing many of us of what some have labeled "affluenza," or unhealthy consumerism.[45] We must consume, we tell ourselves, in order to grow the economy. We must do the latter, of course, in order to consume. But what if we approached life differently? What would progress look like if it were not always measured in terms of the production of consumer goods? Also, on a possibly related note, what would desire reduction do for the environment? We may learn from the Cynics that, aside from apparent economic necessity, there is no intrinsic need, and, therefore, no intrinsic desire for more and more wealth and goods and novel sources of pleasure.[46]

That asserted, most ancient Cynics would not have supported any government that forcibly reduced people's desires. Not only that but most looked upon those who were poor as living in the necessary condition for happiness—if only, the Cynics judged, the poor would intentionally choose their poverty even as they themselves did. The Cynics did not mean for this to serve as an excuse for the wealthy to go on their merry way in luxury; rather, they often expressed pity for the wealthy and the powerful, who, they believed, were enslaved to what they desired and what they possessed. For those of us who are comfortably wealthy, the idea can serve as a point of reflection: in what way can I reduce my own desires so as to increase my sense of satisfaction and happiness?

There's far more we can learn from the Cynics. In brief, they have something to say to us about the intrinsic value of hard work and suffering in establishing in us the habit of endurance—what many now call "grit," the ability to stick with something no matter how challenging and painful it is. Along with this is the significance of practice or training related to cultivating those excellent habits that will carry us through life—the realization that such habits do not always come naturally, and that most of us have to work at forming them. Finally, we may learn to speak the truth frankly and cleverly. Because the Cynics lived a life of chosen poverty judged by them to be incredibly rich, they had very little to lose in speaking their minds to the political and other leaders or powers of their day. When Alexander the Great stood over Diogenes while he was sunbathing and asked him what he could grant him, Diogenes said, "I would like you to stop blocking the light"—this because he wanted nothing. Another time, when a man derisively reminded Diogenes of the fact that he had been sentenced to exile by the citizens of Sinope, his home town, he responded, "And I sentenced them to stay there."[47]

It is this creative, inside-out way of looking at life that allowed the Cynics to live and freely speak as they did and to be content as they reportedly were.

But who were the Cynics? Let's turn now to a few basic facts about this influential group of ancient Greek and Roman philosophers.

BASIC FACTS ABOUT THE CYNICS

What is Cynicism? As we have noted, Plato judged Diogenes of Sinope a "Socrates gone mad (*mainomenos*)." As we have also noted, this was not intended as a compliment. Rather, it was meant to undercut what Diogenes was doing, to say that he was everything denoted by *mainomenos*, a Greek word related to the English words "mania" and "maniac." He was crazy! insane! a lunatic! a man drunk! a man frenzied (as in the sort of frenzy inaugurated by Dionysus and his secret rites)! For Plato, Diogenes—and thus Cynicism—was an extreme version of the far healthier, moderate, and *sane* Socrates.

If Diogenes was a "Socrates *mainomenos*," then what was it about Socrates that Diogenes and Cynicism took too far? The answer primarily has to do with the Socratic art of endurance—Socrates' self-control and indifference to suffering.[48] But it is also related to Socrates' frank and open search for the meaning of reality and human life and his free questioning of the conventional terms used to describe the same. It also has to do with his habitual inattention to his own appearance, and his emphasis on frugality and living a simple life. Diogenes and the Cynics took all of these to an extreme (begging, of course, the Aristotle-inspired question about whether a virtue or an excellence can even be an extreme). The Stoics later said that "the Cynic philosophy and way of life is a shortcut to virtue." This "shortcut" element of Cynicism also seems to imply an extreme. It is not the steady-as-you-go climb to the mountaintop; rather, it is going straight up, off the trail. In this way we might say that the ancient Cynics were off-roaders. So, if philosophers like Plato advocated the road less travelled followed by the few—which they did relative to the many who were focused, they judged, on things like getting rich, building a reputation, and having the fullest possible range of pleasures—the Cynics trudged along an empty road travelled by very, very few to none at all, a feat that took immense courage, intense focus, and, yes, a fair measure of madness. You're going up *that* way?

Here's how the tenth century AD Byzantine *Suda* (a historical dictionary and encyclopedia covering the ancient Greek and Roman and Byzantine worlds) defined Cynicism:

> A school of philosophy. It's definition is 'a short path to virtue.' The goal of Cynicism is to live according to virtue, in the manner of Diogenes and Zeno of Citium. The Cynics held that one should live frugally, eating sufficient food to support oneself and looking down on wealth and reputation and nobility of birth. Some of them were vegetarians, using plants for food, and they drank cold water and utilized whatever shelter they happened to find, even large wine-jars. They used to say that it was a unique characteristic of a god neither to need nor want anything—and those who need and want few things are like a god. They also hold that virtue is teachable and that it cannot be lost.[49]

In summary, then, Cynicism was a shortcut—the short path to virtue or excellence (*arete*). It was the diet plan that most doctors would advise against, the one where you lose three or more pounds per week versus the far more steady—and surely, Plato would argue, sane and healthy—one to two pounds. Nevertheless, the few who truly practiced Cynicism seemed to get it done. In some measure they became virtuous men and women, champions in the contest against pleasure and pain. But they were the few—the very few.

Who were the major Cynics? Some of the most significant Cynics were Antisthenes of Athens, Diogenes of Sinope, Crates of Thebes, Crates' wife, Hipparchia of Maroneia, Teles of Megara, Demetrius, Dio Chrysostom, and Demonax.[50]

Who founded Cynicism? There are two positions regarding who founded Cynicism. The traditional view held by scholars through antiquity and by many if not most scholars today is that the Athenian Antisthenes (c. 445-365 BC) founded Cynicism.[51] There have been those, however, who have doubted this position. They hold that Diogenes of Sinope (c. 410-323 BC) was the actual founder. It was only later, they claim, that others labeled Antisthenes a Cynic in order to connect Zeno of Citium (c. 334-262 BC), the founder of Stoicism, to Socrates (c. 469-399 BC). This strategy of connection worked because Zeno of Citium was the student of the Cynic Crates of Thebes (c. 365-285 BC), who was the student of Diogenes of Sinope, who was (it was supposed) the student of Antisthenes. Regardless of the view one takes on the matter, it seems safe to conclude that in some way both Antisthenes and Diogenes inspired and influenced the founding of Cynicism—Antisthenes as a "Socratic" philosopher, and Diogenes, who was, as Dudley states, the original *dog*. But what does *that* mean—to call Diogenes a dog?

What does the name "Cynic" mean? How did the Cynics get their name? The name Cynic means "dog" (from the Greek *kuōn* or *kyōn*, dog). There are two major accounts for why the Cynics came to be called "dogs." One is stated by Diogenes Laertius in his *Lives* (6.13):

> Antisthenes used to lecture in the gymnasium of the White Dog (*Cyno-sarges*). He did so not far from the gymnasium's gates. Some people say that the Cynic school received its name from the White Dog. And Antisthenes himself was simply called "Dog."

Most, however, accept the other account. It has to do with the intentional shamelessness of the Cynics and its similarity to the shamelessness of dogs. People called them "dogs" or "dog-like" (*kunikos*) because they behaved like dogs. To expand on this, Diogenes was nicknamed dog "because of his rejection of conventions, his adoption of poverty, and his practice of shamelessness."[52] A scholium on Aristotle gives the following explanation for why the Cynics were called dogs:

> The Cynics, or Dogs, have their name for four reasons. First, it is for the detached carelessness of their way of life, for they emphasize a general indifference, and, like dogs, they eat and have sex in public spaces, and they go barefoot and sleep in wine-jars and tubs and along the way. . . . The second reason is that the dog is a shameless animal, and Cynics praise shamelessness as being superior to decorum and respectability. . . . The third reason is that the dog is good at keeping watch, and they guard the canons of their philosophy. The last reason is that the dog is a perceptive animal that can discriminate between its friends and enemies. . . . Accordingly, Cynics recognize those who are suited to philosophy as friends, and they welcome them kindly, while they bark like dogs at those who are ill-equipped for the pursuit of wisdom.[53]

Finally, we are told in an anecdote that Diogenes himself called himself "the dog." The story goes that "One day Alexander the Great stood by Diogenes and said, 'I am Alexander, the great and mighty king.' In response, Diogenes said, 'And I am Diogenes, the dog.'"[54]

What was it like to practice the Cynic way of life? Cynic practice consisted of two major aspects. One was about becoming truly free or independent by means of ongoing training—the practice of endurance by reducing desires, embracing hardship and suffering, and living a self-sufficient and simple or frugal life centered on necessity alone. The other had to do with a mission to others to help them see through human vanity and the apparent value of many human conventions in order to live a more authentic and virtuous life according to nature. Alongside Cynic training and practice, frankness or truth-telling and preaching was the central way that Cynics reached others.

What are the major ancient sources for the Cynics and the nature of Cynicism? Diogenes Laertius' *Lives and Opinions of Eminent Philosophers* (third century AD) is one of the most significant sources for identifying who the major Cynics were and what they believed. The problem is that it requires judicial reading against other sources to discover what is accurate and what is not. This is particularly true regarding biographical details furnished by the *Lives*. Nevertheless, as others have judged, Diogenes Laertius' general presentation of the Cynics and their approach to life seems fairly accurate.

Aside from Diogenes Laertius, there were many others who wrote about the Cynics and Cynicism.[55] Unfortunately, most if not all of what they had to say is now lost. Others, whose writings we still possess, include Xenophon of Athens, Teles of Megara, Dio Chrysostom, Epictetus, Apuleius, Lucian of Samosata, and Julian (the Roman emperor). Aside from Diogenes Laertius, their works make up the content of this present collection of Cynic texts.

What major works did the Cynics write?—or those who wrote from a Cynic perspective? And who favorably wrote about Cynicism? Of the earliest Cynics, we possess only fragments. The longest passages are "The Speech of Ajax" and "The Speech of Odysseus" by Antisthenes. Both emphasize the Cynic virtues of each Homeric hero. Nothing significant survives from Diogenes of Sinope. A collection of ancient Cynic letters exists, the letters of Diogenes and Crates, among others, but, though they are Cynic in spirit and counsel, they are not considered genuine.[56] Later writers either wrote favorably about Cynicism or from a Cynic perspective. Though he himself was not a Cynic, in his *Symposium*, Xenophon allows Antisthenes to speak in his own Cynic voice about the wealth of the soul and the frugal life of simplicity. Dio Chrysostom, who lived and practiced the Cynic way of life for many years, wrote several orations with Cynic themes centering on Diogenes of Sinope. One, *Oration* 6, demonstrates the blessings of the Cynic way of life compared to the suffering brought on by the usual pursuit of ease and pleasure. Another, *Oration* 8, explores Diogenes of Sinope's turn to what amounts to Cynicism under the tutelage of Antisthenes, and offers a speech by Diogenes given at the Corinthian games that explains his own ongoing contest with hardship and pleasure. Epictetus, a Stoic philosopher and instructor, wrote a discourse surveying what it truly means to live a Cynic life. Lucian of Samosata, or someone who imitated his style, penned a dialogue, *The Cynic*, in which a Cynic philosopher defends his way of life. We have passages from Apuleius, author of the *Metamorphoses* (*The Golden Ass*), that give us some idea about Crates of Thebes and his practice of Cynicism. The Roman emperor Julian, though not himself a Cynic, wrote a few orations addressing Cynic themes. Finally, Joannes Stobaeus preserved long passages of the Cynic Teles of Megara, including "On Self-Sufficiency," "A Comparison of Poverty and Wealth," and "On Pleasure Not Being the Goal of Life."

THE BIG IDEAS, GOALS, AND PRACTICES OF THE CYNICS

The Cynic outfit. One ancient Cynic claimed that the Cynic outfit was the "uniform for a good man."[57] Certainly it was an outfit for the man who wished to live a simple, frugal life. "Cynics," Diogenes Laertius explains, "teach that a man should live simply . . . wearing only one piece of clothing, a worn garment."[58] When asked to defend himself and the way he appeared—his long beard and hair, his bare feet, and particularly his dirty old cloak—one Cynic answered, "It meets my needs. It was easy to come by, and it gives its owner no trouble. It is the cloak for me." Later he added that "the whole outfit that you ridicule . . . enables me to live a quiet life, doing what I want."[59]

The outfit itself was a simple one consisting of a doubled-over, tattered cloak (*tribōn*), a leather bag (*pēra*), and a staff (*baktron*). The first we hear of it is in reference to Antisthenes. "Antisthenes wore only one garment. He was the first to fold or double over his cloak, which was rather threadbare. He carried a staff and a leather bag."[60] Later men suggested the Cynics dressed the way they did in imitation of Heracles, one of their heroes. Crates, for example, was compared to the hero in that he "also went about half-naked and was distinguished by the club he carried."[61] Heracles himself, we are told, "was clad in a dirty skin."[62] Diogenes of Sinope called Heracles' clothing—that is, the lion skin—"virtue's clothing."[63]

The Stoic Epictetus was careful to point out that the Cynic outfit did not a Cynic make. To be a Cynic one had to act like a Cynic. It's to that—to the goals and practice of the Cynic—we now turn.

Cynic Goals

Living life according to virtue. "The Cynics hold that the goal of life is to live according to virtue."[64] We have already noted several times that many in the ancient world considered Cynicism to be a "shortcut to virtue"—to excellence, the good life. And it is true. But virtue, here, must be understood correctly. Although it had to do with elevating the soul above the body and valuing internal goods over things external, we mustn't overlay other or later Greek ideas onto the Cynic conception of virtue, which was something radical, even excessive—"Socrates gone mad," as Plato contended.

For the Cynic, virtue—which, according to Antisthenes "is the same for a woman as it is for a man"—is sufficient for happiness. Happiness itself is a matter of the drastic reduction of desire, or even the absence of desire, and the psychological freedom that follows from such—a freedom from all wants. It is self-control and the self-sufficiency or independence that results therefrom.[65] What is the guiding star that may lead one to this life of virtue? The answer is nature. Living virtuously means living according to nature.

Living life according to nature. For the Cynics, living according to nature entails two major points. One is the opposition to convention, the way humans customarily feel and think, seek and do things. By convention we humans eat, have sex, and relieve ourselves in private; we pursue gold, wear fashionable clothing, contract marriages, put on lavish feasts, worship many gods, form into rival parties and polities, and fight wars. But it doesn't have to be so. We are told that "Diogenes [the Cynic] asserted that he could counter . . . convention with nature." Accordingly, he reevaluated all human customs, "granting nothing at all . . . to human custom and law, but following nature." For example, we are informed that

"Diogenes was in the habit of doing everything in public—both the business of Demeter [eating] and Aphrodite [having sex]."[66] How may we know what it means to follow nature? We may by observing the way animals behave—dogs, lions, and mice, for instance. Though meant to be a criticism, one ancient observer notes that Cynics "utilize [the] good things [of the earth] no more than the beasts. Your drink is water, just like theirs. You eat what you pick up, like a dog. And the dog's bed is as good as yours—straw is enough for . . . you." In short, says this observer, the Cynics reject "all the wonderful paraphernalia of civilization." Of course, any Cynic in his right mind would have nodded in agreement. In fact, the Cynic criticized eventually declares, "My prayer would be . . . that I might need bedding no more than the lion, and costly food no more than the dog. Let my sufficient bed be the whole earth, my house this universe, and my chosen food the easiest to procure."[67] The story goes that Diogenes learned how to follow nature by watching a mouse:

> Theophrastus declares in his work the *Megarian* that it was by watching a mouse—how it didn't long for a marriage bed, and how it didn't care about the dark, and how it didn't long for things that have a reputation for causing pleasure—that Diogenes discovered the means of adapting himself to circumstances.[68]

Desire reduction. As already mentioned, the life of virtue for the Cynic was closely tied to the radical reduction of desire. Diogenes Laertius recounts that "when someone extolled a luxurious life" in the presence of Antisthenes, that is, a life that would satisfy every conceivable desire, "he said, 'May the sons of your enemies have a luxurious life!'" He is also reported to have said, "I would rather go insane than enjoy myself with pleasure." Similarly, Diogenes told a man "who was earnestly entreating a prostitute" with every hope of success, that "it would be better for [him] to be unsuccessful."[69] The point seems to have hinged upon the fact that such satisfaction never fully comes; desire always leaves one desiring more, and the pursuit of pleasure often leaves one in pain or suffering hardship.

"Pleasure," writes Dio Chrysostom, "after overpowering and taking possession of her victims, delivers them over to the most hateful and most difficult hardship." He presents Diogenes of Sinope as one who battles with pleasure and those desires that longingly stretch out for pleasure. But, Diogenes declares, a man "should flee from pleasure as far as possible and only have unavoidable dealings with her."[70]

The Cynic view was that the desires are a plague that torment the human soul. Diogenes averred that "bad men obey their desires as house slaves obey their masters."[71] These were not only what we might term positive desires, such as the desire *for* pleasure of any kind, lust *for* sex, or greed *for* wealth, but also negative desires, those desires *against* something—the desire that seeks to avoid (and is thus *against*) pain and suffering, the desire of anger *against* personal injury, and the desire of fear that *flees* death, and the like.[72] When accused of not having any true victories to speak of, Diogenes claimed that he had vanquished "many and mighty antagonists" including "anger, pain, desire, fear, and the most redoubtable beast of all, treacherous and cowardly, I mean pleasure."[73]

If bad men are enslaved by their desires, then what about good men? What are they to do? Epictetus explains that desire must be completely taken away.[74] If the master is desire, and the master causes untold suffering, then there must be a revolt. Desire must be overturned. But what will happen, we may ask, when desire is reduced in this manner? Diogenes asserts that something remarkable occurs. A new kind of pleasure appears, as it were, in the sky. It's as if one leaves the city and its light pollution behind and moves out into the countryside where the stars are finally revealed in all their majestic number and brilliance. "According to Diogenes, contempt for pleasure is, if we get used to it, quite pleasant itself. And just as those who are accustomed to living with pleasure feel nauseous when they have to give this life up, so too do those who have practiced the opposite life feel pleasure when they look down on pleasure."[75] Diogenes judges that "the gods had given men an easy life" — one according to reduced desire. "But," he said, "the easy life had become obscure over time by their seeking honey-cakes and perfumes and like things."[76] The Cynic in Lucian's dialogue expresses what may be the desire-reducing Cynic's motto: "May I never wish for more than my share but be content with less."[77]

Self-control (enkrateia). "When Phryne the prostitute set up a golden statue of Aphrodite in Delphi, Diogenes is said to have written on it, 'From Greece's lack of self-control.'"[78] So reports Diogenes Laertius, giving us insight into the nature of self-control—that when desire is present (desire for things like the "works of Aphrodite," as sex was commonly called), self-control is often absent.

Key to desire reduction is self-control. In fact, it may fairly be said that self-control *is* desire reduction or to be without desire altogether. St. Basil of Caesarea, a Christian bishop who had great admiration for Diogenes of Sinope and who betrays his own Cynic leanings (if we may call them such) in his letters and other writings, wrote that "God seems to be self-control because he desires nothing." He goes on to write, "Desire is a disease of the soul, whereas its health is self-control."[79] Self-control as health, then, is the opposite of desire as disease. To become healthy, to become self-controlled, a person must necessarily reduce his or her desires. The greater the reduction, the greater the health. Diogenes is reported to have said that "it was characteristic of the gods to need nothing, and that, consequently, when a man needs very little or nothing at all, he is like the gods." It was a judgment repeated by later Cynics.[80]

Diogenes Laertius notes that Diogenes of Sinope exhibited *apatheia*, impassibility or freedom from desire and other emotions, and Crates was known for his self-control (*enkrateia*). Cynic *apatheia* and *enkrateia* are closely related.

Self-sufficiency (autarkeia) "You alone revealed to mortal men the teaching that self-sufficient living is a way of life that is not burdensome."[81] Such was the inscription written on the bronze statue set up to celebrate Diogenes in his hometown of Sinope. The self-sufficient man is the one who is easily able to provide for himself everything he desires—the easy life that the gods originally supplied. And what he desires lines up with simple necessity. "A man's sufficiency is that which meets his needs."[82] Warmth? The Cynics' tattered cloak is enough. Defense? His staff. A storehouse? His leather bag. A dwelling? The wine-jar that Diogenes lived in or some public space. Food? Lupin beans, olives, and other simple foods. Drink? Water or inexpensive wine. Explaining how Diogenes taught self-sufficiency, Diogenes Laertius informs us that he "used to teach the boys in his care to supply their own needs, and to be content with simple food and water to drink."[83] The Cynic in Lucian's dialogue states, "I enjoy what comes to hand, use what is cheap, and have no yearning for the elaborate and exotic."[84]

The wise man, argued Antisthenes, "is self-sufficient."[85] While this has to do with the fact that the wise man is easily able to provide for his needs, it also—or perhaps mostly—has to do with the fact that the wise man is the virtuous man, the man whose life is in accord with nature. Virtue is "sufficient in itself for happiness." To put it another way, "Virtue is self-sufficient for happiness."[86] Accordingly, Crates knew that if his sons became philosophers, men in love with wisdom, they "would need nothing."[87]

Freedom (*eleutheria*) Seen in another light, self-sufficiency is freedom. "The character of a Cynic," writes Epictetus, it that "of a free man," that "of a man who lives under the open sky."[88]

Such freedom releases the Cynic from the anxiety and subservience that many experience in the presence of others, particularly in the presence of those who have and wield great power. Such unfree men worry about what the powerful may do to them or whether they will give them what they want. Rather than being free and independent, they are entirely others-dependent. When may they eat? Only when the powerful eat. As Diogenes pointed out to Callisthenes, a man who "shared extravagance at the side of Alexander [the Great]," he was only allowed to eat "when Alexander [chose to eat]."[89] Likewise, we are told that when Plato "approached [Diogenes] and quietly said to him, 'If you had paid court to Dionysus [the tyrant of Syracuse], you would not now be washing vegetables,'" Diogenes countered, "'If you had washed vegetables, you wouldn't have paid court to Dionysus.'"[90]

When asked "what he gained from philosophy," Crates answered, "A measure of lupin beans and no one to worry about." In doing so, he concretely reduced Cynicism to two of its most essential goals: to have enough and to be free from worry about others.

Crates declared "that obscurity and poverty were his own home-land, which Fortune could never take captive."[91] Of his outfit, one Cynic explained, "it enables me to live a quiet life, doing what I want and keeping the company I wish to keep."[92] Finally, Diogenes "declared that his manner of life was the same as that of Heracles. He preferred freedom more than everything else."[93]

Cynic heroes (hērōs). The mention of Heracles highlights another goal the Cynics had—to be like certain heroes, certain great human beings (some who were eventually deified). To name the most prominent from mythology, there were Heracles, Theseus, Odysseus, and the Amazons.[94]

The Cynic in Lucian's dialogue declares that Heracles "was the best man that ever lived. . . . He had self-control and fortitude. He wanted power and not luxury." There was also Theseus, who was Heracles' disciple, says the same Cynic. He was "the best of his generation—he too chose to go naked and without shoes. It was his pleasure to let his hair and beard grow." "Well," he concludes, "I admire those ancients and would gladly be like them. By contrast, I do not have the smallest admiration for the present generation's wonderful felicity—tables! clothes! bodies artificially polished all over! no hair growing in any of the places where nature plants it!"[95]

The Roman writer Apuleius compares the Cynic Crates of Thebes to Heracles (in this case, the Latin version Hercules) in this way:

> The poets tell that Hercules of old by his valor subdued all the wild monsters of legend, beast or man, and purged all the world of them. Even so our philosopher Crates was truly a Hercules in the conquest of anger, envy, avarice, lust, and all the other monstrous and shameful things that plague the human soul. He expelled all these pests from their minds, purged households, and tamed vice. Not only that, but he too went half-naked and was distinguished by the club he carried. And he sprang from that same Thebes where men say that Hercules was born.[96]

More recent heroes (relative to the origin of Cynicism) were the Persian king Cyrus, who cherished the value of hard work and human effort, and Socrates, who was—in the Cynic mind any-way—the prototypical Cynic.

Cynic Practice

Cynic shamelessness (anaideia). Form in your mind the picture a large dog hunched over in a grassy park doing his business. (An unpleasant image, yes, but in this case necessary.) He glances around with a strained look on his face as if somewhat defenseless. Then, nature having taken its course, he pads away smiling—sniffing the grass, chasing a squirrel, wagging his tail, all the while oblivious to others. The Cynics wanted to be no different than this dog. In a word, they wished to be shameless in what they did and where they did it. Accordingly, whereas most Greeks ate, made love, and used the restroom in private, they advocated doing these acts wherever they happened to be, even in the most public of all locations, the marketplace. There is no natural function that is truly shameful, they argued; rather, such functions have only become shameful thanks to human convention.

Take farting, for example, something that seems naturally embarrassing, even shameful. On the contrary, for the Cynic, the act of passing gas is quite natural and, therefore, not truly or naturally shameful in any way or in any situation. We see this illustrated in a story Diogenes Laertius relates about Crates and his student Metrocles.

> One day, in the midst of others, Metrocles of Maroneia farted when he was practicing a speech. He was so despondent because of what he had done that he shut himself up in his house, fully intending to starve himself to death. When Crates learned about this and was summoned, he visited Metrocles. First, he ate a bowl of lupin beans—*on purpose*. Then he tried to persuade Metrocles that he had done nothing bad. For it would have been a miracle if he had not, following nature, relieved himself of such a blast of wind. Finally, when Crates himself farted, he renewed Metrocles' strength, encouraging him by means of similar actions.[97]

Take another example—that of going to the restroom. According to a story told by Dio Chrysostom, Diogenes once did his business in public during the Isthmian games. Imagine him there, speaking to a crowd about his own successful battles with hardship and pleasure. To illustrate his struggles, he mentions the example of Heracles, who, he contends, heroically labored in a similar manner. Diogenes says that

> to avoid creating the opinion that he [Heracles] did only impressive and mighty deeds, he went and cleaned out the dung in the Augean stables, that immense accumulation of many years. For he thought that he should fight stubbornly and war against opinion as much as against wild beasts and wicked men.

Ordinarily, such gruesome labor would have been the work of a shameless slave. But not in Heracles' case! Dio Chrysostom explains that the crowd listening to Diogenes truly enjoys what he is saying—until, that is, Diogenes behaves in a shameful manner that defies every sensible norm (and with this we get to Cynic shamelessness, that of performing an "inglorious act" in public):

> While Diogenes spoke in this manner, many stood around and listened to his words with great pleasure. Then—possibly with this thought of Heracles in his mind—he stopped speaking and, squatting on the ground, he performed an inglorious act. Seeing this, the crowd straightway scorned him and called him crazy.[98]

To give one last example, most of us might find tripping before others or making a loud noise or doing something apparently subservient in public embarrassing. Not the Cynics.

> Someone dropped a loaf of wheat bread [in a public space] and was ashamed to pick it up. Seeing this, Diogenes wished to offer him a lesson, and so he tied a rope to the neck of a wine-jar and dragged it across the Ceramicus.[99]

Rather than cowering with shame, Diogenes positively welcomed all the popped eyeballs and open mouths expressing astonishment. Similarly:

> Someone wished to study philosophy with Diogenes, so he gave the man a big fish to carry [in a public space] and told him to follow after him. Eventually, thanks to the shame he felt, the man threw the fish away and departed. Sometime later, Diogenes encountered him, and laughing, he said, "Our friendship ended thanks to a big fish!"[100]

Moreover, the Cynics held that the whole notion of reputation was bunk, something unnatural, a matter of human convention alone. Somewhat paradoxically, therefore, they held that "a bad reputation is a good thing."[101] The point was not that a bad reputation was something good in itself (they were not establishing a new convention), but to counter the idea that a good reputation—which depends in part at least on others rather than on oneself alone—was something inherently good. Additionally, a bad reputation assisted the Cynic in his efforts to let go of convention and to follow nature. Consequently, they held that the laughter of others directed at oneself is itself laughable and something to embrace and overcome:

> When someone said, "Most people laugh at you," [Diogenes'] reply was, "Yes—and it is likely that asses laugh at them. But even as they pay very little attention to asses, so do I not pay attention to them."[102]

> One man said to [Diogenes], "The many laugh at you." He replied, "But I am not laughed down."[103]

Training, practice, exercise (askēsis). Since ancient times there has been the debate over whether Cynicism was a school of philosophy or a way of life.[104] If nothing else, the Cynic emphasis was always on training, practice, and exercise rather than mere theories and ideas. Diogenes made the point to the Cynic Hegesias when the latter asked him to lend him one of his writings. "You are a vain and thoughtless man," Diogenes judged. "For in the case of figs, you would not choose painted figs but real ones, yet in this case you pass over genuine practice for what is merely written."[105]

We are told that "Diogenes said that absolutely nothing in life is successful without training, which has the power to conquer anything."[106] Training of the soul, he said, "gives rise to perceptions that facilitate virtuous deeds."[107] What sort of training did he have in mind? The following anecdotes give some idea.

Diogenes Laertius tells us that "in summertime, Diogenes used to roll in his wine-jar house over hot sand. And in wintertime, he used to hug statues of men covered with snow. He practiced endurance in every way." And "he would walk in the snow barefoot." And "Diogenes once begged alms from a statue. When asked why he did this, he said, 'To practice being rejected.'" And "Diogenes was going into a theater while everyone else was going out in the opposite direction. When someone asked him why, he said, 'This is what I practice doing every day of my life.'" Diogenes was not the only one to practice in this manner. "Crates," we're informed, "used to revile prostitutes on purpose in order to practice getting used to the profanity they would give him in return."[108]

Endurance (karteria). In many ways, Cynicism as a way of life can be reduced to the ability to endure whatever may happen. "When someone asked him what result he obtained from philosophy, Diogenes said, 'If nothing else, this: I am prepared for every turn of fortune.'"[109] The report is that Antisthenes would walk some ten miles round trip each day to be with and listen to Socrates in Athens. From him he "learned the art of endurance . . . imitating his indifference to suffering." It was because of this education in endurance, we are told, and imitation of Socrates' example "that [Antisthenes] began the Cynic philosophy and the Cynic way of life."[110] Remarking on Cynic endurance, Epictetus states, "The Cynic should also have such power of endurance that he seems insensible to the common sort, like a stone."[111]

We have already seen how individual Cynics trained to endure. Now let's turn to how they positively embraced hardship.

Toil, hard work, hardship, suffering (ponos). "Antisthenes argued that hard work, with all its toil and suffering, is something good. He did so by pointing to the examples of great Heracles and Cyrus."[112] The Cynic logic was something along these lines: if the ability to endure is something positive, and hard work and its consequent suffering as well as other hardships are the means by which one develops the ability to endure, then hard work, suffering, and hardship are something positive. In *Oration* 8, Dio Chrysostom has Diogenes put it this way:

> But the noble and excellent man believes that his hardships are his greatest opponents, and always wants to battle with them day and night—not to win a sprig of parsley, as so many goats might do, nor for a bit of wild olive, or of pine, but to win happiness and virtue throughout all the days of his life . . . He is afraid of none of those opponents nor does he pray to draw another, but he challenges them one after another, grappling with hunger and cold, withstanding thirst, and disclosing no weakness even though he must endure the lash or give his body to be cut or burned. Poverty, exile, loss of reputation, and the like have no terrors for him.[113]

Raising the example of Heracles, as Cynics liked to do (as mentioned above), Epictetus expounds, "When Heracles was exercised by Eurystheus, he did not think that he was wretched, but without hesitation he attempted to execute all that he had in hand." Later on in the same discourse, he presents Diogenes calling out to passersby "to see the battle between a fever and a man." Instead of going to a friend's house to nurse his illness, he suggests that a Cynic should "look around for some convenient dunghill on which you will endure your fever."[114]

Pleasure (hēdonē). Interestingly, these hardships are not the only kind that Diogenes faces with determination. Rather, he also battles pleasure, which, he points out, deceives and bewitches and imprisons. "For it is impossible to dwell with pleasure or even to linger with her for any length of time without being wholly conquered and enslaved." To remain free, therefore, one must again and again decline pleasure. "He should flee from pleasure as far as possible and only have unavoidable dealings with her."[115] The experience of pleasure in itself serves to weaken and gradually enslave a man rather than freeing him.

This ultimate hardship of being enslaved to pleasure is one the Cynic cannot embrace because it inherently entails weakness, the erosion of the ability to endure. As such, the difference between the one enslaved and the Cynic is immense: the addict (the one enslaved to pleasure) suffers enslavement by force (by the force of desire for pleasure, which powerfully demands satisfaction), whereas the Cynic endures deprivation by choice. The difference between the two is vast—that of choice versus a lack of freedom. Putting up with hard work and suffering is not about being a masochist. Rather, in the end, it is about contentment—the ability to endure anything in order to be content with anything. The Cynic in Lucian's dialogue states, "I can put up with cold and heat and be content with the works of God." Not those, he counters, who pursue an easy life full of pleasure. They are "displeased with everything that happens and grumble without ceasing. What is, is intolerable. What is not, [they] pine for. In winter [they] want summer; in summer, winter. In heat [they] pine for cold; in cold, for heat."[116]

Things indifferent (adiaphoros). For the Cynics, those things that contribute to virtue and being virtuous are good, and those that contribute to vice and being vicious are bad. Anything else is "indifferent," that is, something that neither contributes to being virtuous or vicious. As Diogenes Laertius summarizes it, "Cynics teach that whatever is between virtue and vice should be counted as indifferent, that is, neither good nor bad."[117] Accordingly, hard work and suffering and the ability to endure are good, whereas a life of ease and pleasure are not. Things like human customs or fine clothing are things indifferent.

Poverty (penia). As with hard work and suffering, the Cynics viewed poverty as something to be welcomed. They did so because when a person embraces poverty, he or she has nothing to lose and is consequently secure. Crates declared that "obscurity and poverty were his own homeland," his own walled city, "which Fortune could never take captive"[118]—Fortune, or Luck, which was notorious for invading a man's life, sacking it, as it were, and taking everything. In Xenophon's *Symposium*, Antisthenes observes,

A man's wealth or lack of wealth is not a matter of household goods but of soul goods. . . . As for me, my possessions are so great that I can hardly find them myself. I have enough to eat so that I'm not hungry and enough to drink so that I'm not thirsty. And I have enough clothing so that when I'm outside, I'm no colder than Callias is. . . . I do not purchase highly prized items in the marketplace since they are very expensive, but I withdraw wealth from my soul.[119]

Simplicity, frugality (euteleia)—simple, frugal (euteles) living, living simply (litōs). If the reduction of desire and self-sufficiency are two of the most significant Cynic goals, both ordered to freedom, then simplicity is one of the most powerful practices by which these goals are achieved. To live simply, to be satisfied with what is necessary and to disregard the inessential, is to be fully content. To live in such as state is to be like the gods, who are completely satisfied.

Here's how Diogenes Laertius sums up the Cynic position, a summary that contains the goal (to be satisfied like the gods), the disregard of inessentials (things like wealth and reputation), and the means by which (living simply):

Cynics also teach that men should live simply, procuring for themselves only necessary food and wearing only one piece of clothing, a worn garment. They think very little of wealth and reputation and noble birth. Some Cynics get by on herbs and vegetables and cold water. They live in any kind of shelter, or even large wine-jars, just as did Diogenes, who used to say that it was characteristic of the gods to need nothing, and that, consequently, when a man needs very little or nothing at all, he is like the gods.[120]

Diogenes Laertius further tells us that upon being accepted by Antisthenes, Diogenes "set out to live a simple and frugal life."[121] The simplicity or frugality he practiced was one of bare necessity, the attempt to live life with the fewest needs or possessions possible—needs and possessions that paradoxically implied being possessed, that the owner was possessed by the possessions themselves in that he depended on them.

One time Diogenes saw a child drinking out of his hands. Consequently, he pulled the cup from his leather bag and tossed it away, saying, "A child has outdone me in frugality." Another time, when he similarly observed a child who had broken his own spoon taking up lentil soup with a hollow crust of bread, he threw away his spoon.[122]

If the ancient athlete's objective was to give his life over to training in order to win victory and glory, the Cynic's goal was to live simply, to live in such a way so as to radically reduce desires and thus become self-sufficient and ultimately free.

The Cynic's fundamental intention and resolution toward living simply is that found in Lucian's dialogue: "Let my sufficient bed be the whole earth, my house this universe, and my chosen food the easiest to procure."[123] The key word is "sufficient."

Citizen of the world (*kosmopolitēs*) Part of a Cynic's practice was the act of releasing himself from all unnecessary externals, including that most important of ancient Greek possessions, citizenship in a particular city-state. Citizenship gave the Greek security and power in the form of walls and numbers. But it also bound him. In exchange for these "goods," he had to get involved in what was oftentimes the turbulent political life of the city, an involvement that in turn created other apparent needs and commitments—not to mention the frequent need to fight on behalf of the city. All of this was judged unnecessary by the Cynic.[124]

Because of this desire for release and consequent liberty, Cynics viewed themselves as citizens of nowhere (we might say) or everywhere (as they said), the whole cosmos, rather than citizens of a particular place. Hence, "When someone asked him where he came from, Diogenes said, 'I am a citizen of the world.'" He believed "the only true citizenship is that which is a citizenship in the whole cosmos."[125]

Living in the world—the Cynic mission

Telling the truth—frankness, outspokenness, freedom of speech (*parrhēsia*). "When someone asked Diogenes what was the most beautiful thing among men, he said, 'Freedom of speech.'"[126] With this brief anecdote, we might think, *Ah, so the Cynics were early proponents of the First Amendment of the Constitution of the United States of America.* Not quite. Although there are similarities between Cynic *parrhēsia* and more modern political freedom of speech and expression in that people are at liberty to say what they truly think, the Cynic emphasis was far broader.

To understand, we must grasp what speech is and does for human beings. In essence, it reveals the mind or thoughts and feelings of a person. Therefore, speech is truly beautiful in that it connects persons, one to another, in a manner that is otherwise hard to achieve. But this is only in theory. In reality, speech can serve as the bars of a prison if it is deceptively utilized to present a person falsely or for some other unspoken motivation and goal. Cynics wanted nothing to do with such an imprisonment. Nor did they wish for such a one for others. Rather, they struggled to speak freely and frankly, to present things in the fullest light rather than allowing things to be overshadowed by the opinion of "the many," by unnecessary courtesies, by deceits, by things like reputation or wealth or power (which may all be viewed as speech in that they present a person in a certain light).

We see frankness or freedom of speech in action with a number of anecdotes having to do with Diogenes' relationship with Alexander the Great, the one man who was the wealthiest and most powerful man in his corner of the world at the time. Again and again Diogenes attempts to identify and speak in terms of how things actually are rather than surrendering to appearances:

> One day Alexander the Great stood by Diogenes and said, "I am Alexander, the great and mighty king." In response, Diogenes said, "And I am Diogenes, the dog."[127]

> When the Athenians voted to call Alexander, "Dionysus," Diogenes said, "You can make me, 'Sarapis.'"[128]

> Alexander stood opposite him and asked, "Are you not afraid of me?" Diogenes replied, "Why? Are you good or bad?" When Alexander said,

"Good," Diogenes replied, "Who then would fear something good?"[129]

One day, when Diogenes was sitting in the sun nearby the Craneum grove of Corinth, Alexander stood over him and said, "Ask me for anything you desire." Diogenes replied, "I would like you to stop blocking the light."[130]

The goal of Cynic freedom of speech or frankness was not merely to be obnoxious. Rather, as with their whole life, the goal was freedom—a freedom that hinged upon the realization that one does not require a certain response from others in order to be free. Consequently, they did not recognize the need to say what others wanted to hear—speech that ended up entrapping rather than liberating.

But more, Cynic frankness served as well to set others free. When asked who he would rather be if he were not himself, the wealthy and powerful Alexander declared he would like to be Diogenes.[131] Apparently he recognized the great value of Cynic freedom. Moreover, by their free speech, the Cynics were able to admonish and advise others who knew that a Cynic would never deceive or be indirect about what was best. We are told that "Crates was nicknamed the 'Door-opener' because he was in the habit of entering every house in order to admonish the inhabitants."[132] Here's how Epictetus expressed the fundamental job of the Cynic:

It is [the Cynic's] responsibility, then, to be able with a loud voice, if the occasion arises, and appearing on the tragic stage, to say like Socrates: "Where are you hurrying? What are you doing, you miserable men? Like blind people you are wandering up and down. You are going by another road and have left the true road. You search for prosperity and happiness where they are not."[133]

Dealing with delusion or vanity (tuphos). To look for happiness where it is not is a matter of delusion. Such delusion or vanity is the smoke or mere appearance of the fire of happiness, we might say, rather than the fire itself. *Tuphos* is an imposter, a pretense, a conceit. It is seeming or appearance rather than being or actuality. Diogenes, we are told, used to say that when he saw ship captains and physicians and philosophers living life, he regarded humans the wisest and most intelligent of all living beings. But when he saw interpreters of dreams and diviners, and those who paid attention to them, or those who were puffed up with their own outward appearance or wealth, he acknowledged that there was no more thoughtless and empty creature than a human being.[134]

More, Diogenes "would generally chide men for the way they prayed, declaring that they asked for the seemingly good rather than the truly good." And he "ridiculed noble birth and reputation and all such distinctions, calling them the showy ornaments of vice."[135]

Other Cynics similarly shed light on *tuphos*. Crates wrote that "much wealth is prey to vanity."[136] It is liable, as the expression goes, to go up in smoke. The Cynic Monimus declared that "all opinion"—that is, unfounded supposition—"is vanity."[137]

Altering the currency (paracharattein to nomisma). Any state's currency is a medium of exchange created to signify value. Once established, such a currency has value or is valuable. The truth, however, is that the currency is only valuable by convention. Gold has no inherent value. Nor does silver. The Cynics concluded the same about all human conventions. Wanting to follow nature, or that which is inherently valuable, they wished to reevaluate "human custom and law"—conventions regarding birth, reputation, marriage, eating, education, politics, and, in short, whatever was traditionally considered valuable. Regarding Diogenes' words and deeds, Diogenes Laertius reports that "it was evident that [he] acted accordingly [that is, in accord with his sayings and teachings]—altering the currency, as it were, or reevaluating human customs, granting nothing at all in this way to human custom and law, but following nature."[138]

Distinguishing between true and false happiness. We've already seen how, according to Epictetus, it is the Cynic's job to speak freely about what makes for happiness and what does not. Like Socrates, the Cynic must call out to others, asking, "Where are you hurrying? What are you doing, you miserable men? . . . You are going by another road and have left the true road. You search for prosperity and happiness where they are not." For the Cynic, true happiness is not found among external goods, things such as wealth and power or even bodily goods. "Most of the precious instruments of happiness that you so pride yourselves on," notes a Cynic, "are won only by vexation and worry." He goes on:

Give a moment's thought, if you will, to the gold you all pray for, to the silver, the costly houses, the elaborate dresses. And do not forget all the trouble and toil and danger they cost—the blood and death and ruin. Not only do large numbers of men perish at sea on their account, but many endure miseries in producing them. Moreover, they're very likely to be fought for—the desire for them makes friends plot against friends, children against parents, wives against husbands. How pointless it all is! Embroidered clothes have no more warmth in them than others. Gilded houses do not do better in keeping out the rain. A drink is no sweeter out of a silver cup—or a gold one for that matter. An ivory bed makes sleep no softer; on the contrary, your fortunate man on his ivory bed between his delicate sheets constantly finds himself calling on sleep in vain. And as to the elaborate dressing of food, I hardly need to say that instead of aiding nutrition it injures the body and produces diseases in it.[139]

True happiness is simple, consisting of simple things. Unhappiness, or false happiness, by contrast, is complex. "Diogenes often declared that the gods had given men an easy life. But the easy life had become obscure over time by their seeking honey-cakes and perfumes and like things."[140]

Going back as far as Homer, the "easy life" was synonymous with the happy life. The problem for the many was that when most imagined the happy, easy life, they envisioned the one lived by the gods—full of pleasure and every desirable thing.

True, said the Cynics. The easy life *is* the life lived by the gods. But the true, real happiness of the gods has everything to do with desiring nothing rather than having every imaginable desire satisfied.

LET'S GO!

As we have seen, Cynicism is very much about going and doing rather than merely, for instance, sitting in a comfortable armchair reading, thinking, and understanding. Whether or not it was an ancient school of philosophy in the sense of a unique perspective on things, Cynicism was certainly a "way of life"—an exercise, a practice. As was said by many, it was a "shortcut to virtue."

The Classics Cave invites you to enter upon the rugged but rewarding path of the ancient Cynics. Come train with them. Listen to the many anecdotes told about their lives, and to what they have to say to us about the happy life that follows nature—about desiring, enduring, and living well. And then get busy *doing*.

As for the latter, you may wish to turn to Part 3, "Points of Wisdom & Ways of Practice." There you will discover "A Plan of Life Following the Cynics," a ten-point list of what may be considered some of the chief practices of living a truly Cynic life. There are also Cynic points of wisdom, as well as three workbook and journal-like prompts and exercises intended to motivate the reader to act toward happiness like a Cynic.

Whatever you do, be prepared to reduce your desires to know greater satisfaction, and to embrace whatever is hard in life in order to make things easier. And more, of course.

Note: As you read along, observe that you will always know where you are in The Classics Cave's *The Best of the Cynics* in a few ways. First, the very top of the righthand page will let you know what chapter you are in, along with the chapter's title. For instance, THREE • ANTISTHENES—ANECDOTES & SAYINGS. Parenthetically, you should be aware that the chapter divisions and titles do not hail from the ancient world. Instead, they are provided by The Classics Cave to facilitate your reading, understanding, and recall. This is true for Diogenes Laertius' presentation of the Cynics from Book 6 of his *Lives* as well as the other selections. As for the material taken from Diogenes Laertius, we have arranged it in such a way that should, again, make easier your approach to the lives, sayings, and practices of the Cynics. You will always know where you are in Diogenes Laertius by means of the bracketed numbers found in the text, such as [2], the numbered section that begins this book's third chapter.

NOTES

[1] Luis E. Navia, *Cynicism – Bibliography*. From http://science.jrank.org/pages/7612/Cynicism.html.

[2] *Webster's New Collegiate Dictionary*, 3rd ed., s.v. "cynic" and "cynical."

[3] David Mazella, *The Making of Modern Cynicism* (Charlottesville: University of Virginia Press, 2007), 21. See also John Christian Laursen, "Cynicism Then and Now," *Iris, European Journal of Philosophy and Public Debate* 1, no. 2 (2009): 475.

[4] "Sallustius, who is referred to in Damasius' *Life* of his friend Isidorus, is the last [Cynic] known to us by name in the long line of followers of Diogenes [of Sinope]." Donald R. Dudley, *A History of Cynicism—From Diogenes to the 6th Century A.D.* (Strand: Methuen & Co. Ltd.), 207.

[5] Raffaella Cribiore, *Gymnastics of the Mind: Greek Education in Hellenistic and Roman Egypt* (Princeton: Princeton University Press, 2001), 128.

[6] See, for instance, the Stoic Apollodorus' remark from his *Ethics*: "The Stoics say that the wise man will play the Cynic since the Cynic philosophy and way of life is a shortcut to virtue," cited in Diogenes Laertius, *Lives and Opinions of Eminent Philosophers* 6.121 (from now on *Lives*).

[7] Diogenes Laertius, *Lives* 6.54.

[8] Dudley, *A History of Cynicism*, 14.

[9] Ibid., 19.

[10] See Diogenes Laertius, *Lives* 6.104, where he recognizes a "certain community between the two schools"—the Stoic and Cynic schools. See also Dudley, *A History of Cynicism*, 96: "Cynicism was to contribute to a more enduring system, that of Zeno of Citium [Stoicism]."

[11] Dudley, *A History of Cynicism*, 103.

[12] Regarding Stoicism's influence on the Neoplatonism of Plotinus, Frederick Copleston offers the example of the *logoi spermatikoi* (the ideas in the World Soul) as "an obvious adoption of Stoic doctrine." See Frederick Copleston, *Greece and Rome: From the Pre-Socratics to Plotinus*, vol. 1, *A History of Philosophy* (Westminster: Newman Press, 1946), 468. But this conception would not have come from the Cynics. Rather, to take a different example, as Dudley points out, the *spoudaios* (the excellent and thus happy man) in contrast with the *phaulos* (the sorry and thus unhappy man—a contrast maintained by Plotinus) may be traced to the Cynics. See Dudley, *A History of Cynicism*, 97. Another Stoic concept originating with the Cynics was that of "things indifferent (*adiaphoros*)"—that is, those things that neither contribute to virtue or being virtuous nor to vice or being vicious. For more on Stoicism, see *The Best of Early Stoicism* (Sugar Land: The Classics Cave, 2021).

[13] See Dudley, *A History of Cynicism*, 104.

[14] According to Dudley, the diatribe was developed by Bion of Borysthenes. ". . . Diatribe as a literary genre appears to have been the work of Bion." See ibid., 65-66; 111.

[15] Hermogenes, *Greek Rhetoric* (Rhet. Graec.) III, p. 406, quoted in Dudley, *A History of Cynicism*, 111.

[16] Dudley, *A History of Cynicism*, 111.

[17] Ibid., 111.

[18] Ibid., 70. Menippus of Gadara was a third century BC Cynic.

[19] Cited in Bracht Branham, "Cynicism," in Anthony Grafton, Glenn W. Most, and Salvatore Settis, eds. *The Classical Tradition* (Cambridge: The Belknap Press of Harvard University Press, 2010), 247.

[20] Dudley, *A History of Cynicism*, 128.

[21] Ibid., 186. According to Dudley, the point comes from the argument of the German scholar Paul Wendland.

[22] Basil, *Letter* 366. Roy J. Deferrari notes that the "letter seems to be spurious," though others have attributed it to Basil. See Roy J. Deferrari, Basil: *Letters 249-368, On Greek Literature* (Cambridge: Harvard University Press, 1934), 350- 351 footnote. For "St. John's declaration" that God is the Word and love, see John 1.1 and 1 John 4.8.

[23] See Frederick Copleston, *Greece and Rome: From the Pre-Socratics to Plotinus*, 441, and Dudley, *A History of Cynicism*, 204.

[24] Gregory of Nazianzus, *Oration* 23, quoted in Dudley, *A History of Cynicism*, 205.

[25] Dudley, *A History of Cynicism*, 174.

[26] See Robert Dobbin, *The Cynic Philosophers from Diogenes to Julian* (London: Penguin Books, 2012), xxxix.

[27] Bracht Branham, "Cynicism," in Anthony Grafton, Glenn W. Most, and Salvatore Settis, eds. *The Classical Tradition*, 247.

[28] Ibid., 247.

[29] Dudley, *A History of Cynicism*, 145. See Epictetus *Discourse* 3.22.

[30] Julian *Oration* 6. For a discussion of his admiration of the Cynicism of Diogenes, see Robert Dobbin, *The Cynic Philosophers from Diogenes to Julian* (London: Penguin Books, 2012), xxxvi.

[31] Diogenes Laertius, *Lives* 6.104. For virtue as the road to happiness, see *Happiness: What the Ancient Greeks Thought and Said about Happiness* (Sugar Land: The Classics Cave, 2021) and *Aretē: Excellence or Virtue—What the Ancient Greeks Thought and Said about Aretē* (Sugar Land: The Classics Cave, 2021).

[32] Strabo, *Geography* 12.3.

[33] Pliny the Elder, *The Natural History* 7.18.

[34] Diogenes Laertius, *Lives* 6.54.

[35] Dudley, *A History of Cynicism*, 118.

[36] Cicero, *On Duties* 1.148.

[37] Lactantius, *Epitome of the Divine Institutes* 39.

[38] Augustine, *City of God* 14.20.

[39] Tatian, *Discourse against the Greeks* 25. Apparently Epicurus, the founder of Epicureanism, held something similar—that "the wise [Epicurean] man will not live like a Cynic . . . nor will he beg for alms." See Diogenes Laertius, *Lives* 10.119.

[40] Lactantius, *Epitome of the Divine Institutes* 39.

[41] Lucian of Samosata, *The Cynic* 5.

⁴² See Frederick Copleston, *Greece and Rome: From the Pre-Socratics to Plotinus*, 439.

⁴³ Diogenes Laertius, *Lives* 6.104.

⁴⁴ Ibid., 2.24-25.

⁴⁵ See John de Graaf, David Wann, and Thomas H. Naylor, *Affluenza: How Overconsumption Is Killing Us—and How to Fight Back* (San Francisco: Berrett-Koehler Publishers, 2014).

⁴⁶ The Cave makes the suggestion fully recognizing the complexity of the economy and the many goods, both material and spiritual, a healthy economy contributes to human living. Even so, the Cynic position is worth considering.

⁴⁷ Ibid., 6.38, 49.

⁴⁸ See ibid., 6.2. "[Antisthenes] learned the art of endurance from [Socrates], imitating his indifference to suffering. So it was that he began the Cynic philosophy and the Cynic way of life."

⁴⁹ *Suda, kunismos* (Cynicism), kappa 2712. Given the similarity of their definition and description of Cynicism, it is clear the author of the *Suda* had an eye on the work of Diogenes Laertius, *Lives* 6.104.

⁵⁰ For more on the major Cynics, see "The Cast of Significant Cynics" in the "Other Matters of Interest Related to the Cynics" section toward the end of this book.

⁵¹ See William John Kennedy, *Antisthenes' Literary Fragments: Edited with Introduction, Translations, and Commentary* (Sydney: University of Sydney, 2017), http://hdl.handle.net/2123/16595.

⁵² James Longrigg, "Cynics," in Graham Speake, ed., *Dictionary of Ancient History* (London: Penguin Books, 1995), 186.

⁵³ See *Scholia in Aristotelem* (Commentary on Aristotle), gathered by Christianus Augustus Brandis (Berolini, apud G. Reimerum, 1836), in Dudley, *A History of Cynicism*, 5.

⁵⁴ Diogenes Laertius, *Lives* 6.60.

⁵⁵ Among those cited by Diogenes Laertius, there were Achaicus, Antisthenes of Rhodes, Cleomenes, Demetrius of Magnesia, Diocles of Magnesia, Dionysius the Stoic, Eratosthenes, Eubulides, Eubulus, Favorinus, Hecaton (Hecato) of Rhodes, Hermippus, Hippobotus, Lysanias, Menander, Metrocles of Maroneia, Menippus, Neanthes of Cyzicus, Olympiodorus of Athens, Polyeuctus, Satyrus, Sosicrates, Sotion, Theophrastus, Theopompus, Timon, and Zeno of Citium.

⁵⁶ The others are the Cynic letters are Anacharsis, Heraclitus, and Socrates or various Socratics. For an introduction to these and their texts, see Abraham J. Malherbe, ed., *The Cynic Epistles: A Study Edition* (Atlanta: Society of Biblical Literature, 1977).

⁵⁷ Lucian, *The Cynic* 16.

⁵⁸ Diogenes Laertius, *Lives* 6.104.

⁵⁹ Lucian, *The Cynic* 1 and 19.

[60] Diogenes Laertius, *Lives* 6.13. Diogenes Laertius' source is Diocles of Magnesia.

[61] Apuleius, *Florida* 22.

[62] Dio Chrysostom, *Oration* 8.

[63] Diogenes Laertius, *Lives* 6.45.

[64] Ibid., 6.105.

[65] See Frederick Copleston, *Greece and Rome: From the Pre-Socratics to Plotinus*, 119.

[66] Diogenes Laertius, *Lives* 6.38, 71, 69.

[67] Lucian, *The Cynic* 5, 15.

[68] Diogenes Laertius, *Lives* 6.22.

[69] Ibid., 6.8, 3, 66.

[70] Dio Chrysostom, *Oration* 8.

[71] Diogenes Laertius, *Lives* 6.66.

[72] For a sampling of various desires, see Apuleius, *Florida* 22: "Even so our philosopher Crates was truly a Hercules in the conquest of anger, envy, avarice, lust, and all the other monstrous and shameful things that plague the human soul."

[73] Dio Chrysostom, *Oration* 9.

[74] See Epictetus, *Discourse* 3.22, where, in inviting one to radically change, he states, "You must take away desire altogether."

[75] Diogenes Laertius, *Lives* 6.71.

[76] Ibid., 6.44.

[77] Lucian, *The Cynic* 15.

[78] Diogenes Laertius, *Lives* 6.60.

[79] Basil of Caesarea, *Letter* 366. On whether or not Basil actually wrote this letter, see the related note above (in short, some say yes; others say no). Regardless, it expresses Cynic judgments.

[80] For Diogenes of Sinope, see Diogenes Laertius, *Lives* 6.104. For "later Cynics," see, for instance, Lucian, *The Cynic* 12: "Accordingly, the gods have no needs, and those men who have the fewest needs are nearest the gods."

[81] Diogenes Laertius, *Lives* 6.78.

[82] Lucian, *The Cynic* 3.

[83] Diogenes Laertius, *Lives* 6.31.

[84] Lucian, *The Cynic* 11.

[85] Diogenes Laertius, *Lives* 6.11.

[86] Ibid., 6.11.

[87] Ibid., 6.88.

[88] Epictetus, *Discourse* 3.22.

[89] Diogenes Laertius, *Lives* 6.45.

[90] Ibid., 6.58.

[91] Ibid., 6.93.

[92] Lucian, *The Cynic* 19.

[93] Diogenes Laertius, *Lives* 6.71.

[94] For the Amazons, see Crates, *Letter* 28 To Hipparchia.

[95] Lucian, *The Cynic* 13-14.

[96] Apuleius, *Florida* 22.

[97] Diogenes Laertius, *Lives* 6.94. In place of "Metrocles of Maroneia farted when he was practicing a speech," one early twentieth century, and thus very late Victorian, translation reads, "When he had made a breach of good manners . . ." Nevertheless, the verb *apoperdomai* (to break wind, fart) clearly appears in the text—twice.

[98] Dio Chrysostom, *Oration* 8.

[99] Diogenes Laertius, *Lives* 6.35.

[100] Ibid., 6.36.

[101] Ibid., 6.11.

[102] Ibid., 6.58.

[103] Ibid., 6.54.

[104] See ibid., 6.103, where Diogenes Laertius obliquely refers to the debate when he says, regarding the Cynics, ". . . if, that is, we decide that the [Cynic] school is a kind of philosophy and not, as some declare, a way of life."

[105] Ibid., 6.48.

[106] Ibid., 6.71.

[107] Ibid., 6.69.

[108] Ibid., 6.23, 34, 49, 64, 90.

[109] Ibid., 6.63.

[110] Ibid., 6.2.

[111] Epictetus, *Discourse* 3.22.

[112] Diogenes Laertius, *Lives* 6.2.

[113] Dio Chrysostom, *Oration* 8.

[114] Epictetus, *Discourse* 3.22.

[115] Dio Chrysostom, *Oration* 8.

[116] Lucian, *The Cynic* 17.

[117] Diogenes Laertius, *Lives* 6.105.

[118] Ibid., 6.93.

[119] Xenophon, *Symposium* 4.34-41.

[120] Diogenes Laertius, *Lives* 6.104.

[121] Ibid., 6.21.

[122] Ibid., 6.37.

[123] Lucian, *The Cynic* 15.

[124] We would be remiss *not* to note that, although he would have been very young, Antisthenes fought on behalf of Athens on at least one occasion, the battle of Tanagra (426 BC). And Diogenes of Sinope may have taken part in the action of the battle of Chaeronea (338 BC).

[125] Diogenes Laertius, *Lives* 6.63, 72.

[126] Ibid., 6.69. We are also told that Antisthenes "took delight in *parrhēsia*" (Dio Chrysostom, *Oration* 8).

[127] Diogenes Laertius, *Lives* 6.60.
[128] Ibid., 6.63. The one (Dionysus) was a Greek god; the other Greco-Egyptian, the combination of the Egyptian gods Osiris and Apis.
[129] Ibid., 6.68.
[130] Ibid., 6.38.
[131] Ibid., 6.32.
[132] Ibid., 6.86.
[133] Epictetus, *Discourse* 3.22.
[134] Diogenes Laertius, *Lives* 6.24.
[135] Ibid., 6.42, 72.
[136] Ibid., 6.86.
[137] Ibid., 6.83.
[138] Ibid., 6.71.
[139] Lucian, *The Cynic* 8-9.
[140] Diogenes Laertius, *Lives* 6.44.

PART 1

THE CYNICS
FROM DIOGENES LAERTIUS' *LIVES*

SUMMARY OF THE CYNIC
WAY OF LIFE & TEACHINGS

IN BRIEF: *Diogenes Laertius offers a synopsis of the Cynic philosophy and way of life. For one, they reject logic and other subjects. The goal is to live a simple life according to virtue. In this way, Cynicism and Stoicism are similar. Whatever does not contribute to virtue or vice is indifferent. One should leave nothing to Fortune. The wise man is worthy of love.*

L ET US ADD . . . the philosophical teachings that the Cynics held in common—if, that is, we decide the school is a kind of philosophy and not, as some declare, a way of life.

Whatever the case, like Ariston of Chios,[1] they were pleased to strip philosophy of logic and the study of nature in order to devote themselves solely to ethics. Moreover, what some record about Socrates, Diocles[2] writes about Diogenes, having him say, "We must look into the good and bad done in our own households."

Cynics also reject the subjects of a more general education. Anyway, Antisthenes asserted that those who had become sensible and moderate were better off not studying literature. Otherwise, he said, they may be perverted by strange things. [104] And so they strip philosophy of geometry and music and every subject of that kind.

Anyway, when someone showed Diogenes a clock, he said, "Its function is useful—one won't be late for dinner." And when a man played a piece of music for him, he said, "City-states and households are managed well by means of intelligence, not by the sounds of the harp and a flute's whistle."

Cynics hold that the goal of life is to live according to virtue. Antisthenes says as much in his *Heracles*—just like the Stoics.[3] There

is, after all, a certain community between the two schools. Therefore, some have said that Cynicism is a shortcut upon the path of
virtue. Zeno of Citium passed his own life in this way.[4]

Cynics also teach that men should live simply, procuring for
themselves only necessary food and wearing only one piece of
clothing, a worn garment. They think very little of wealth and reputation and noble birth. Some Cynics get by on herbs and vegetables and cold water. They live in any kind of shelter, or even large
wine-jars, just as did Diogenes, who used to say that it was characteristic of the gods to need nothing, and that, consequently, when a
man desires very little or nothing at all, he is like the gods.

[105] They further hold that virtue can be taught, just as Antisthenes declares in his *Heracles*.[5] Also, that once it is acquired it cannot be lost.

They also teach that the wise man is worthy of love. He is a man
without fault, and a friend to similar men.

Cynics teach that we should entrust nothing to Fortune.

In agreement with Ariston of Chios,[6] Cynics teach that whatever
is between virtue and vice should be counted as indifferent, that is,
neither good nor bad.

NOTES

[1] Ariston of Chios was a third century BC Greek philosopher, who studied with
Zeno of Citium (c. 334-262 BC), the founder of Stoicism. Zeno himself had practiced philosophy with the Cynic Crates of Thebes. This accounts, perhaps, for
the mixture of Stoic and Cynic elements in Ariston's own philosophy that em-
phasized a fairly stark ethics over epistemology (logic and the like) and physics
or natural philosophy.

[2] Diocles of Magnesia (second or first century BC) was an ancient historian and
writer of biography and summaries. He concentrated on the views, sayings,
and lives of the earliest philosophers.

[3] Stoicism was an ancient school of philosophy founded by Zeno of Citium (c.
334-262 BC). The Stoics held that the good or happy life is one lived in conformity with nature. Such a life is, for human beings, a rational life, which is, in turn,
a virtuous life. To learn more about ancient Stoicism, see *The Best of Early Stoicism* (Sugar Land: The Classics Cave, 2021).

[4] Zeno of Citium (c. 334-262 BC) initially practiced philosophy, or a life of radical virtue, with the Cynic Crates of Thebes. He went on to found his own school, Stoicism, named after a covered colonnade (*stoa*) in Athens. Zeno taught that all of reality consists of matter and mind, or divine reason, which makes, orders, and governs that which is natural. To live well is to live naturally, which is to say rationally or virtuously.

[5] The question whether virtue can be taught was a very live one in the ancient world, with significant proponents on either side or somewhere in between. For more, see Hugh Mercer Curtler, "Can Virtue Be Taught?" *Humanitas* 7, no. 1 (1994): 43-50. For more on the various views of virtue (*aretē*), see *Aretē: Excellence or Virtue—What the Ancient Greeks Thought and Said about Aretē* (Sugar Land: The Classics Cave, 2021).

[6] For Ariston of Chios, see the note about him above.

ANTISTHENES
LIFE & ACCOMPLISHMENTS

IN BRIEF: *Diogenes Laertius relays the details of Antisthenes' mixed ancestry, his education, the founding of the Cynic school, his appearance and manner, his writings, and his death. Thanks to his father, Antisthenes was an Athenian citizen. He first studied under the sophist Gorgias before attaching himself to Socrates, from whom he learned the art of endurance. He later lectured at the White Dog gymnasium, wearing a worn-out cloak, doubled over, and carrying a staff and a leather bag. His beard was long. He was clever and a witty conversationalist. His written works were many—some sixty plus, divided into ten volumes. When Diogenes offered suicide as a way to avoid the suffering of his last illness, Antisthenes refused.*

ANTISTHENES, THE SON of Antisthenes, was an Athenian. It was said, however, that he was not legitimately an Athenian. When someone taunted him because of this, he said, "The mother of the gods is also a Phrygian." He said this because his mother was supposedly from Thrace.[1]

So it was that when he had distinguished himself in the battle of Tanagra,[2] he presented Socrates with the occasion to say that if both of Antisthenes' parents had been Athenians, he would not have been so noble and brave.

Antisthenes himself mocked the Athenians who bragged about being sprung from the earth. He said that being "earth-born" made them no more well-born than spiral-shelled snails or wingless locusts.

ANTISTHENES' EDUCATION, SCHOOL & MANNER

Antisthenes first listened to the lectures of Gorgias the rhetorician.[3]

This explains the rhetorical style that Antisthenes employs in his dialogues—particularly in his *Truth* and in his *Exhortations*.

[2] According to Hermippus,[4] Antisthenes originally hoped to speak to the public gathering at the Isthmian games.[5] His plan was both to criticize and praise the Athenians, the Thebans, and the Lacedaemonians for their flaws and virtues. Upon seeing the great crowds of spectators arriving from those cities, however, he abandoned his plan.

Sometime later, he encountered Socrates. He used to benefit so much from him that he counseled his own students to become fellow-students of Socrates. Making his home in the Piraeus,[6] Antisthenes used to walk about five miles to Athens every day in order to hear Socrates. He learned the art of endurance from him, imitating his indifference to suffering. So it was that he began the Cynic philosophy and the Cynic way of life.

[13] Antisthenes used to lecture in the gymnasium of the White Dog (Cynosarges). He did so not far from the gymnasium's gates. Some people say that the Cynic school received its name from the White Dog. And Antisthenes himself was simply called "dog."

According to Diocles,[7] Antisthenes wore only one garment. He was the first to fold or double over his cloak, which was rather threadbare. He carried a staff and a leather bag. Neanthes[8] also affirms that Antisthenes was the first to fold over his cloak. Sosicrates,[9] however, in the third book of his *Philosophers' Successors*, declares that Diodorus of Aspendos was the first one to let his beard grow long and to use a staff and leather bag.[10]

[14] Of all the Socratic philosophers, Theopompus[11] praises Antisthenes alone both for his cleverness and his ability to win over everyone by means of his witty conversation. Both are evident in his own writings and in Xenophon's *Symposium*.[12]

ANTISTHENES' INFLUENCE

It seems that the manliest section of the Stoic school of philosophy originated with Antisthenes. Athenaeus the epigrammatist[13] writes the following about the Stoics:

You experts in Stoic counsel, you who inscribe the best teachings of all upon sacred pages—that virtue alone is the good of the soul, that virtue alone preserves the lives and cities of men. It is not so with the enjoyment of the flesh. This is the favorite goal of other men, accomplished by one of the daughters of Memory.

[15] Antisthenes led the way in terms of Diogenes' indifference to suffering, Crates' self-control, and Zeno's patient endurance. He himself proposed the principles that served as the foundations for the Stoic commonwealth.

Referring to his conversations, Xenophon[14] declares that Antisthenes was the most delightful of men. Otherwise, he was firm and self-controlled.

ANTISTHENES' WRITINGS

Antisthenes' writings exist in ten volumes. The first volume includes: *On Expression*, or *Styles of Speaking*; *Ajax*, or *The Speech of Ajax*; *Odysseus*, or *On Odysseus*; *A Defense of Orestes*, or *On Forensic Writers*; *Similar Writing*, or the *Lysias and Isocrates*; a reply to Isocrates speech called, *Without Witnesses*.

The second volume includes: [16] *On the Nature of Animals*; *On the Procreation of Children*, or *On the Amatory Affairs of Marriage*; *On the Physiognomy of the Sophists*; *On Justice and Courage*—an exhortation in three books; *On Theognis*—parts four and five.

The third volume includes: *On the Good*; *On Courage*; *On Law*, or *On the Constitution of a Republic*; *On Law*, or *On the Noble and Justice*; *On Freedom and Slavery*; *On Trust and Good Faith*; *On the Guardian*, or *On Obedience*; *On Victory*—an economic work.

The fourth volume includes: *Cyrus*; *The Greater Heracles*, or *On Strength*.

The fifth volume includes: *Cyrus*, or *On Kingship*; *Aspasia*.

The sixth volume includes: *Truth*; *On Discussion*—a debate handbook; *Satho*, or *On Debating*—in three books; *On Discourse*.

[17] The seventh volume includes: *On Education*, or *On Names*—in five books; *On the Use of Names*—a controversy; *On Questioning and Answering*; *On Opinion and Knowledge*—in four books; *On Dying*;

On Life and Death; On Those in Hades; On Nature—in two books; *A Question about Nature*—two books; *Opinions*, or *The Controversialist; Problems Relative to Learning.*

The eighth volume includes: *On Music; On Commentators; On Homer; On Injustice and Impiety; On Calchas; On the One Who Reconnoiters; On Pleasure.*

The ninth volume includes: *On the* Odyssey; *On the Magic Wand; Athena*, or *On Telemachus; On Helen and Penelope; On Proteus; Cyclops*, or *On Odysseus;* [18] *On the Use of Wine*, or *On Strong Wine and Drunkenness*, or *On the Cyclops; On Circe; On Amphiaraus; On Odysseus and Penelope and the Dog.*

The tenth volume includes: *Heracles*, or *Midas; Heracles*, or *On Practical Wisdom*, or *On Strength; Cyrus*, or *The Beloved; Cyrus*, or *The Scouts and Spies; Menexenus*, or *On Ruling; Alcibiades; Archelaus*, or *On Kingship.*

And so, this is the list of his writings. Timon[15] criticizes Antisthenes for writing so much and calls him a "prolific babbler."

Antisthenes' Death

Antisthenes died of disease. And when he was ill, Diogenes came to visit him, and said, "Don't you require a friend?"

He was carrying a dagger. Antisthenes replied, "Who will release me from this suffering?"

And Diogenes, showing him the dagger, said, "This will."

But the other countered, "From this suffering, I said, not from life!"

[19] In this way, Antisthenes seemed to bear the illness in a cowardly fashion thanks to his love of life. Here are my verses on him:

You were a dog in life, Antisthenes, born to bite the heart with words, if not with teeth. You perished by means of the wasting disease. Perhaps someone will inquire, "What difference does it make? We must all have some guide to Hades."

Notes

[1] The ancient Greeks identified the non-Greek goddess Cybele (Kybele), the Phrygian mother of the gods (Phrygia was in western Asia Minor, present-day

Turkey). During Antisthenes' life, Thrace would have been counted as a non-Greek land (mostly in present-day Bulgaria and Turkey, though a small portion covers the north-eastern portion of Greece). Antisthenes is simply making the point that even if his mother is non-Greek (i.e., from Thrace), it is not so bad.

² The battle of Tanagra (in Boeotia) was part of the Peloponnesian War (between Athens and Sparta and their respective allies). It took place in 426 BC. See Thucydides, *History of the Peloponnesian War* 3.91.

³ Gorgias the rhetorician (c. 483-c. 375 BC) was a Presocratic sophist from Leontini in Sicily. He is known for his rhetorical exercise arguing that nothings is.

⁴ Hermippus of Smyrna (today, Izmir, Turkey) was a third century BC biographer who wrote about the lives and sayings of eminent men.

⁵ The Isthmian games were held at Corinth every two years in honor of the god Poseidon.

⁶ The Piraeus was Athens' chief harbor. The walk from the Piraeus to Athens, as Diogenes Laertius indicates, was forty *stadia* (the pl. of *stadion*)—about five miles.

⁷ Diocles of Magnesia (second or first century bc) was an ancient historian and writer of biography and summaries. He concentrated on the views, sayings, and lives of the earliest philosophers.

⁸ Neanthes of Cyzicus was a third century BC historian and biographer.

⁹ Sosicrates was a second century BC writer who concentrated on the various schools of philosophy, their founders, and the founders' successors.

¹⁰ Diodorus of Aspendos was a fourth century BC Pythagorean who, according to Sosicrates and contrary to other ancient sources (Diocles of Magnesia and Neanthes of Cyzicus), was the first to dress and equip himself as a Cynic (long beard, staff, and leather bag).

¹¹ Theopompus of Chios was a fourth century BC Greek historian and rhetorician.

¹² For example, see Antisthenes' response to Socrates in Xenophon's *Symposium* 3.8; 4.34-4.44—Chapter 9 in this present volume. For Xenophon, see the note below.

¹³ Aside from the few citations made by Diogenes Laertius (6.14 and 7.30), we know nothing else about Athenaeus the *epigrammatopoios* (literally, the epigram- or inscription-maker).

¹⁴ Xenophon (c. 430-354 BC) was an Athenian historian and statesman. He was slightly younger than Antisthenes. Aside from the *Anabasis*, or *The Expedition Up* (the account of the harrowing escape of the Ten Thousand, a Greek mercenary force, after the battle of Cunaxa), Xenophon is known for a number of writings centered on Socrates.

¹⁵ Timon of Phlius was a mostly third century BC Pyrrhonist (skeptic) philosopher and writer. He wrote the collection of satirical poems, called the *Silloi*.

ANTISTHENES
ANECDOTES & SAYINGS

IN BRIEF: *Diogenes Laertius offers a string of short stories about Antis-thenes. Each one includes a pithy observation or saying. Broadly speaking, Antisthenes' orientation is toward the good life or happiness. For him, the greatest happiness is to die well, which means to live well. Virtue, includ-ing the key virtues of wisdom, courage, justice, piety, and a simple non-luxurious life, are the means by which we may live well. Life is not about seeking pleasure or a good reputation. Nor does our ancestry matter. Ra-ther, we must work hard and welcome the criticism of others, ordering our own thoughts so that they are like an impregnable fortress. As such, we may stand with the virtuous few against the not-so-virtuous many.*

A NTISTHENES ARGUED THAT hard work, with all its toil and suf-fering, is something good. He did so by pointing to the exam-ples of great Heracles and Cyrus—drawing the one from the Greeks and the other from the non-Greek barbarians.[1]

[3] Antisthenes was the first to define *logos* by saying that "logos is an account that clearly explains what a thing was or what it is."

Again and again he said, "I would rather go insane than enjoy myself with pleasure."

He also said, "We should only associate with those women who will be thankful."

An older boy from Pontus asked Antisthenes what he required to learn with him. The latter replied, "Bring a new book, a new writ-ing utensil, and new writing tablets." He meant that he should bring and have on display a new mind.

When someone inquired what sort of wife he should marry, he

said, "If she is beautiful, you will never have her to yourself. And if she is ugly, you will pay for it dearly."

When he was told that Plato[2] was abusing him, he said, "It is a royal privilege to do what is noble and to hear bad things said about what I do."

[4] When Antisthenes was being initiated into the Orphic mysteries, the priest said that whoever is initiated has a share of many good things in Hades.[3] In response, he said, "Why, then, don't you die?"

When he was reproached because his parents were not both freemen, he said, "Neither were they both wrestlers. Even so, I am a wrestler."

When someone asked him why he only had a few students, he replied, "Because I cast them out with a silver wand."

When he was asked why he was so sharp in admonishing his students, he declared, "Physicians are just the same with those who are ill."

One day, when he saw an adulterer running for his life, he said, "Wretched man! What a great amount of danger you might have avoided at the price of an obol."

We learn from Hecaton[4] in his *Anecdotes and Sayings* that Antisthenes used to declare that it is better to fall in with carrion crows than with flatterers, since the one eats the dead, while the other devours the living.

[5] When someone asked him what the greatest happiness was among human beings, Antisthenes said, "To die happy."[5]

When a friend complained to him that he had lost his notes, Antisthenes said, "You should have written them on your mind instead of on paper."

"As iron is devoured by rust," he said, "so are jealous people consumed by their own jealous disposition."

He declared that those who wish to be immortal must live piously and justly.

He said that city-states are destroyed when they are unable to judge the difference between good and bad men.

Once, when he was applauded by bad men, he said, "I'm afraid that I have done something wrong."

[6] Antisthenes said that when brothers agree, no fortress is as strong as their common life.

He said that the right travelling supplies for a journey are such that, even if you are shipwrecked, you will be able to swim with them.

One day when he was reproached for keeping company with worthless men, he declared, "And physicians are also with the ill without becoming ill."

"It is odd," he said, "that we weed out certain grasses from the grain and the unfit in war, but we do not excuse worthless men from the business of the city-state."

When he was asked what result he obtained from philosophy, he said, "The ability to be in my own company and to be acquainted with myself."

When someone called on him for a song over the wine, he said, "Then you must accompany on the flute."

When Diogenes asked him for a tunic, he directed him to fold over his cloak instead.

[7] When someone asked him what sort of learning is the most necessary, Antisthenes said, "The learning that strips away anything that must be unlearned."

He advised that when men are slandered, they should bear with it more courageously than if they were pelted with stones.

He used to taunt Plato with being arrogant. Accordingly, when he once saw a spirited horse during a procession, he turned to Plato and said, "If you were a horse, you would similarly be proud and showy." He said this all the more when Plato kept praising the horse. And one day when he visited Plato, who was ill, he looked into the basin into which he had vomited and remarked, "I see the bile but not the vanity."

[8] Antisthenes used to advise the Athenians to vote that asses are horses. When they judged the proposal irrational, he said, "And yet there are generals among you who have had no training but are merely elected."

One man said to him, "The many praise you." In response, he said, "Why? What wrong have I done?"

Upon turning the torn part of his tattered cloak so that it came into view, Socrates saw it and said, "I can see your love of fame through your tattered cloak."

In his work *On the Socratic Philosophers*, Phanias[6] relates how someone asked Antisthenes what he must do to be noble and good, and he said, "You must learn from those who well know that your vices must be rejected."

When someone extolled a luxurious life, he said, "May the sons of your enemies have a luxurious life!"

[9] To the youth who was posing fantastically as an artist's model, Antisthenes said, "Tell me, if the bronze could speak, on what do you believe it would pride itself most?" The youth replied, "On its beauty." Antisthenes said, "Are you not, then, ashamed of taking pride in the same thing as a lifeless thing?"

When a young man from Pontus promised to take good care of him as soon as his boat came in with its cargo of salt fish, Antisthenes took him and an empty sack to a flour seller's shop. He had the sack filled and moved to go away. When the woman asked for his payment, he said to her, "The young man will pay when his boatload of salt fish arrives."

It seems that Antisthenes was responsible for the exile of Anytus and the execution of Meletus.[7] [10] For when he encountered some youths from Pontus who had come to Athens thanks to the fame of Socrates, he led them off to Anytus, ironically declaring him to be wiser than Socrates. Those standing around Anytus were full of indignation. Therefore, they chased him out of the city.

Whenever Antisthenes saw a woman beautifully adorned, he would go to her house and direct her husband to bring out his horse and arms. Then, if a man owned these, he would say nothing more, leaving the woman's luxurious clothing and jewelry alone since the man could defend himself with his horse and arms. But if he didn't have them, then he called on him to strip her adornment.

The following teachings were pleasing to Antisthenes:

He showed that virtue can be taught.

He taught that the well-born and the virtuous are one and the same.

[11] He held that virtue was sufficient for happiness. Virtue requires nothing more than the strength of Socrates.

Antisthenes held that virtue is something you do—it's a matter of deeds. It doesn't require a stockpile of arguments or much learning.

He held that the wise man is self-sufficient since all the goods of others are his.

He believed that a bad reputation is a good thing. He believed the same about hard work.

He believed that the wise man would be guided in his public acts not by the established laws but by the law of virtue. He also believed that the wise man would marry in order to have children with those women who possess a good natural disposition. Moreover, he would love her since only the wise man knows those who are worthy of love.

[12] Diocles[8] records the following of Antisthenes' sayings:

Nothing is strange or helpless to the wise man.

A good man is worthy of love. Excellent men—serious men of character—are friends.

Make allies of men who are at once courageous and just.

Virtue is a weapon that cannot be taken away.

It is better to fight with a few good men against everyone who is bad than to fight with a multitude of bad men against the few who are good.

Pay attention to your enemies, for they are the first to notice your faults.

Honor a just man more than a kinsman.

Virtue is the same for a woman as it is for a man.

Good deeds are beautiful, whereas bad deeds are shameful. Consider every worthless act foreign.

[13] Practical wisdom is a sturdy wall that will neither fall down nor be betrayed. We must build such walls by means of our own impregnable thoughts and reasonings.

DIOGENES LAERTIUS: [19] We may now move on to those Cynics and Stoics who owe their origins to Antisthenes.

NOTES

[1] The Cynics admired the Greek hero Heracles (famous for his twelve labors) and the non-Greek king of Persia Cyrus (the sixth century BC founder of the Persian empire) for their positive attitude toward toil and hardship (*ponos*).

[2] Plato (c. 427-347 BC) was a Greek philosopher from Athens. He is known for his many dialogues and letters. Some explore the definition of terms (such as virtue or piety), and others offer Plato's understanding of the cosmos, knowledge, the Forms or Ideas (such as the Good or Beauty), pleasure, human excellence, happiness, and political well-being.

[3] The Orphic mysteries centered on the teachings of the legendary Greek poet Orpheus. They were based on the myth of Dionysus Zagreus. Initiation promised "good things in Hades," the realm of the dead.

[4] Hecaton (or Hecato) of Rhodes was a second and first century BC Stoic philosopher and writer, who wrote about various philosophical topics (virtue and the goal of life, for example).

[5] Compare Antisthenes' reply to what Solon famously has to say about happiness to the Lydian ruler Croesus in Herodotus, *Histories* 1.32. "O king, whoever possesses the most while passing through life and then dies agreeably is the one who, in my view, deserves to bear the name 'happy.'"

[6] Phanias of Eresos was a fourth century BC Greek Peripatetic (Aristotelian) philosopher and writer, who collaborated with Theophrastus, the successor to Aristotle.

[7] The Athenians Anytus and Meletus were responsible for bringing Socrates to trial on the charges of impiety and corrupting the youth of Athens. The trial resulted in Socrates' death in 399 BC.

[8] Diocles of Magnesia (second or first century bc) was an ancient historian and writer of biography and summaries. He concentrated on the views, sayings, and lives of the earliest philosophers.

DIOGENES

LIFE & ACCOMPLISHMENTS

IN BRIEF: *Diogenes Laertius first gives various accounts having to do with the exile of Diogenes from his hometown of Sinope. They all center on a coinage debasement scandal. Once exiled, Diogenes went to Athens and became Antisthenes' follower, living a simple life. At some point, Diogenes was taken and sold into slavery to a man called Xeniades in Corinth. He managed his master's household and educated his children. Over time he taught others as well and gained a following. One account has him growing old in his master's house and dying there—though there is some controversy over the manner of his death, whether by colic or by voluntarily holding his own breath. Lastly, Diogenes Laertius provides a list of possible writings.*

D IOGENES OF SINOPE was the son of Hicesias, who was a banker and money-changer.

CONTROVERSY AND EXILE FROM SINOPE

Diocles[1] relates that Diogenes went into exile because his father was entrusted with the public money of the state and subsequently debased the coinage. But in his book on Diogenes, Eubulides[2] says that Diogenes himself did this and was forced to leave his home along with his father. Moreover, Diogenes himself actually confesses in his *Pordalus* that he debased the coinage.

Others say that Diogenes had been appointed to supervise the mint artisans, who persuaded him to debase the coinage. In order to learn whether or not he should do what he was urged to do, he went to Delphi[3] or to the Delian oracle in his own land. When the god gave him permission to alter the "political currency," Diogenes did not exactly understand what this meant—that he could alter the political customs. Instead, he adulterated the smaller coins. When his act was discovered, some say that Diogenes was exiled, while others say that he voluntarily fled the city in fear.

[21] Some say that Diogenes himself corrupted the money when he took over the coinage operation from his father. As a result, his father was imprisoned and died. Meanwhile, Diogenes fled the city and came to Delphi, hoping not to learn whether he should debase the coinage but what he should do to acquire the greatest reputation—and that's when he received the oracle.

TURN TO PHILOSOPHY AND A SIMPLE LIFE

When Diogenes came to Athens, he approached Antisthenes. The latter sent him away since he did not accept students. Still, he wore Antisthenes down by his sheer persistence.

One day, when Antisthenes raised his staff against him, the student offered his head to him and said, "Strike it!—you will find no wood hard enough to keep me away from you as long as I think you have something to say."

From that moment on, Diogenes was Antisthenes' student. And being an exile, he set out to live a simple and frugal life.

[22] Theophrastus[4] declares in his work the *Megarian* that it was by watching a mouse—how it didn't long for a marriage bed, and how it didn't care about the dark, and how it didn't long for things that have a reputation for causing pleasure—that Diogenes discovered the means of adapting himself to circumstances.

Some say that Diogenes was the first to fold over his cloak. This was necessary because he slept in it. He carried a leather bag that held his food. He used any place for any purpose—eating, sleeping, and talking with others. And pointing at the colonnade of Zeus and the building that housed the sacred processional vessels, he would say that the people of Athens had furnished him with places to live.

[23] Diogenes did not use a staff until he was sick and weak. After he recovered, however, he carried the staff everywhere. He didn't carry it in the city, though. He only had it when he was out walking along a road with his leather bag. That's what Olympiodorus, a former magistrate in Athens, says, as well as Polyeuctus, the orator, and Lysanias, the son of Aeschrio.

Diogenes wrote a letter to someone asking him to provide a small house for him. He himself explains in his letters that, when the man delayed, he took for his abode a large wine-jar in the Temple of Cybele.

In summertime, Diogenes used to roll in his wine-jar house over hot sand. And in wintertime, he used to hug statues of men covered with snow. He practiced endurance in every way.

DIOGENES ENSLAVED

[74] When Diogenes was sold as a slave, he endured it most nobly. He was captured by pirates under the command of Scirpalus when on a voyage to Aegina. They carried him off to Crete and put him up for sale. When the herald asked him what he knew how to do, he said, "I know how to rule men." Having said this, Diogenes pointed to a certain Corinthian man, one whose garment had a fine purple border, a man named Xeniades . . . , and he said, "Sell me to this man — he needs a master."

So it was that Xeniades came to buy him. He then took him to Corinth and set him over his own children and entrusted his whole household to him. Diogenes managed his property in such a manner that Xeniades used to go around saying, "A good man possessed by a god has come into my house."

[75] In his work *On Pedagogues*, Cleomenes[5] says that the friends of Diogenes wanted to ransom him. But he told them that they were silly. "Lions are not the slaves of those who feed them," he said. "Rather, those who feed them are enslaved to the lions. Slaves fear men, whereas men fear wild animals."

And again, [29] in his *Sale of Diogenes*, Menippus[6] tells us how Diogenes was asked what he could do when he was captured and put up for sale. In reply he said, "I govern men." Consequently, the man said to the crier, "Announce this man—he's good if someone wants to buy a master for himself." When he was prevented from sitting down, he said, "It makes no difference—for fish are sold in whatever position they are."

[30] Diogenes marveled that before we buy a pot or a dish we test it to see whether it rings true, but if it is a man, we are content merely to look at him.

When Xeniades purchased him, Diogenes said to him, "You must obey me even though I am a slave. For if a physician or a helmsman were slaves, they would be obeyed."

And again, [36] When Xeniades purchased him, Diogenes said to him, "Come, do what you are ordered to do." And when Xeniades quoted the line, "Tributary streams flow backwards, up and away from rivers," Diogenes asked him, "If you had been sick and had purchased a physician, would have you then, instead of obeying him, said, 'Tributary streams flow backwards, up and away from rivers.'"

DIOGENES THE PEDAGOGUE AND TEACHER

[30] In his book *The Sale of Diogenes*, Eubulus tells us that Diogenes trained the sons of Xeniades in the following manner. After their other studies, he taught them to ride, to shoot with the bow, to sling stones, and to hurl javelins. Later, when in the wrestling school, he would not allow the physical trainer to train them like athletes, but only enough to keep them looking healthy and to train them in good habits.

[31] The boys used to memorize many passages from poets and prose writers and from the writings of Diogenes himself. And he would make them practice various short cuts and approaches to make these passages easier to remember.

Diogenes used to teach the boys in his care to supply their own needs, and to be content with simple food and water to drink. He further accustomed them to cutting their hair close to the skin, and to shun fashionable adornments, and to go out with fewer clothes on and no shoes, and to walk along the way silently and without looking around. He also used to take them out hunting with the dogs.

As for the boys, they had a great regard for Diogenes and always paid attention to him, speaking fondly of him to their parents. [75] It is true that Diogenes had an amazing gift of persuasion. He could easily conquer anyone with words. It is said that a certain man from Aegina named Onesicritus sent Androsthenes, one of his two sons, to Athens. And when he listened to Diogenes, he stayed there. Eventually, the father sent his older son, Philiscus, the one I've already mentioned, to Athens in order to search for Androsthenes.[7] But he was kept there in the same way. [76] Finally, when the father himself arrived, he was equally attracted to the pursuit of philosophy, just as his sons were. And so he joined his sons—so magical was the charm in Diogenes' words.

Among those who listened to him, there was Phocion, surnamed the Honest, and Stilpon the Megarian,[8] and many other men involved in public life.

DEATH AND BURIAL

[31] The same Eubulus relates that Diogenes grew old in the house of Xeniades. And that when he died, he was buried by his sons. And that while he was still living with him, Xeniades once asked him how he wished to be buried. To this query he replied, "On my face." [32] When he asked why, he said, "Because in a little while everything will be turned upside down." He said this because the Macedonians were already attaining power. From a low position, they had risen high.

[76] Diogenes is said to have been nearly ninety years old when he died. Regarding his death there are several different accounts:

One is that he was seized with colic after eating raw octopus. And so he died.

Another is that he died voluntarily by holding his breath. This account was followed by Cercidas of Megalopolis,[9] or of Crete, who, in his meliambics writes:

No more is the man who was from Sinope—the famous one who carried a
staff, doubled over his cloak, and lived in the open air. [77] But pressing his
lips against his teeth and holding his breath, he departed. He was rightly
called Diogenes, the offspring of Zeus, and the heaven-dwelling dog.

Another version is that, while Diogenes was trying to divide an
octopus among the dogs, he was so severely bitten through the ten-
don of his foot that it caused his death.

His friends, however, according to Antisthenes in his *Successions
of Philosophers*, speculated that it was due to the retention of his
breath. At the time, he happened to be living in the Craneum, the
gymnasium at the gates of Corinth.[10] When his friends came to him,
as was their habit, and found him all wrapped up, they guessed he
was sleeping, even though they knew he was not in the habit of
giving himself over to drowsiness and sleep. Thereafter, they drew
aside his cloak and found that he was dead. They supposed that he
had done this on purpose in order escape from the rest of his life.

[78] And so a quarrel arose among his friends as to who should
bury Diogenes. They even came to blows over it! Nevertheless,
when their fathers and other men of influence arrived, he was buried under their direction beside the gate that leads into the Isthmus.
They set up a pillar over his grave, with a dog in Parian marble
topping it.[11]

Later on, his fellow citizens honored him with bronze statues,
on which the following was inscribed:

Time makes even bronze grow old. But your glory, Diogenes, will endure
through every age. You alone revealed to mortal men the teaching that self-
sufficient living is a way of life that is not burdensome.

[79] I too have written him an epigram in the proceleusmatic
meter:

A. Diogenes, come tell me what fate took you to Hades.
B. It was the bite of a wild dog.

But some say that when he was dying, Diogenes left instructions that they should throw him out unburied so that every wild animal might feed on him. Or they should toss him into a ditch and sprinkle a little dust over it. According to others, however, his instructions were that they should throw him into the Ilissus so that he might be useful to his brothers.

Demetrius,[12] in his work *On Men of the Same Name*, asserts that Diogenes died in Corinth on the same day that Alexander died in Babylon. He was already an old man by the time of the 113th Olympiad.

WRITINGS

[80] The following books are attributed to Diogenes.

Dialogues: the *Cephalion*; the *Ichthyas*; the *Jackdaw*; the *Leopard*, the *Athenian People*; the *Republic*; the *Art of Ethics*; *On Wealth*; the *Love Matters*; the *Theodorus*; the *Hypsias*; the *Aristarchus*; *On Death*; the *Letters*.

Seven tragedies: the *Helen*; the *Thyestes*; the *Heracles*; the *Achilles*; the *Medea*; the *Chrysippus*; the *Oedipus*.

Sosicrates,[13] in the first book of his *Philosophers' Successors*, and Satyrus, in the fourth book of his *Lives*, allege that Diogenes left nothing in writing. Satyrus declares that the tragedies are by Philiscus, his friend from Aegina. Sotion,[14] in his seventh book, declares that the following alone are the genuine works of Diogenes: *On Virtue*; *On the Good*; the *Love Matters*; the *Beggar*; the *Tolmaeus*; the *Leopard*; the *Casandrus*; the *Cephalion*; the *Philiscus*; the *Aristarchus*; the *Sisyphus*; the *Ganymede*; the *Anecdotes and Sayings*; and the *Letters*.

NOTES

[1] Diocles of Magnesia (second or first century bc) was an ancient historian and writer of biography and summaries. He concentrated on the views, sayings, and lives of the earliest philosophers.

[2] Some have identified this Eubulides with Eubulides of Miletus, who was a fourth century BC student of Euclides (also Euclid) of Megara. That said, aside

from the information that Diogenes Laertius provides, that this Eubulides wrote a life of Diogenes of Sinope, we know nothing with any certainty.

[3] That is, to the Greek Oracle of Delphi, or the Temple of Apollo, where the god Apollo offered responses to visitors' queries.

[4] Theophrastus of Eresos was a fourth and early third century BC philosopher, researcher, and writer. He was Aristotle's successor as the head of the Peripatetic school. Diogenes Laertius (*Lives* 5.43) reports that he wrote a compendium of the writings of Diogenes.

[5] Cleomenes was a fourth and third century BC Cynic philosopher. He was the student of Crates of Thebes.

[6] Menippus was a third century BC Cynic who wrote satires.

[7] For more on Onesicritus and Philiscus, see Chapter 6 in this volume or Diogenes Laertius, *Lives* 6.84.

[8] Stilpon (Stilpo) of Megara was a fourth century BC Greek philosopher. He was part of the Megarian school, which was founded by Euclides (also Euclid) of Megara, a student of Socrates.

[9] Cercidas of Megalopolis was a third century BC Greek poet, statesman, and lawgiver.

[10] The Craneum was a grove of cypress trees just outside Corinth. It was, as Diogenes Laertius puts it, "at the gates."

[11] "Parian marble" was a very fine white marble that was quarried on the Greek island of Paros.

[12] Demetrius of Magnesia was a first century BC biographer.

[13] Sosicrates was a second century BC writer who concentrated on the various schools of philosophy, their founders, and the founders' successors.

[14] Sotion of Alexandria was a third and second century BC Peripatetic, who wrote about the succession of philosophers in each school of philosophy.

DIOGENES
ANECDOTES & SAYINGS

IN BRIEF: *Diogenes Laertius conveys a leather bagful, as it were, of stories about Diogenes of Sinope—stories that often include a pithy, witty observation or saying. Many have to do with Diogenes' criticism and ridicule of the philosopher Plato, illustrating Diogenes' general ability to scorn others. Diogenes also ridiculed the orator Demosthenes and shrugged off the self-importance of Alexander the Great, whom he termed "wretched." Many of his comments have to do with ordinary men and women who are, he observes, thoughtless, unwise, weak. They behave in contradictory or superstitious ways, pursuing everything—ease, pleasure, wealth, reputation, power—but that which is truly good. Diogenes longed to find a real man, that is, one who behaved as one rather than as a slave or worse. Diogenes himself sought wisdom and trained hard in order to endure hardship. He lived a simple life of self-control and contentment. Moreover, he offered himself as an example of how not worry about others. His words and behavior were meant to "alter the currency," that is, reevaluate human customs and values.*

D IOGENES WAS GREAT at pouring scorn on his contemporaries. He said the school of Euclides[1] was full of black bile. And Plato's discourses were exhausting. And the performances at the Dionysia a great marvel for morons.[2] And the demagogues the servants of the mob.

He also used to say that when he saw ship captains and physicians and philosophers living life, he regarded humans the wisest and most intelligent of all living beings. But when he saw interpreters of dreams and diviners, and those who paid attention to them, or those who were puffed up with their own outward appearance or wealth, he acknowledged that there was no more thoughtless and empty creature than a human being.

Diogenes would continually say that for the conduct of life we need either reason or a bridle.

[25] Observing Plato one day eating olives at a costly banquet, Diogenes said, "How is it that you, the philosopher who sailed to Sicily for the sake of these dishes, do not enjoy them now that they are in front of you?" Plato replied, "By the gods, while I was there I mostly ate olives and similar things as well." "Why then," Diogenes said, "did you go to Syracuse? Was it that Attica did not grow olives at that time?" But in his *Miscellaneous History*, Favorinus attributes this to Aristippus.[3]

Another time Diogenes was eating dried figs when he encountered Plato and offered him a share of them. When Plato took them and ate them, he said, "I said that you might have a share of them — not that you might eat them all."

[26] And one day, when Plato invited friends coming from Dionysius into his house, Diogenes trampled on his carpets and said, "I trample on vain and frivolous pursuits." Plato's reply was, "How much vanity you reveal by not appearing to be vain." Others tell us that what Diogenes actually said was, "I trample on the vanity of Plato." And the latter said, "Yes, Diogenes, with another kind of vanity."

Moreover, in his fourth book, Sotion[4] declares that the Cynic said the following to Plato. Diogenes once asked Plato for some wine and later on for some dried figs. Plato sent him a whole jar full. In reply, Diogenes said, "If someone asks you how many are two plus two, will you answer, twenty? Thus it seems you neither give as you are asked nor answer as you are questioned." In this way, Diogenes ridiculed Plato as one who talked and talked without end.

[27] When Diogenes was asked where he saw good men in Greece, he said, "Good men? Nowhere. But there are good boys in Lacedaemon."

One day, while he was giving a serious lecture and no one came to listen to him, he began to hum and whistle. When at that point people began to gather around him, he criticized them for eagerly arriving to listen to nonsense, whereas they carelessly delayed coming for something serious.

Diogenes would say that men strive in punching and kicking to outdo one another, but no one strives to become a noble and good man. He was amazed that literary scholars investigate Odysseus' misfortunes while they are ignorant of their own. And that musicians tune their lyre's strings while their soul's disposition and habits are out of tune. [28] And that mathematicians gaze at the sun and the moon but overlook matters close at hand. And that orators are so zealous and serious when they speak about justice, but they never practice it. And that those who are greedy blame everything on money while loving it excessively.

Diogenes used to condemn those who commended just men for being above their property and money while being jealous of the very rich.

He was moved to anger by the fact that men sacrifice to the gods to ensure health, but during the sacrifice they feast in a manner that harms health.

He was astonished that when slaves saw that their masters were greedy gluttons that they still did not snatch any of the food for themselves.

[29] Diogenes would praise those who were about to marry—and didn't. And those who were going to go on a voyage—and didn't. And those who were about to engage in politics—and didn't. And those who were going to have and raise a family—and didn't. And those who were about to move in with rulers—and didn't.

He used to say, moreover, that we should hold out our hands to our friends without closing the fingers. . . .

[32] Someone took Diogenes into a magnificent house and told him that he must not spit therein. Subsequently, when he cleared his throat, he spit in the man's face since he was unable, he said, to find a worse place to spit. Others say this is Aristippus' story.[5]

One day Diogenes called out for men to come to him. When they gathered around him, he struck them with his staff, saying, "I called for men, not for trash!" Hecaton[6] tells this story in the first book of his *Anecdotes and Sayings*.

Alexander [the Great] is reported to have said, "If I had not been Alexander, I would have liked to have been Diogenes."

[33] Diogenes held that the word that means "impaired or disabled" should not be used for those who cannot speak or hear or see, but for those who have no leather bag.

As Metrocles[7] declares in his *Anecdotes and Sayings*, one day, with his head half shaved, Diogenes went to a party where everyone was young, and he was seized and beaten by them. Later on he wrote the names of those who had struck him on a white writing tablet and hung it around his neck until they were stricken with judgment and reprimanded for their behavior.

Diogenes used to say that he himself was the dog of those men who were praised, but that none of them dared to go out hunting with him.

Someone said to him, "I conquered men at the Pythian games."[8] Diogenes responded, "In fact, I conquer men. You merely conquer slaves."

[34] To those who said to him, "You are an old man, you should take a break and rest," Diogenes replied, "Why? If I were running a long race, should I slow down when I was near the finish line? Should I not endure to the end?"

When he was invited to dinner, he said that he would not go. The reason? The day before, he said, no one had thanked him for coming.

He would walk in snow barefoot and do the other things mentioned above. Moreover, he attempted to eat meat raw, but he could not digest it.

On one occasion he found the orator Demosthenes[9] dining at a tavern. When he withdrew within, Diogenes said, "All the more you will be inside the tavern." When some foreigners wished to see Demosthenes, he stretched out his middle finger and said, "This man is the demagogue of the Athenian people."

[35] Someone dropped a loaf of wheat bread and was ashamed to pick it up. Seeing this, Diogenes wished to offer him a lesson, and so he tied a rope to the neck of a wine-jar and dragged it across the Ceramicus.[10]

He used to say that he imitated the chorus masters. They also set the note a little high so that the rest would hit the right note.

Most people, he said, are within a finger's breadth of being out of their minds—for if you walk along with your middle finger stretched out, someone will believe you mad, but if it is the fore finger, he will not.

He said that very valuable things were sold for worthless things—and the other way around. Accordingly, a statue goes for three thousand, while a choenix measure of barley meal is sold for two copper coins.

[36] Someone wished to study philosophy with Diogenes, so he gave the man a big fish to carry and told him to follow after him. Eventually, thanks to the shame he felt, the man threw the fish away and departed. Sometime later, Diogenes encountered him, and laughing, he said, "Our friendship ended thanks to a big fish!" The version given by Diocles,[11] however, is as follows. When someone asked Diogenes to tell him what to do, he led him away and gave him a half obol's worth of cheese to carry. But the man refused. Consequently, Diogenes said, "Our friendship ended thanks to a block of cheese worth a half obol."[12]

[37] One time Diogenes saw a child drinking out of his hands. Consequently, he pulled the cup from his leather bag and tossed it away, saying, "A child has outdone me in frugality." Another time, when he similarly observed a child who had broken his own spoon taking up lentil soup with a hollow crust of bread, he threw away his spoon.

Diogenes used to make this argument: "All things belong to the gods. The wise are friends of the gods, and friends hold all things in common. Therefore, all things belong to the wise."

According to Zoilus of Perga,[13] Diogenes once saw a woman supplicating the gods in an unseemly manner. Wishing to release her from her superstition, he stepped up to her and said, "Woman, are you not afraid that a god may be standing behind you and that you may disgrace yourself? I say this because every place is full of god."

[38] Diogenes dedicated to Asclepius[14] a striker—a man whose job it was to run up to and beat all those who prostrate themselves before the gods with their faces to the ground.

He was in the habit of saying that all the curses and calamities found in tragedy had befallen him —

> Without a city and a house, robbed of his own fatherland,
> A beggar, a wanderer, enduring life each day.

Nevertheless, Diogenes asserted that he could counter Fortune with courage, convention with nature, and emotion with reason.

One day, when Diogenes was sitting in the sun nearby the Craneum grove of Corinth, Alexander stood over him and said, "Ask me for anything you desire."[15] Diogenes replied, "I would like you to stop blocking the light."

Some man had been reading aloud for a very long time, and when he drew near to the end of the scroll and pointed to a space with no writing, Diogenes said, "Take courage, men. I see land."

When a man demonstrated by a syllogism that he had horns, Diogenes touched his forehead and said, "I don't see them." [39] Similarly, when someone declared that there is no such thing as motion, Diogenes stood up and walked back and forth.

When a man was giving an address about those things hanging in the sky, Diogenes asked, "How many days has it been since you've come down from the sky?"

A wicked eunuch inscribed on his house, "May nothing evil enter." Diogenes asked him, "How, then, is the master of the house supposed to enter?"

When Diogenes had anointed his feet with sweet smelling oil, he declared that the sweet smelling oil went from his head up into the air, but from his feet into his nose.

The Athenians urged Diogenes to be initiated into the mysteries.[16] They told him that in the nether world, initiates enjoy special privileges. "It would be laughable," he said, "if the Spartan king Agesilaus and the Theban general Epaminondas continue on in the mud while some worthless jokes who have been initiated will be in the Islands of the Blessed."[17]

[40] When a mouse crept onto the table, Diogenes declared, "Ah, I am now feeding a freeloader."

When Plato called him a dog, Diogenes said, "Yes—since I return to those who sold me."

When he was leaving the public baths, someone asked whether there were many human beings bathing. Diogenes said, "No." Yet when another man asked him whether there was a great crowd of bathers, he said, "Yes."

Plato defined a human being as "a featherless animal with two feet," and he was applauded for this. Diogenes then plucked a chicken, brought it to Plato's school, and said, "This is Plato's man." As a result, "and with broad, flat nails" was added to the definition.

When someone asked him what the proper time for lunch was, he said, "If you're a rich man, whenever you want. If you're poor, whenever you can."

[41] When he was in Megara and saw the sheep covered with leather garments while the children were naked, he said, "It is better to be a Megarian man's ram than his son."

A man hurled a gate's crossbar at him and said, "Keep watch!" In reply, Diogenes said, "What, are you about to strike me again?"

He used to call demagogues the servants of the crowd and the wreathes crowning them the flowering of popularity.

He lit a lamp in the middle of the day and walked around saying, "I'm searching for a human being."

Once, Diogenes was made to stand still while someone poured water over him. When those standing around pitied him, Plato said, "If you want to pity him, stand back"—referring to his love of fame.

When someone struck him with his fist, he said, "Heracles! How did I forget to wear a helmet when I walked out?" [42] But when Meidias assaulted him and said, "There are three thousand for your credit," the next day, Diogenes wrapped his own hands with boxing straps, beat him up, and said, "There are three thousand for yours."

When Lysias the apothecary asked him if he believed in the gods, Diogenes said, "How can I not believe in them when I suspect you are hated by the gods?" Others attribute this reply to Theodorus.[18]

Observing someone purify himself, Diogenes said, "Unhappy man! Don't you know that you cannot get rid of sins by means of purification rites any more than you can get rid of grammar errors?" He would generally chide men for the way they prayed, declaring that they asked for the seemingly good rather than the truly good.

[43] As for those who were terrified by their dreams, Diogenes would say that they did not pay attention to what they did while they were awake, but were curious busybodies about all the images they see while asleep.

At Olympia, the herald announced, "Dioxippus is victorious over men!"[19] Diogenes said, "More exactly, he is victorious over slaves—I over men."

The Athenians were fond of Diogenes. When a young boy broke the wine-jar in which he lived, they beat the boy and gave Diogenes another jar.

Dionysius the Stoic reports that after the battle of Chaeronea, Diogenes was dragged off to Philip and questioned. Upon being asked who he was, he answered, "I am a scout spying on your insatiable greed." Hearing this, Philip admired him and set him free.[20]

[44] Once when Alexander had sent a letter to Antipater at Athens by the hands of a man called Athlios, Diogenes, who was present, said, "Wretched man from a wretched man by means of a wretched man to a wretched man."[21]

When Perdiccas[22] threatened to put Diogenes to death if he did not come to him, Diogenes said, "That's not surprising since a scorpion or a tarantula would do the same." Instead of that, Diogenes expected the threat to be something like, "If you live apart from me, I will live happily."

His voice resounding, Diogenes often declared that the gods had given men an easy life. But the easy life had become obscure over time by their seeking honey-cakes and perfumes and like things. Accordingly, to a man who had his servant put on his shoes, he said, "You won't be happy until he wipes your nose. And that won't happen until your hands are disabled."

[45] Once Diogenes saw some temple officials leading away someone who had stolen a libation bowl belonging to the treasurers, and he said, "The great thieves are leading away the little thief."

Another time, when he watching a young boy throwing stones at a cross used for executions, he said, "Well done, one day you will hit the target."

When some young boys stood around him and said, "Look out that he doesn't bite us." In response, Diogenes said, "Take courage, boys! A dog doesn't eat beetroot."

To the man who was proud of wearing a lion's skin, his words were, "Stop dishonoring virtue's clothing."

When someone was pronouncing Callisthenes[23] happy and talking about the extravagance he shared at the side of Alexander, Diogenes said, "So then the man is unhappy since he takes his morning and evening meals when Alexander chooses."

[46] When he was in need of money, Diogenes told his friends that he was reclaiming it from his friends, not begging for it.

One day when Diogenes was masturbating in the marketplace, he declared, "I wish I could rub my belly in the same way and relieve my hunger."

When he saw a young man going off to dine with some satraps, he dragged him away to his friends and called on them to watch over and protect him.

When a young man who was beautifully adorned asked him some question, Diogenes said he would not answer until he first pulled up his clothes and showed him whether he was a man or a woman.

A young man was playing kottabos[24] in the baths. Diogenes said to him, "The better you play, the worse it is for you."

During a feast, some people kept throwing bones at him as if he were a dog. Consequently, he urinated on them just like a dog.

[47] Diogenes used to call all rhetoricians and those who spoke for fame "three times human," by which he meant, "three times wretched."

He called an ignorant rich man "a sheep with golden wool."

When he spotted the announcement "For sale" written on the house of a profligate man, Diogenes said, "I knew that after such carousing and feeling sick you would readily vomit up your owner."

To the young man who complained about the number of people who annoyed him by their attentions, he said, "Stop hanging out a sign of invitation."

Addressing a public bath that was very dirty, he said, "Where do people wash after they have bathed here?"

When everyone was criticizing a thick-witted harp player, Diogenes alone praised him. When asked why, he said, "Even though he is as he is, he plays the harp and he doesn't steal."

[48] To the harpist whose audience was always leaving him, he saluted, "Rejoice, rooster!" When the man asked him why he called him that, Diogenes replied, "Because your song makes everyone get up."

A young man was showing himself off, delivering a set speech to a crowd of people, when Diogenes, having filled the front fold of his garment with lupin beans, stood opposite him eating the beans. When the crowd began to look at him instead of the young man, he said that he was astonished that they had stopped looking at the young man in order to look at him.

A very superstitious man said to him, "I will split open your head with one blow." Diogenes replied, "And I will make you tremble with a sneeze from the left."[25]

When Hegesias asked Diogenes to lend him one of his writings, he replied, "You are a vain and thoughtless man, Hegesias. For in the case of figs, you would not choose painted figs but real ones, yet in this case you pass over genuine practice for what is merely written."

[49] When someone criticized him for his exile, Diogenes said, "No, unhappy man. It was because of my exile that I began to pursue philosophy."

And when someone reminded him that the citizens of Sinope had sentenced him to exile, he said, "And I sentenced them to stay there."

Diogenes once saw an Olympic victor tending sheep, and said to him, "My excellent man, you've gone too quickly from Olympia to Nemea."

When he was asked why athletes are so senseless, he said, "Because they are built up of swine and cattle flesh."

Diogenes once begged alms from a statue. When asked why he did this, he said, "To practice being rejected."

Once, when he was begging—as he did at first when he was in need—he said to someone, "If you have already given to anyone else, give to me also. If you have not, begin with me."

[50] When a tyrant asked Diogenes what kind of bronze is best for making a statue, he replied, "The kind from which Harmodius and Aristogiton[26] were made."

When someone asked him how he treated his friends, Diogenes said, "Like bags—as long as they are full he hangs them up, but when they are empty, he throws them away."

A newlywed put this inscription on his house: "Hercules the noble victor, the son of Zeus, dwells here. May nothing evil enter." To which Diogenes added, "After the battle, an alliance."

He said that the love of money is the mother-city or origin of all evils.

Seeing a profligate man eating olives in a tavern, he said, "If you had eaten breakfast in this way, you would not be eating dinner in this way."

[51] Diogenes called good men images of the gods.

He said that love was the business of those with nothing to do.

When someone asked him what was wretched in life, he said, "An impoverished old man."

When he was asked what animal's bite is the worst, he said, "Of wild animals, the sycophant's. Of tame animals, the flatterer's."

Once, when he saw two poorly painted centaurs, Diogenes said, "Which of these is Chiron?"[27]

He compared flattering speech to honey used to gag you.

He called the belly "the Charybdis"[28] of one's livelihood.

Hearing once that Didymon the flute player had been caught in the act of adultery, he said, "His name alone is sufficient to hang him."

When he was asked why gold is pale, he said, "Because gold has so many people plotting against it."[29]

Seeing a woman carried along in a litter, he said, "The cage is not well-matched to the animal."

[52] And seeing once a runaway slave sitting on the edge of a well, he said, "Be careful, young man, that you do not fall in."

Seeing a young man stealing clothes at the public baths, he said, "Is it for unguents or for other clothes?"

Once, when he saw some women hanging from an olive tree, he said, "I wish that every tree bore such fruit."

When he saw a thief stealing clothes, he quoted Homer, saying, "What are you doing, good man? Are you stripping the corpses of the dead?"[30]

When he was asked if he had a young girl or boy, he said, "No." The person further asked, "So then, when you die, who will carry you out?" To which, he replied, "Whoever needs the house."

[53] Seeing a handsome young man sleeping without a guard, he poked him and said in imitation of Homer, "Wake up! May someone not plant a spear in your backside while you're sleeping!"[31]

Similarly, to someone who was buying very expensive delicacies in the marketplace, he said, "You are doomed to a speedy death, my child, from your purchase in the marketplace."

When Plato was conversing about the forms using the terms "tableness" and "cupness," Diogenes said, "I can see a table and a cup, Plato, but I cannot see your tableness and cupness." Plato replied, "That's reasonable enough since you have eyes to look at a cup and a table, but you do not have the mind to see tableness and cupness."[32]

[54] When someone asked Plato, "In your mind, what kind of a man does Diogenes seem to be?" He said, "A Socrates gone mad."

When Diogenes was asked about the right time to marry, he said, "For a young man, not yet. For an old man, nevermore."

When asked what he would take to let a man punch him on the head, he said, "A helmet."

Seeing a young man beautifying himself, he said, "If it is for men, you are unfortunate. If it is for women, you do wrong."

He once saw a young man blushing, and said, "Take courage— such is the color of virtue."

One day after listening to two lawyers argue a case, Diogenes condemned both sides, saying that the one man had stolen but the other had not lost anything.

When he was asked what wine he found pleasant to drink, he replied, "Wine that another man provides."

One man said to him, "The many laugh at you." He replied, "But I am not laughed down."

[55] When someone said that life is bad, Diogenes said, "Not life, but living badly."

When people were advising him to search for his runaway slave, he said, "It would be laughable if Manes is able live without Diogenes, but Diogenes is unable to live without Manes."

When Diogenes was eating a breakfast of olives among which he found a cake, he flung the olives away and declared, "Away, stranger, from the royal road." Another time, "He lashed an olive."[33]

When he was asked what kind of a dog he was, he said, "When hungry, I'm a Maltese lapdog. When I'm full, I'm a Molossus. Most people praise these dogs, though they do not venture out hunting with them because of the hard work involved. So neither can you live with me because of your fear of suffering."

[56] When he was asked if wise men eat cakes, Diogenes said, "They eat everything, just as the rest of mankind."[34]

When he was asked why people give to beggars and not to philosophers, he said, "Because they fear that one day they may become disabled or blind, but they never expect to become a philosopher."

Diogenes was begging from a greedy man who was slow to respond. "Man," he said to him, "I'm begging for nourishment not for burial expenses."

When he was once criticized for having debased the coinage, he said, "That was when I was such as you are now. But as I am now, you will never be."

Another time, when he was reproached for the same thing, he said, "And I used to piss sitting down, but now I don't."[35]

[57] When he came to Myndus and saw large gates but a small city, he said, "Men of Myndus, shut your gates—or your city will get away!"[36]

When he once saw a man who had been caught stealing purple dye, he said, "Carried off by a purple death and by mighty Fate."

When Craterus demanded that he come and visit him, Diogenes said, "I would rather live on a few grains of salt in Athens than enjoy a table full of costly food with Craterus."[37]

Diogenes went up to the orator Anaximenes, who was a fat man, and said, "Give some of your belly to us beggars. You will relieve yourself and benefit us."[38]

And once, when the same man was giving a lecture, Diogenes held up some pickled fish and thus distracted the audience. This annoyed the orator, and Diogenes said, "An obol's worth of pickled fish has ended Anaximenes' lecture."

[58] Being once criticized for eating in the marketplace, Diogenes said, "I did so since it was in the marketplace that I became hungry."

Some authors attribute the following to him. Plato saw him washing greens. So he approached him and quietly said to him, "If you had paid court to Dionysus, you would not now be washing vegetables." Equally quiet, Diogenes replied, "If you had washed vegetables, you wouldn't have paid court to Dionysus."[39]

When someone said, "Most people laugh at you," his reply was, "Yes—and it is likely that asses laugh at them. But even as they pay very little attention to asses, so do I not pay attention to them."

When Diogenes once saw a young man studying philosophy, he said, "Well done, inasmuch as you are leading those who admire bodily things to the beauty of the soul."

[59] When someone marveled at the votive offerings set up in Samothrace, Diogenes said, "There would have been far more if those who were not saved had set them up." Others attribute this remark to Diagoras of Melos.[40]

To a handsome young man who was going to a drinking party, he said, "You will return a worse man." When the young man came back and said, "I went and became no worse," Diogenes remarked, "You're no Chiron; rather, you're Eurytion."[41]

Diogenes was begging from a discontented man. The man said to him, "If you can persuade me." Diogenes replied, "If I could persuade you, I would have persuaded you to hang yourself."

When Diogenes was returning from Lacedaemon to Athens, someone asked him, "Where are you coming from and where are you going?" He replied, "I'm going from the men's part of the house to the women's part."

[60] When he was returning from Olympia, someone asked him whether there was a large crowd. "Yes," he replied, "there was a great crowd but very few men."

He compared profligates to fig trees growing on a cliff. Their fruit is not enjoyed by any man, but is eaten by ravens and vultures.

When Phryne the prostitute set up a golden statue of Aphrodite in Delphi, Diogenes is said to have written on it, "From Greece's lack of self-control."

One day Alexander the Great stood by Diogenes and said, "I am Alexander, the great and mighty king." In response, Diogenes said, "And I am Diogenes, the dog."

When someone asked him what he had done to be called a dog, he said, "I wag my tail for those who give me something, and I bark at those who don't, and I bite worthless men."

[61] Diogenes was gathering figs. When the watchman told him that earlier a man had hanged himself from the same tree, Diogenes said, "Well then, I will clean the tree of its fruits."

When Diogenes saw a man who had been a victor at the Olympian games looking again and again at a prostitute, he said, "Look at that warlike ram who is overpowered by the first girl he happens to meet."

He compared prostitutes to deadly honeyed potions.

Diogenes was eating breakfast in the marketplace, and those standing around gathered around him calling out, "Dog!" In return, he said, "But you are the dogs, standing around and watching me eat breakfast."

When two effeminate men hid themselves from him, he said to them, "Don't be afraid! A dog doesn't nibble on beetroot."

When someone asked him where a boy was from who had become a prostitute, he said, "He is from Tegea."

[62] After seeing an unschooled and rather dull wrestler making rounds as a physician, Diogenes said, "What is this? Do you now want revenge from those who defeated you?"

Seeing the son of a prostitute throwing stones at a crowd of people, he said, "Take care that you do not hit your father!"

When a boy showed him a dagger he had received from a man who admired him, he remarked, "It is a beautiful and noble blade with an ugly and shameful handle."

When some people were praising someone who had giving him something, he said, "Why don't you praise me, the one who was worthy to receive it."

When someone asked Diogenes to return his cloak to him, Diogenes said, "If it was a gift, then it is now mine. If it was a loan, then I'm now using it."

When a child told him that he had gold tucked away in his cloak, Diogenes said, "Yes, that's why you sleep with it under your head."

[63] When someone asked him what result he obtained from philosophy, he said, "If nothing else, this: I am prepared for every turn of fortune."

When someone asked him where he came from, Diogenes said, "I am a citizen of the world."

When a couple was sacrificing to the gods so that a son might be born to them, he said, "Why don't you sacrifice to ensure what kind of man your son will be?"

When someone asked him for a contribution for a common meal, he said to the presiding collector, "Collect from the rest—keep your hands off Hector."

He used to say that courtesans were the queens of kings since they make them do their bidding.

When the Athenians voted to call Alexander, "Dionysus," Diogenes said, "You can make me, 'Sarapis.'"[42]

When someone criticized him for going into impure places, he said, "The sun shines into a bathroom without losing its shine."

[64] Diogenes was eating in a temple when some dirty loaves of bread were set before him. Taking them up and throwing them away, he declared that nothing dirty should enter a temple.

To the man who said to him, "You know nothing, even though you are a philosopher," Diogenes replied, "If I aspire to wisdom, this is being a philosopher."

When someone brought a child to him and declared that his disposition was good and that he had excellent character traits, Diogenes said, "So then, why does he need me?"

Those who express weighty sentiments without doing anything, Diogenes used to compare to a harp. For like them, the harp can neither hear nor feel.

Diogenes was going into a theater while everyone else was going out in the opposite direction. When someone asked him why, he said, "This is what I practice doing every day of my life."

[65] Once when Diogenes saw a young man behaving effeminately, he said, "Are you not ashamed that the plans you have for yourself are worse than what nature has for you? For nature made you a man and you are forcing yourself to be a woman."

Observing a foolish man tuning a harp, he said, "Are you not ashamed to give this piece of wood harmonious sounds while you fail to harmonize your soul with your life?"

To the one who said, "I am unfit for doing philosophy," Diogenes replied, "Why then do you live if you do not care to live happily?"

To the one who looked down on his father in contempt, Diogenes said, "Are you not ashamed to look down on the very one without whom you would not be here to exhibit such pride?"

Noticing a handsome young man chatting in an inappropriate manner, he said, "Are you not ashamed to draw a lead dagger from an ivory scabbard?"

[66] When someone criticized him for drinking in a tavern, Diogenes said, "I also get my hair cut in a barber's shop."

When he was criticized for receiving a cloak from Antipater, he quoted Homer, saying, "The glorious gifts of the gods are not to be thrown away."[43]

A man shook a gate's crossbar at him and said, "Keep watch!" In response, Diogenes struck the man with his staff and said, "Watch out!"

To the man who was earnestly entreating a prostitute, he said, "Why, miserable man, do you want success when it would be better for you to be unsuccessful?"

To the man with perfumed hair, he said, "Be careful that your sweet-smelling head doesn't make for a foul-smelling life."

He said that bad men obey their desires as house slaves obey their masters.

[67] When someone asked him why slaves were called footmen, Diogenes said, "Because they have the feet of men but a soul such as my interrogator has."

Diogenes asked a profligate man for a mina, a rather large sum of money. When the man asked him why he asked others for an obol, or a smaller amount, but he asked him for a mina, Diogenes said, "Because I hope to receive something from others again, but whether I get anything from you again is up to the gods."

When Diogenes was criticized for begging when Plato did not beg, he said, "He does. But when he does, he holds his head down close so that none may hear him."

Seeing an untalented archer, Diogenes sat down next to the target and said, "I'm sitting here so I won't get hit."

He said that the pleasure shared by lovers is their own misfortune.

[68] When someone asked him if death is something bad, he said, "How can it be bad if, when it is present, we do not feel it?"

Alexander stood opposite him and asked, "Are you not afraid of me?" Diogenes replied, "Why? Are you good or bad?" When Alexander said, "Good," Diogenes replied, "Who then would fear something good?"

According to Diogenes, education is a source of moderation for the young, diversion for the old, wealth for the poor, and ornamentation for the wealthy.

When the adulterer Didymon was once treating a girl, Diogenes said to him, "Be careful that in caring for the eye you do not destroy the pupil."

When someone said that his own friends were plotting against him, Diogenes said, "What will you do if you have to treat your friends and your enemies alike?"

[69] When someone asked Diogenes what was the most beautiful thing among men, he said, "Freedom of speech."

Entering a school, Diogenes saw many statues of the Muses but few students. And he said, "Together with the gods, you have many students."

Diogenes was in the habit of doing everything in public—both the business of Demeter and Aphrodite. Accordingly, he used to make the following arguments. "If to eat breakfast is not at all unnatural, then neither is it unnatural to eat breakfast in the marketplace. But it is not unnatural to eat breakfast; therefore, it is not unnatural to eat breakfast in the marketplace. And continually masturbating in public, he said, "I wish I could rub my belly in the same way and stop hunger."

And many other sayings are attributed to him—so many that it would take too long to recount them.

[70] Diogenes declared that there are two kinds of exercise—training of the soul and training of the body. And that the latter exercise gives rise to perceptions that facilitate virtuous deeds. Each practice is incomplete and ineffectual without the other. Good health and strength have to be present with whatever else is important, whether for the soul or for the body. He offered positive proof for how easily we arrive at virtue by means of physical exercise. One can see that craftsmen acquire hand-speed with careful practice. And flute players and athletes excel by means of their own labor. And if these transferred the practices to the soul, then the exercises would not be without profit and incomplete.

[71] Diogenes said that absolutely nothing in life is successful without training, which has the power to conquer anything. Rather than unprofitable, toilsome exercises, men should prefer those which follow nature in order to live happily. Men are unhappy because of a lack of understanding.

According to Diogenes, contempt for pleasure is, if we get used to it, quite pleasant itself. And just as those who are accustomed to living with pleasure feel nauseous when they have to give this life up, so too do those who have practiced the opposite life feel pleasure when they look down on pleasure.

Such were Diogenes' sayings and conversations. And it was evident that he acted accordingly—altering the currency, as it were, or reevaluating human customs, granting nothing at all in this way to human custom and law, but following nature. He declared that his manner of life was the same as that of Heracles. He preferred freedom more than everything else.

[72] Diogenes argued that all things belong to the wise by arguing in such a way that I mentioned before. "All things belong to the gods. The wise are friends of the gods, and friends hold all things in common. Therefore, all things belong to the wise."

And about the law, he argued the following: "It is impossible for society to exist without the law. For without a city, no advantage can be derived from that which is civilized. But the city is civilized, and there is no advantage in the law without a city. Therefore, the law is something civilized."

Diogenes ridiculed noble birth and reputation and all such distinctions, calling them the showy ornaments of vice.

The only true citizenship is that which is a citizenship in the whole cosmos.

Diogenes argued that women should be held in common. He recognized no other marriage than the union of a man who persuades and the woman who is persuaded. For this reason, he also held that sons should be held in common.

[73] Diogenes said there was nothing monstrous in taking anything from a temple or in eating the flesh of any animal—nor was there anything impious about taking and eating even human flesh. He said this was clear from the customs of other nations. Moreover, according to right reason, he said that every element is contained in everything and pervades everything. Meat is in bread. And bread is in vegetables. And all other bodies also, by means of certain invisible passages and particles, find their way into and unite with all substances in the form of vapor. He makes this clear in the *Thyestes*—if the tragedies are really his and not the work of his friend

Philiscus of Aegina or the work of Pasiphon, the son of Lucian, who, according to Favorinus in his *Miscellaneous History*, wrote them after the death of Diogenes.[44]

Diogenes held that we should abandon music, geometry, astronomy, and the like as useless and unnecessary.

[74] He was very successful in replying to arguments, as is clear from what we have already gone over.

NOTES

[1] That is, the school of Euclides (also Euclid) of Megara, the Megarian school. Euclides was a student of Socrates.

[2] The Great Dionysia was the ancient Athenian spring festival during which various forms of drama—tragedies, satyr plays, and comedies—were competitively performed.

[3] Favorinus of Arelate (present-day Arles, France) was a second century AD Roman philosopher and sophist. Aristippus (c. 435-356 BC) was a philosopher from Cyrene (present-day Libya). Originally a companion of Socrates, Aristippus is known as the founder of Cyrenaicism (called such after his home city), a philosophy that promotes pleasure as the chief goal of life.

[4] Sotion of Alexandria was a third and second century BC Peripatetic, who wrote about the succession of philosophers in each school of philosophy.

[5] For Aristippus, see the note above.

[6] Hecaton (Hecato) of Rhodes was a second and first century BC Stoic philosopher and writer, who wrote about various philosophical topics (virtue and the goal of life, for example).

[7] Metrocles of Maroneia, the Cynic philosopher and brother of Hipparchia.

[8] The Pythian games were held at Delphi every four years in honor of the god Apollo.

[9] Demosthenes was a highly regarded fourth century BC Athenian statesman and orator known for his anti-Macedonian stance.

[10] The Ceramicus (*Kerameikos*) was the potter's quarter in Athens, a public space filled with many people, and so one would wish to avoid any embarrassing behavior.

[11] Diocles of Magnesia (second or first century bc) was an ancient historian and writer of biography and summaries. He concentrated on the views, sayings, and lives of the earliest philosophers.

[12] An obol was a silver coin. Six obols were worth one drachma.

[13] Aside from Diogenes Laertius' reference to Zoilus of Perga, nothing more remains from or about him from antiquity.

[14] The son of Apollo, and educated by the centaur Chiron, Asclepius was the Greek god of medicine.

[15] The Craneum was a grove of cypress trees just outside Corinth, as Diogenes Laertius puts it, "at the gates." Alexander is Alexander the Great.

[16] The "mysteries" here refer to the Eleusinian Mysteries, those celebrated at Eleusis (nearby Athens) in honor of the goddess Demeter and her daughter Persephone. For an early narrative of the institution of the Mysteries, see *Homeric Hymn 2 to Demeter* 473 ff.

[17] The Islands of the Blessed were judged a location of immense happiness in the ancient world. For more on the Islands of the Blessed, see Hesiod, *Works and Days* 167-173; Pindar, *Olympian* 2.69-74; Plato, *Gorgias* 523b-c; and Drinking Song (Scolia) 894. For a collection of texts regarding the Islands, see *Happiness: What the Ancient Greeks Thought and Said about Happiness* (Sugar Land: The Classics Cave, 2018).

[18] Theodorus, called "the Atheist," was a fourth and fifth century BC Cyrenaic philosopher—a member of the Cyrenaic school of philosophy founded by Aristippus of Cyrene. For more on Aristippus and Cyrenaicism, see the note above.

[19] Dioxippus of Athens was victor in the pankration at the Olympic games of 336 BC.

[20] Philip II of Macedon defeated the Greeks, led by Thebes and Athens, at the battle of Chaeronea in 338 BC. As noted before, Diogenes may have taken part in the battle.

[21] One meaning of the word or name *athlios* (Athlios) is "wretched" or "struggling, miserable." Antipater (397-319 BC) was a Macedonian general and regent. He served under both Philip II and Alexander the Great. For several letters sent by Diogenes (pseudo-Diogenes) to Antipater, see Twelve, letters 4, 14, and 15.

[22] Perdiccas was a mid-fourth century BC Macedonian king. For several letters sent by Diogenes (pseudo-Diogenes) to Perdiccas, see Twelve, letters 5 and 45.

[23] Callisthenes of Olynthus, a relative of Aristotle, was a fourth century BC Greek historian, who accompanied Alexander the Great's expedition of conquest as its official historian.

[24] Kottabos was an ancient drinking game in which players flicked wine (its sediments) at a target with an amorous or erotic intention or wish in mind.

[25] In Homer, good omens (such as a flying eagle) appear on the right, whereas bad ones appear on the left. Sneezes also serve as a sign from the gods indicating good or ill. We see this in the *Odyssey* when Telemachus sneezes, confirming the impending doom of the suitors.

[26] Harmodius and Aristogiton were responsible for the 514 BC assassination of Hipparchus, and the attempted assassination of his brother, the Athenian tyrant Hippias. Hipparchus and Hippias were the sons of the longtime Athenian tyrant Pisistratus (Peisistratus).

27 The son of Kronos (in the form of a horse) and Philyra, Chiron was a centaur (part human and part horse), who dwelled in a cave on Mount Pelion. Among others, Chiron brought up and educated the heroes Jason and Achilles, and the god Asclepius.

28 For the all-consuming monster Charybdis, see Homer, *Odyssey* 12.103-106: "On one of its lower rocks is a great and wild fig tree, blooming with leaves. Beneath this tree, wondrous Charybdis sucks down the deep, black water. Three times a day she releases the water, sending it up. But three times she sucks it down again—it's a terrible sight! May you not happen to be there when she noisily sucks down the water!"

29 In Homer's *Iliad* and *Odyssey*, "pale" (*chlōros*) is oftentimes given as the color of fear. See, for example, *Iliad* 7.479 and *Odyssey* 24.450.

30 See Homer, *Iliad* 10.343, 387.

31 See, for instance, Homer, *Iliad* 5.40 and 11.447. In Homer, the brave man encounters the enemy face-forward, while the coward runs away offering his back as an easy target.

32 The reference is to Plato's teaching about the forms or ideas, those absolute realities in which all other dependent realities participate—such as Beauty itself and beautiful things, the Good itself and good things.

33 Both lines refer to earlier Greek literature. The first is a play on Euripides, *Phoenician Women* 40, "Stranger [Friend], make way for the tyrant!" (when Laius' charioteer orders Oedipus, Laius' son, out of the roadway). In speaking the line, Diogenes recognizes the tyrannical part that cakes (or really, anything not simple) play relative to simple things, such as olives, which Diogenes calls *xenos* or friend (stranger). The other line points to Homer, *Iliad* 5.366 and 8.45, though in reference to horses that willingly take the charioteer where he wishes to go.

34 Athenaeus of Naucratis reports that once, when Diogenes "was eagerly eating a cake at a feast," he said to someone who questioned him about this that he was merely "eating bread that was made quite well" (*Deipnosophists* 3.80). Elsewhere, Diogenes highlights the fact that philosophers eat everything, "but not," he says, "like everyone else" (see *Gnomologium Vaticanum* 188). So, yes, they eat what everyone eats—just not *like* everyone. And they see through what a thing is. Rather than "cake," it is just "bread" (wheat bread or *artos*).

35 Perhaps a reference to Hesiod's advice: "Do not stand upright facing the sun when you take a piss. . . . A scrupulous man who has a wise heart sits down or goes to the wall of an enclosed court" (*Works and Days* 727, 731-732).

36 Myndus was a city along the western coast of Asia Minor (present-day Turkey).

37 Craterus was a fourth century BC Macedonian general, who helped to rule after Alexander the Great's death.

38 Anaximenes of Lampsacus was a fourth century BC Greek rhetorician.

[39] Dionysus II, the Younger, was the fourth century BC tyrant of the Greek city-state of Syracuse in Sicily.

[40] Samothrace is a Greek island in the Aegean Sea. Diagoras of Melos was a fifth century BC Greek sophist and poet, who had the reputation for atheism.

[41] For Chiron, see the above note. Eurytion was another centaur who did not have the good reputation enjoyed by Chiron.

[42] Dionysus was the Greek god of wine. Serapis was a Greco-Egyptian god associated with the sun, healing, and fertility.

[43] For Antipater, see the note above. Diogenes is paraphrasing the Trojan hero Paris, who, in Homer's *Iliad* 3.64-65, states that "the lovely gifts of golden Aphrodite" should not "be thrown away."

[44] Pasiphon was a third century BC writer. For Favorinus, see the note above.

MONIMUS, ONESICRITUS & OTHERS
SOME OF DIOGENES' STUDENTS

IN BRIEF: *Diogenes Laertius gives some details about a few of Diogenes of Sinope's notable followers. Among them are Monimus, a slave who pretended madness in order to follow Diogenes, and Onesicritus, who joined Alexander (the Great) on his expedition and wrote about him. Others are Menander, Hegesias, and Philiscus.*

MONIMUS OF SYRACUSE was Diogenes' student. According to Sosicrates,[1] Monimus was the house slave of a certain Corinthian banker. Xeniades, the man who bought Diogenes, frequently visited this man and extolled Diogenes' virtue in word and deed. He did this so much, in fact, that he excited in Monimus a passionate admiration for Diogenes so that he immediately feigned madness, flinging away from the banker's table all the small coins and other money. He did this until his master finally dismissed him. And Monimus went directly to Diogenes and became his student. He also followed Crates the Cynic, devoting himself to the same pursuits. Seeing this behavior, he seemed even more mad to his master.

[83] Monimus came to be a notable man, so much so that he is even mentioned by the comic poet Menander.[2] In one of his plays, *The Groom*, he says the following:

There was a man, Philo, whose name was Monimus. He was a wise man, but not exactly famous.

A. The one who carried the leather bag?

B. Not just one bag but three. He never spoke a single word, so help me Zeus, to match the saying, "Know yourself," or any other such sayings.

Far beyond these he went, your dusty mendicant, saying that all opinion is vanity.

Monimus was a man of such gravity that he thought very little of reputation and was eager for the truth.

Aside from some playful stuff mixed with a few covert serious points, he wrote two books . . . *On Impulses* and an *Exhortation to Philosophy*.

Onesicritus. [84] Some report that Onesicritus was from Aegina. But Demetrius of Magnesia[3] says that he was a native of Astypalaea. He was also one of the notable students of Diogenes.

His career seems to have resembled that of Xenophon since Xenophon joined the expedition of Cyrus and Onesicritus that of Alexander. And Xenophon wrote the *Education of Cyrus*, while he wrote about how Alexander was educated.[4] The one was an encomium of Cyrus; the other of Alexander—except the imitator fell short of the model.

Among the other students of Diogenes, there was Menander, nicknamed Oakwood (*Drymus*), who was a great admirer of Homer. There was also Hegesias of Sinope, nicknamed "Dog Collar" (*Kloios*). And there was Philiscus of Aegina, mentioned above.

NOTES

[1] Sosicrates was a second century BC writer who concentrated on the various schools of philosophy, their founders, and the founders' successors.
[2] Enormously popular in the ancient world, Menander (c. 342-291 BC) was a comedic playwright from Athens and the leading proponent of the New Comedy. He is known for one complete play of some one hundred that remain— *The Grouch* (or *Dyskolos*).
[3] Demetrius of Magnesia was a first century BC biographer.
[4] Xenophon (c. 430-354 BC) was an Athenian historian and statesman. He was slightly younger than Antisthenes. Aside from the *Anabasis*, or *The Expedition Up* (the account of the harrowing escape of the Ten Thousand, a Greek mercenary force, after the battle of Cunaxa), Xenophon is known for a number of writings centered on Socrates. Xenophon also wrote—as Diogenes Laertius notes—the *Cyropaedia* or the *Education of Cyrus*. As mentioned in the Introduction, Cyrus was an exemplar to the Cynics, given his penchant for hard work.

CRATES
LIFE, ANECDOTES & SAYINGS

IN BRIEF: *Diogenes Laertius reports that Crates was a relatively wealthy Theban man who gave up all his wealth in order to live the simple life of a Cynic. There are several stories relating how this remarkable change of life occurred and who it was he followed, whether Bryson the Achaean or Diogenes of Sinope. Crates practiced endurance by seeking hardship, flouting convention, and securing an independent life free from the approval of others. He assisted others by admonishing them.*

CRATES, THE SON of Ascondas, was a Theban. He was one of the most notable Cynic students. Hippobotus,[1] however, reports that he was the student of Bryson the Achaean rather than Diogenes. . . . [86] Crates was nicknamed the "Door-opener" because he was in the habit of entering every house in order to admonish the inhabitants.

Here's an example of one of his compositions:

How much I have learned and considered,
the noble lessons taught me by the Muses.
But much wealth is prey to vanity.

The following line tells us what he gained from philosophy: "A measure of lupin beans and no one to worry about."

This is also given as his: "Hunger puts a stop to sexual desire. And if not hunger, then time. And if both these fail, then a noose."

[87] Crates flourished in the one hundred thirteenth Olympiad.

According to Antisthenes in his *Successions*, Crates was led to the Cynic philosophy when he was watching a certain tragedy and

saw Telephus in an altogether wretched state, carrying a little bas-
ket. Consequently, he converted his property into money—for he
belonged to a distinguished family. And having collected about
two hundred talents, he distributed the sum among the citizens.

Crates devoted himself to philosophy with such strength that
even the comic poet Philemon mentions him. He says, at any rate,
"To be like Crates, he would wear a cloak thick with hair during the
summer and a tattered one during the winter."

But Diocles[2] reports how Diogenes persuaded Crates to give up
his property and sheep, and throw his money into the sea.

[88] He further reports that Alexander stayed in his house just
as Philip had once stayed in Hipparchia's house.[3] Crates frequently
used his staff to drive away some of the family members who tried
to turn him away from his purpose. Still, his resolution remained
unshaken.

Demetrius of Magnesia[4] tells a story that Crates deposited his
money with a banker, making the following agreement with him. If
his sons became ordinary people, then he was to give the money to
them. But if they became philosophers, then he was to apportion it
among the people, since his sons would need nothing if they were
philosophers.

Eratosthenes[5] tells us that Crates had a boy named Pasicles with
Hipparchia. I'll say more about her in a moment. When Pasicles had
grown up, Crates took him to a brothel and told him that's how his
own father had taken on a lover.

[89] Adulterous relationships, he said, belong to the realm of tragedy. They end with exile and murder. That said, relationships with
prostitutes belong to the realm of comedy. From extravagance and
drunkenness they end in madness. . . .

Crates used to say that it was impossible to find a flawless person, just as pomegranates always have one rotten seed.

When Crates provoked Nicodromus the harp player, Nicodromus struck him on the face. So then, he inscribed on his forehead,
"Nicodromus did this."

[90] Crates used to revile prostitutes on purpose in order to practice getting used to the profanity they would give him in return.

When Demetrius of Phalerum[6] sent him loaves of bread and some wine, Crates reproached him, saying, "If only the springs delivered bread as well as water." It was clear from this remark that Crates was a water drinker.

When certain Athenian magistrates penalized him for clothing himself with fine linen, Crates said, "I'll show you that Theophrastus[7] also wears fine linen." They didn't believe him, so Crates led them to a barber's shop and showed them Theophrastus being shaved.

At Thebes, Crates was once flogged by the master of the gymnasium. Another version of the story is that he was flogged by Euthycrates at Corinth. And being dragged by his feet, he called out, as if he could care less, "Seized by the foot and dragged over heaven's high threshold."

[91] Diocles,[8] however, says that he was dragged in this manner by Menedemus of Eretria.[9] Since Menedemus was handsome and was useful, as it were, to Asclepiades the Phliasian, Crates grabbed him by the thighs and said, "Is Asclepiades in here?" Unable to endure this abuse, Menedemus dragged Crates by the feet and the latter said what was quoted a moment ago.

In his *Anecdotes and Sayings*, Zeno of Citium[10] relates that, without even really thinking about it, Crates stitched a sheepskin inside his tattered cloak.

Crates was ugly in his appearance, and so people laughed at him when he was exercising. When he raised his hands, he was in the habit of saying, "Take courage, Crates, on behalf of your eyes and the rest of your body. [92] You will see these men, the ones who are laughing at you, shriveled up by disease, acknowledging your own happiness and blaming themselves for laziness."

He used to say that we should study philosophy until generals appear the same as donkey-drivers.

He used to say that those who live with flatterers are as helpless as young cows among wolves, for neither these nor the others have anyone fitting to assist them. Rather, there are only those who plot against them.

Sensing that he was dying, Crates sung to himself, saying, "You are marching off to the house of Hades, dear hunchback, stooped over by old age." He said this because time had bent him over.

[93] When Alexander inquired whether he wished to see his homeland rebuilt, Crates said, "Why should it be rebuilt? Perhaps another Alexander will come and raise it to the ground again."

He went on to declare that obscurity and poverty were his own homeland, which Fortune could never take captive. Moreover, Diogenes was his fellow-citizen, and man who was not given over to plotting inspired by envy.

Menander[11] mentions Crates in the *Twin Sisters* in the following lines:

> Wearing a tattered cloak, you will go out with me, as once the Cynic Crates went out with his wife. His daughter, too, as he himself said, he gave away for a thirty day trial.

[. . .]

[98] There still exists a volume of Crates' letters, in which he wrote his best philosophy in a style that sometimes resembles that of Plato.

He has also written tragedies that are characterized by a very lofty philosophy, such as the following line:

> My fatherland has neither defensive tower nor roof, but it is as wide as the whole earth, its buildings and house ready and near at hand for us to dwell in.

Crates died when he was old and was buried in Boeotia.

[. . .]

[93] But now let's move on to Crates' own students.

NOTES

[1] Hippobotus was a late third to early second century BC historian of philosophy.

[2] Diocles of Magnesia (second or first century BC) was an ancient historian and writer of biography and summaries. He concentrated on the views, sayings, and lives of the earliest philosophers.

³ Alexander the Great of Macedon and his father, Philip II.

⁴ Demetrius of Magnesia was a first century BC biographer.

⁵ The third century BC director of the library at Alexandria, Eratosthenes of Cyrene carried out research in many areas of study. He is most famous for measuring the circumference of the earth.

⁶ Demetrius of Phalerum was a fourth and third century BC Athenian orator, statesman, and philosopher. The Macedonian general Cassander appointed him the governor of Athens in 317.

⁷ Likely Theophrastus, the fourth century BC successor of Aristotle in the Peripatetic school of philosophy.

⁸ For Diocles of Magnesia, see the note above.

⁹ Menedemus of Eretria was the fourth and third century BC Greek philosopher who founded the Eretrian school of philosophy. Asclepiades the Phliasian (of Phlius) was Menedemus' friend and participated in the Eretrian school.

¹⁰ Zeno of Citium (c. 334-262 BC) initially practiced philosophy, or a life of radical virtue, with the Cynic Crates of Thebes. He went on to found his own school, Stoicism, named after a covered colonnade (*stoa*) in Athens. Zeno taught that all of reality consists of matter and mind, or divine reason, which makes, orders, and governs that which is natural. To live well is to live naturally, which is to say rationally or virtuously.

¹¹ Enormously popular in the ancient world, Menander (c. 342-291 BC) was a comedic playwright from Athens and the leading proponent of the New Comedy. He is known for one complete play of some one hundred that remain—*The Grouch* (or *Dyskolos*).

METROCLES, HIPPARCHIA & OTHERS
ANECDOTES & SAYINGS

IN BRIEF: *Diogenes Laertius offers an account of Metrocles, who was one of Crates' students. He recounts how Crates helped him overcome an embarrassing situation, as well as a few other details of his life, sayings, and death. As for Hipparchia, the sister of Metrocles, Diogenes Laertius tells the story about how she fell in love with Crates' teachings and way of life and eventually married him in order to follow the Cynic path with him. Finally, Diogenes Laertius reports the names of other Cynic philosophers.*

METROCLES OF MARONEIA, the brother of Hipparchia, was at first the student of Theophrastus the Peripatetic.[1] That Theophrastus weakened him is illustrated by the following story:

One day, in the midst of others, he farted when he was practicing a speech. He was so despondent because of what he had done that he shut himself up in his house, fully intending to starve himself to death. When Crates learned about this and was summoned, he visited Metrocles. First, he ate a bowl of lupin beans—*on purpose*. Then he tried to persuade Metrocles that he had done nothing bad. For it would have been a miracle if he had not, following nature, relieved himself of such a blast of wind. Finally, when Crates himself farted, he renewed Metrocles' strength, encouraging him by means of similar actions. . . .

[95] Metrocles divided things in the following manner: those things that are obtained with money, such as a house, and those things that are obtained with time and care, such as an education. He said that wealth is harmful if it was not used in a worthwhile manner.

Metrocles died when he strangled himself. He was an old man.

Theombrotus and Cleomenes were his students.

Demetrius of Alexandria was Theombrotus' student.

Timarchus of Alexandria and Echecles of Ephesus were Cleomenes' students—that said, Echecles also listened to Theombrotus' lectures. Menedemus, whom we will address in a moment, also listened to his lectures. Moreover, Menippus of Sinope was also renowned among them.

HIPPARCHIA

[96] Hipparchia, the sister of Metrocles, was also captured by the teachings of the Cynics. They were both from Maroneia. Hipparchia fell in love with the teachings and life of Crates—so much so that she would not pay attention to any of her suitors, nor to their wealth, nor to their nobility of birth, nor to their beauty. No, Crates was everything to her. She would even threaten her parents with suicide if she were not given in marriage to him. Accordingly, they called on Crates to talk her out of it. He did all he could. But when he failed to persuade her, he got up, took off his clothes right in front of her, and said, "This is the man you hope to marry. Here are his possessions. Deliberate and make your choice with these facts in mind since you will not be my partner unless you share in my pursuits."

[97] The girl made her choice. She adopted his manner of dressing and went around with him as her husband. She appeared with him in public, and when he dined with others, she went out with him.

Accordingly, Hipparchia went to a drinking party given at Lysimachus' house. It was there that she embarrassed Theodorus, nicknamed "the Atheist,"[2] with the following sophism:

> Any action that would not be called wrong if done by Theodorus would not be called wrong if done by Hipparchia.
> Now, Theodorus does no wrong when he strikes himself.
> Therefore, neither does Hipparchia do wrong when she strikes Theodorus.

The man had no reply for her argument. Rather, he pulled her cloak up. Even so, Hipparchia was neither panic stricken nor thrown into confusion as a woman would usually be.

[98] And when Theodorus quoted Euripides to her, saying, "Is this the woman who has abandoned the loom and the weaver's shuttle?"[3] She said, "I, Theodorus, am that woman. But do you think that I have been ill-advised regarding my affairs if, instead of spending more time on the loom, I have used it for education?"

These anecdotes and countless others are told about this female philosopher.

OTHER CYNIC PHILOSOPHERS

[99] Menippus, who was by descent a Phoenician, was also a Cynic. He was a slave, as Achaicus declares in his *Ethics*. Diocles[4] further informs us that his master was a man named Baton, who was a citizen of Pontus.

[102] There was also Menedemus, though he was originally the student of the *Epicurean* Colotes of Lampsacus.

NOTES

[1] Theophrastus of Eresos was a fourth and early third century BC philosopher, researcher, and writer. He was Aristotle's successor as the head of the Peripatetic school. Diogenes Laertius (*Lives* 5.43) reports that he wrote a compendium of the writings of Diogenes.

[2] Theodorus, called "the Atheist," was a fourth and fifth century BC Cyrenaic philosopher—a member of the Cyrenaic school of philosophy founded by Aristippus of Cyrene.

[3] See Euripides, *Bacchae* 1236.

[4] Diocles of Magnesia (second or first century BC) was an ancient historian and writer of biography and summaries. He concentrated on the views, sayings, and lives of the earliest philosophers.

PART 2

OTHER WRITINGS
ABOUT THE CYNICS & CYNICISM

ANTISTHENES' PRIDE

FROM XENOPHON'S *SYMPOSIUM*[1]

IN BRIEF: *Prodded by Socrates, Antisthenes discusses the soul goods he possesses and the simple life he leads. He always has enough—of food, drink, clothing, and sexual satisfaction. His enjoyment comes from withdrawing wealth from his soul. Thanks to his simple life, he trusts he will always be able to provide himself with whatever he requires. He's honest and generous, willing to share his soul wealth with anyone. Most importantly, he has ample leisure time to be with Socrates.*

SOCRATES SAID, "AND you, Antisthenes, what do pride yourself on?"

"I pride myself on wealth," he declared.

[...]

[34] "Okay, then," Socrates went on, "given the little wealth that you have, tell us how you pride yourself on wealth."

"I do because I believe that a man's wealth or lack of wealth is not a matter of household goods but of soul goods. [35] I observe many private citizens who think of themselves as poor even though they have a pile of money and possessions. For this reason they give themselves over to any toil or danger in order to increase their wealth. And I know of brothers who have an equal share of their inheritance. One of them has plenty, more than enough to meet expenses, while the other is in utter want. [36] And I've observed some tyrants who are so hungry for wealth that they are willing to do terrible things compared with those who are entirely poor. Because they lack things, some people snatch things, others break in and take things, and others follow the slave trade. But there are some tyrants who destroy whole families, kill men by the crowd, and oftentimes enslave even entire cities, all for the sake of money. [37] I deeply pity these men for this oppressive disease. They are like the man who has plenty to eat but can't satisfy himself even though he keeps on eating.

"As for me, my possessions are so great that I can hardly find them myself. I have enough to eat so that I'm not hungry and enough to drink so that I'm not thirsty. And I have enough clothing so that when I'm outside, I'm no colder than Callias is, a man who is remarkably wealthy. [38] And when I go into a house, I look on the walls as exceedingly warm tunics and the roofs as exceptionally thick mantles. And the bedding that I own is so satisfactory that it is actually a hard task to wake me up in the morning. If my body ever stands in need of satisfying the urges of Aphrodite, I am quite satisfied with whomever is nearby. And those I go to are quite fond of me since no one else is willing to be with them.

[39] "All these things seem so pleasant to me that I would never pray for greater pleasure in engaging in any one of them. No, I'd rather pray for less. I would because I regard some of them as being more pleasurable than they are beneficial.

[40] "But the most valuable part of my wealth I count as this, that even if someone robbed me of what I now possess, I see no occupation so humble that it would not furnish me with adequate provisions. [41] For whenever I wish to enjoy myself, I do not purchase highly prized items in the marketplace since they are very expensive, but I withdraw wealth from my soul. And this makes a difference in producing enjoyment—whether I have something only when I truly want it, or when I have something extravagant, like this fine Thasian wine that fortune has presented to me, and I am drinking without the promptings of thirst.

[42] "Yes—and it is natural that those whose eyes are set on frugality are more honest than those whose eyes are fixed on money-making. For those who are most contented with what they have are least likely to covet what belongs to others.

[43] "And it is worth noting that wealth of this kind also makes people generous. My friend Socrates here and I are examples. For

Socrates, from whom I acquired this wealth of mine, did not come to my relief limiting it by number and weight, but he gave me all that I could carry. And as for me, I am now stingy with no one; rather, I openly display my abundance to all my friends and share my soul wealth with anyone who desires it.

[44] "But—most exquisite possession of all!—you observe that I always have leisure, with the result that I can go and see whatever is worth seeing, and hear whatever is worth hearing, and—what I prize the most—I pass the whole day, untroubled by business, in Socrates' company. Like me, he does not bestow his admiration on those who count the most gold, but he spends his time with those who are pleasing to him."

NOTES

[1] The translation that follows is a modified version of O.J. Todd's translation of Xenophon's *Symposium* (1923).

THE DISCOURSES
OF TELES THE CYNIC[1]

IN BRIEF: *Teles' first discourse argues that it is better to actually possess good things and be good than merely to appear to have and be them. The second challenges us to perform the role Fortune has given us well and to be content with our circumstances rather than blaming everything on them. Poverty is no bad thing. We should prepare ourselves for whatever may come our way. The third contends that exile is not truly something bad. The fourth discourses (a and b) argue against the notion that wealth somehow relieves a man of insatiable desire and other negative qualities. Only simplicity will do so, freeing one from scarcity. Moreover, those who have relatively little can often spend more time doing philosophy than those who are rich. The fifth points out that there is far more pain in life than pleasure; thus, pleasure cannot be the goal of life. Six challenges us to make use of circumstances well, playing the part that Fortune assigns us. Finally, seven asserts that the one who is free from passion is the happy one. Such a one doesn't feel grief over the loss of loved ones.*

1. ON APPEARING AND BEING

SOME PEOPLE SAY that appearing to be just is better than actually being just. And yet appearing to be good is not better than actually being good—is it?

Of course not.

Tell me, then, do men play their parts well because they appear to be good actors or because they actually are good?

Because they actually are.

And do men play the lyre well because they appear to be good lyre players or because they actually are good?

Because they actually are.

And, generally, do men do well in all other things because they appear to be good or because they actually are good?

Because they actually are.

Accordingly, living well is better than not living well. Being good, then, is better than appearing good, for the just man is good — not the man who appears just.

And what about the other things that human beings imagine goods?[2] Would you rather . . . possess them or appear to possess them? For instance, would you prefer to see or to appear to see? [4] To be healthy or to appear so? To be strong or to appear so? To be well-off and have friends or to appear so? Again, regarding the goods of the soul, would you prefer to understand and be wise or to appear so? To be without pain and sorrow or to appear so? To be confident, to be without fear, to be courageous or to appear so? Yet when it comes to justice, would you rather appear to be just rather than actually being just?

Well, I would rather appear to be courageous than to actually be courageous.

But is not the courageous man also the one who is actually fearless and free from any pain and grief? Why do you wish to appear courageous?

Because people will honor me.

They will! But they will also position you as the right-hand man in battle. And they will call on you to engage in single combat. . . . Then what do you imagine will happen since you are actually a coward and in danger? . . .

And now, even if you speak the truth, you will not be believed. . . . See how much you will receive by appearing to be courageous and capable of endurance? But you pretend and hide the truth just like politicians do.[3]

2. ON SELF-SUFFICIENCY

[5] Just as a good actor must contend well for the victory with the

mask and role that the playwright gives him, so also must a good man compete with the one that Fortune gives him. For Bion says that Fortune, like a playwright, sometimes gives the mask and role of a first-speaker and sometimes that of a second-speaker.[4] And sometimes a king, and sometimes a wandering beggar. So, when you are a second-speaker, do not wish for the mask and role of a first-speaker. [6] Otherwise, you will do something unsuitable.

[6] *Bion says that we may rule or be ruled well; lead many or only one; be well-off and give freely, or poor and receive things boldly. We may make good use of many things or just a few. The key is moderation and a lack of vanity.*

[7] And Poverty would say to the man who brought a charge against her, "Why do you battle me? Do I rob you of anything good? I don't, do I? Not of moderation. Not of justice. Not of courage—do I? Are you lacking anything necessary for life? Are not the roads full of vegetables and the springs full of water? Do I not furnish you with as many beds as the earth does? As well as leaves for bedding? Or is it not possible to delight in me? Or don't you see old women eating cheap barley cakes and talking away? Or don't I provide you with hunger—a season that costs nothing and is not effeminate? Or is it not the case that a hungry person most enjoys eating and least misses the seasoning?—and that the thirsty person most enjoys drinking and least awaits the drink that is not by his side? [8] Or is anyone hungry for a sweet cake and thirsty for wine from Chios? Instead, don't human beings seek these things thanks to extravagance and lust? Or don't I furnish you with housing that is a gift? In winter there are the baths, in summer the holy places. 'For what kind of summer dwelling place do you have,' Diogenes says, 'such as I have in the Parthenon, sweet smelling and very costly?'"

If Poverty said these things to you, how would you respond? As for me, I suppose I would fall silent.

And yet we blame everything else more than we do our own irritability and unhappiness. We blame old age, poverty, chance encounters, the day, the season, the place. . . . [9] Many mad men lay the blame on circumstances rather than on themselves. Bion puts it this way: just as when you catch a wild animal, you may be bitten, so too if you take hold of a snake by the middle, you'll be bitten, but if you do so by the throat, then nothing will happen. It's the same with circumstances, he says. If you take them one way, you may experience distress. Yet if you take them in the same way as Socrates, you will not suffer. But if in any other way, then you will feel distress, not because of circumstances but because of your own character and your own false views.

[10] Accordingly, one should not attempt to change circumstances; rather, one should get ready for them as they are. Do this as sailors do. They don't try to change the winds and the sea. Instead, they ready themselves so that they are able to respond to these things. The wind is still, the sea is calm? Fine—they move along by means of the oars. The wind is behind the ship? They raise the sails. The wind is blowing against the ship? They lower them and let go.

And you? Take a look at your present circumstances and do what is necessary. You have become old—then do not seek the things of a young person. Again, you have become weak—then do not seek to take on the loads of a strong person. . . . [11] Again, you have become a person without means—then do not seek the way of life of a rich man. Rather, as you respond to the air temperature (you loosen your garments in fair weather and tighten them up in the cold), do so as well relative to the means of living (loosen up with abundance and tighten up with scarcity).

We are not able to be content with our present circumstances when we devote ourselves excessively to luxury and when we judge work a misfortune and death the worst of evils. If you become someone who looks down on pleasure, and someone who doesn't set himself against hard work, and someone who considers equal both good and bad reputation, and someone who doesn't fear death, then it will be possible for you to do whatever you wish without suffering distress. [12] Accordingly, as I say, I do not see how circumstances themselves involve anything troublesome—neither old age nor poverty nor if one is foreign.

[12-13] *We know that circumstances are not troublesome in themselves given the different human responses, positive and negative, to the same circumstances. Teles repeats the observation of Antisthenes found in Xenophon, that two brothers with the same wealth will respond to it in different ways—one distressed and one content. And he offers the example of Diogenes, who showed that a city—Athens in this case—is either very expensive or cheap depending on how one approaches living in it.*

[13] It is not the city that is cheap or very expensive; rather, if one lives one way it is very expensive, and if one lives another way it is cheap. So it is with circumstances. If someone makes use of them in one way, they appear favorable and easy. But if in another way, unmanageable, annoying. . . .

[14] *How is poverty annoying or painful?* Did not Crates and Diogenes easily carry on when they gave up arrogance and became beggars and developed the ability to make use of a cheap and simple way of life.

[14-15] *We tend to respond to things—to old age, wealth, poverty—according to our character. We should willingly leave life when nature calls on us to leave, as though leaving a festal gathering or a drinking party.*

[16] As the good actor performs the prologue well, and the middle part well, and the conclusion well, so also does the good man live the first part of life well, and the middle part well, and the end well.

[16-20] *In the end, Teles admonishes, we should leave life aside just as we do an old cloak. This is how Socrates behaved when he was given the hemlock. He drank it boldly, cheerfully, and contentedly. Moreover, he put up with his difficult wife. She was no more of a bother to him than a wild goose might be—as was demonstrated by his dinner engagements with Alcibiades that were upset on one occasion by his wife and on another by a bird.*

3. ON EXILE

[21-25] *Exile is not bad if we think of it in terms of skills. One's flute*

playing, for example, or ability to act or give counsel is not any worse for being in a foreign land.

Stilpon (of Megara)[5] himself denies that exile robs us of any goods. What soul goods go missing? Courage, justice, or any other virtue? No. And bodily goods? Health, strength, sharp eyesight or hearing? No. What about externals? Again, no.

But some say that exiles don't rule. Nor do they have freedom of speech. Yes, but some are given power. Think of Lycinus, Hippomedon the Spartan, and the Athenians Chremonides and Glaucon.[6] But exiles don't rule in their own homeland. Yes, but consider women and young boys and other young men. None of them rule, and yet they are not annoyed. Not only that but both rulers and private individuals rule—it is just that the number of those they rule are different. Besides, there is use in both.

But you won't be able to enter your own homeland. Yes, but even now I can't go everywhere—into the Thesmophorion[7] or the gymnasium (sometimes) or my own homeland. And women cannot go into the temple of Enyalius[8] and other places.

[25] Regardless, just as I am able to transfer from one ship to another and have a comparably good voyage, so I am able to move from one city to another and be equally happy. *The only problem is dwelling with worthless men.*

But isn't it crazy to be exiled by inferiors? [26-32] *Yes, but it is better than by noble or just men. And the blame belongs to those who vote for these men. And isn't it better to know what your homeland is really like?*

But it seems a great thing to be in the land of one's birth and upbringing? Yes, but would you always stay in your house if it is falling down? Or in a small boat if a larger one were available?

But many reproach metics, those who come from another city. Yes, and yet you admire Cadmus and Heracles,[9] who both settled in a city not their own. For the Spartans, it is not the citizenship that matters but whether or not one shares in their way of life.

But what if it is not possible to be buried in one's own land? Really, though, what difference is there? The road to Hades is the same regardless. And why should you even care if you're not buried. "The struggle over burial," says Bion, "has made many tragedies." *The land of your fathers or a foreign land; buried or not; burned by fire or eaten by a dog or carrion-crows, above ground or by worms below—what's the difference or big deal? Or if you have your eyelids closed?* Does someone close the eyelids of those who die at sea or in battle? *Rather, this seems childish.*

4A. A COMPARISON OF POVERTY AND WEALTH

[33] It seems to me that the acquisition of wealth releases one from scarcity and need.

And how is that? Don't you see that some people have acquired much—as appearances go, anyway—and yet they don't use it because of stinginess and meanness.

[33-35] *Teles cites the examples of Priam, Laertes, and Tantalus.*[10] *The point: though they long for things, many wealthy individuals do not experience their wealth thanks to stinginess and a certain failure to hope. Such a man may enjoy himself at another man's house but not his own.*

[35] The ancients put it well: if a thing doesn't free a man from insatiate desire and stinginess and false pretension, then neither does it free him from need and scarcity. [36] But no amount of wealth frees a man from insatiate desire and stinginess and false pretension since it does not change his character or his habits. For instance, not even poverty will change the character of those who are moderate if they become poor after being rich. It seems to me someone could sooner say that the acquisition of wealth changes skin color, body size, or appearance than it does character. But so long as this man is insatiable, stingy, pretentious, and wretched, he will experience need and scarcity.

[37-38] *To possess wealth without the ability to use it is the same as not having it. So it is with bankers and the daughters of Phorcys.*[11] *Or to have food without the ability to taste it.*

[38] Therefore, in response to the man who asked, "What will it mean for me to do philosophy?" Crates said, "You will easily be able to open your bag and freely give from it rather than, as now,

writhing and irresolute and shaking as men do with disabled hands. . . . If you notice that your bag is empty, you will not suffer distress. . . . You will live satisfied with what you have, neither desiring what is absent nor [39] being displeased with whatever comes your way.

[39-40] *Do not attempt to cure scarcity and need with wealth. Doing so, says Bion, is like trying to cure a man who has dropsy, or edema, with whole rivers of water. This will never relieve the thirst he experiences due to the dropsy. Similarly, giving a man wealth will never relieve him of his yearning as long as he's insatiable and wants to be popular and is superstitious. So, if you want to cure your son, send him not to gain power or wealth with the ruler Ptolemy or other rulers, but to study philosophy with Crates and the other Cynics. The school is important.*

Even the Cynic Metrocles said that, when he studied at certain schools, he felt like he had to have the right shoes, clothes, servants, house, food, wine, and entertainment. [41] But when he switched over to Crates, there was none of these things. Rather, he became simple in his character and habits, satisfied with a tattered cloak and barley bread and vegetables, neither yearning after his earlier way of life nor vexed by the present. *He learned to make due with a doubled-over cloak, previously used bathing oil, simple food, and public shelters. His own satisfaction meant he had no need for servants.*

[42] *Such is not the case for the pretentious, superstitious, popularity-seeking, and insatiable—even the one with much wealth.* As long as this man remains the same, he is neither satisfied nor content. Rather, he will keep his desires and appetites for big things like this. As a result, he will experience need and scarcity.

[42-44] *He'll never desire to be the age he is or who he is. When old, he wants to be young; when young, old. If a slave, he wants to be free. But even freedom won't be enough. He'll need a slave or two, a house, some land, and Athenian citizenship. And more. He'll want to rule, to be a king, to be Alexander himself! He'll want to become immortal! And if it were possible, Zeus himself! How is this not the same as being in a condition of perpetual need? What amount of wealth releases one from these desires? Kings never have enough. They'd be better off stepping down or living*

simply, frugally. As Crates said, the leather bag has great power — that of the lupine bean and anxiety about nothing. It is also a great thing to forget about the need to flatter and be flattered.

4B. A COMPARISON OF POVERTY AND WEALTH

[45] It is not accurate to say that poverty hinders one from doing philosophy whereas wealth is useful. For how many men do you suppose have been kept from the leisure necessary for philosophy thanks to an abundance of wealth as compared to those lacking wealth?

[45-48] *In contrast to wealthy men who are always busy thanks to all they have, poor beggars are much more likely to do philosophy. The truth is those in need are forced to practice endurance, whereas those who are rich don't have to. Such men have no interest in hard work or philosophical inquiry; rather, their wish is for every pleasure.*

According to Zeno (of Citium),[12] *Crates of Thebes told a shoemaker that he had more of an opportunity to practice philosophy than Themison, the Cyprian king, because the shoemaker could listen to a reading about philosophy while stitching shoes whereas the king could hardly do this despite his great riches. So it is that the simple man, and even the household slave, is better off than the free and rich man who has to worry about many things (as he does, for example, during a war).*

As for honor, sometimes even the poor are honored more than the rich. Consider the very poor Athenian man Aristeides, who was given great financial responsibility since he was just, versus the very rich man Callias, whom the Athenians appointed his aid. Or think about the highly honored Spartan Lysander, who didn't even have enough to provide a dowry for his daughters. There are many more examples, of course, of those who are poor yet held in great honor.

5. ON PLEASURE NOT BEING THE GOAL OF LIFE

[49] If the happy life must be measured by the yardstick of excessive pleasure, then no one, says Crates, will be judged happy. Rather, if

anyone wishes to weigh every stage in the whole of life, he will discover that there is a far greater quantity of pain and suffering.[13]

[49-51] *For one, we're asleep half the time. As for the stages of life, we move through the stages of childhood dissatisfied with one thing or another and controlled and even beaten by various teachers. As we move on, we fear various men and have to engage in unpleasant duties, always busy, paying for one thing or another. The older we get, the younger we wish to be. The old man wants to be a youth again, though he's treated more like a very young child.*

[51] So then, I do not see how someone will live a happy life if he really must measure it by an excess of pleasure.

6. ON CIRCUMSTANCES

[52] Fortune, as though a playwright, makes up roles of every kind: a shipwrecked man, a beggar, an exile, a well-regarded man, and one disreputable. A good man should, therefore, contend well with whatever role that Fortune gives him. You have become shipwrecked—play the shipwreck well. From being well-off you have become poor—play the poor man well. . . . Be satisfied with any clothing, food, and service that happen to come along, as was Laertes . . . [53] For these things are enough for living suitably and healthily, unless someone wishes to live luxuriously. *But luxury is not necessarily beneficial.*

Regardless, we should make use of circumstances as sailors make use of the wind and other circumstances. It's the same when there's a military campaign—the man who has a horse contends as a horseman, the man with arms struggles as a hoplite, [54] and the man without armor fights as one bare of armor. And as when the enemy press upon you, hurling their weapons, you retreat to camp since you are fighting bare of armor, so when a war-like fight presses upon you at times—a lack of resources, a poor state of health—retreat to one meal per day, to self-service, to a tattered cloak, and, finally, to Hades.

7. ON FREEDOM FROM PASSION

[55] *People are not called "painless" or "fearless" in the same way that they are called "chestless" or "mindless." The latter merely have a bad chest or mind whereas the former are beyond pain and fear.*

[56] In this way, the happy man will also be free from passion and trouble. But whoever is in distress and pain and fear—how could such a one be satisfied with life? And if not satisfied, how could such a one be happy? Or if pain touches him, how could fear and anguish and anger and pity not do so? For when these things exist, human beings feel pain and distress. *So too with feelings of suspicion, hate, jealousy, envy, and malicious exultation.*

To be free from passion is the very thing that a blessed man should be so that he does not feel grief over the death of a friend or a child [57] or even over the end his own life.

[57-61] *Courage meets death nobly and boldly—like Socrates, who was not vexed. Or like Spartan women, who are pleased when their sons, even though they die, do well in battle, whereas Athenian women merely want their sons to return safely. There was one Spartan woman who even pulled up her clothes when her son retreated from battle and asked, Where are you going? Do you want to return to where you came from? Spartan men are born to be useful and helpful, she said, not merely to survive. Nor should we stop living when a loved one has died. But we should go on. Why do we imagine ourselves unfortunate because someone has died but not fortunate because he has lived?*

[61] Yes, *you say,* but he will no longer exist.

Nor did he exist ten thousand years ago! Nor in Trojan times! Nor even in the time of your great-grandfathers! And yet you are not grieved by this; rather, you are displeased that he will not exist in times to come.

Since I have been robbed of the intimate friendship I had with him. . . .

[61-62] *Yes, but so it was when he was away from you in other circumstances—when serving in the military or as an ambassador, for instance. The point, Teles concludes, is to be a man—not a stupid man.*

NOTES

[1] The chapter could just as well have been titled "Diatribes" or "Sermons." Italics represent a summary of Teles' original text. Translated here are what we at The Classics Cave believe are the best parts of Teles' discourses. Portions in italics provide a summary of the remainder of the discourse.

[2] For the three kinds of goods (goods of the body, external goods, and internal goods or goods of the soul), see Teles' extended comments in his discourse *On Exile*.

[3] The ending seems abrupt, perhaps indicating a missing portion of the discourse.

[4] The distinction is between a leading role and a supporting role.

[5] Stilpon (Stilpo) of Megara was a fourth century BC Greek philosopher. He was part of the Megarian school, which was founded by Euclides (or Euclid) of Megara, a student of Socrates.

[6] Lycinus was an exile from Italy, possibly Tarentum. Hippomedon was the son of the Spartan king Agesilaus. When his father was exiled in 241 BC, Hippomedon joined him in exile. The third century BC brothers Chremonides and Glaucon were the sons of the Athenian man Eteocles. Both were exiled from Athens after the Chremonidean War (c. 267-261), during which the Macedonians retook Athens.

[7] The Thesmophorion was a fall festival for women in honor of Demeter. It was meant to secure an abundant crop. Edward O'Neil argues that the Thesmophorion mentioned here was that of Megara (see *Teles: The Cynic Teacher*).

[8] Enyalius was the son of Ares, the Greek god of war.

[9] Cadmus (Kadmos) was the founder of Thebes. The hero and demigod Heracles wandered about the Greek world (and beyond) and lived in many places.

[10] Priam was the ruler of Troy during the Trojan War. Among many others, his sons were the heroes Paris (who ran off with Helen) and Hector. Laertes was the father of the hero Odysseus. For Tantalus, the king of Sipylus in Lydia, who betrayed the gods and thus suffered thirst and hunger in Hades, see Homer, *Odyssey* 11.582 ff.

[11] The three Graiai, the daughters of Phorcys, shared one eye and one tooth between them. See Apollodorus, *Library* 2.4.2.

[12] Zeno of Citium (c. 334-262 BC) initially practiced philosophy, or a life of radical virtue, with the Cynic Crates of Thebes. He went on to found his own school, Stoicism, named after a covered colonnade (*stoa*) in Athens. Zeno taught that all of reality consists of matter and mind, or divine reason, which

makes, orders, and governs that which is natural. To live well is to live naturally, which is to say rationally or virtuously.

[13] Depending on how we count and label them, the stages are the three of childhood (babyhood, what we might call an elementary schooler, and an advanced
schooler); that of youthhood, the *ephēbos*, the age of one's youthful prime, from
18 up to 20; that of being twenty (*eikosi*) and the years following; that of being
in full bloom or in the prime of life (*akmazō*), what we might call a full-bloomer,
a full-on man or woman; and, finally, that of edging just past prime and moving toward old age (*gēras*), or an old man.

DIOGENES' CONTEST
FROM DIO CHRYSOSTOM'S *ORATION* 8[1]

IN BRIEF: *Dio Chrysostom relays how Diogenes came to Athens when he was exiled from Sinope, and how he attached himself to Antisthenes. Eventually, Diogenes moved to Corinth in order "to convict fools of their folly and correct them." This move presented him with the opportunity to preach to a crowd at the Isthmian games. During his discourse, he describes his own ongoing contest with hardship and pleasure, and offers Heracles as an example of a man who struggled well.*

WHEN DIOGENES WAS exiled from his native Sinope, he came to Athens looking like a beggar. He found there many companions of Socrates, namely Plato, Aristippus, Aeschylus, Antisthenes, and Euclides of Megara.[2] As for Xenophon, he was in exile on account of his campaign with Cyrus.

Now it was not long before Diogenes looked down on them all—all but for Antisthenes. He turned to him not so much because he approved of the man himself as much as he approved of the words he spoke. He held these sayings to be the only true ones, the ones most capable of benefiting mankind.

[2] When he contrasted the man Antisthenes with his words, he sometimes made the criticism that the man himself was much weaker. And so in reproach, Diogenes would call him a trumpet because Antisthenes failed to hear himself no matter how much noise he made.

Antisthenes tolerated this banter since he greatly admired the man's nature. [3] And so, in response to being called a trumpet, he used to say that Diogenes was like a wasp, the buzz of whose wings is slight but whose sting is very sharp. Therefore, he took delight in the outspokenness of Diogenes, just as horsemen, when they get a horse that is high-strung and yet courageous and willing to work, do not object to the difficult temper of the animal, but dislike and have no use for one that is lazy and slow. [4] Sometimes, therefore, he used to stretch and excite Diogenes, while at other times he tried to relax him, letting him down, just as those who twist strings for musical instruments stretch the strings, taking care, however, not to break them.

After Antisthenes' death, Diogenes moved to Corinth since he considered none of the others worth associating with. And there he lived without renting a house or staying with a friend, but camping out in the Craneum.³ [5] He did this because he observed that large numbers gathered at Corinth on account of the harbors and the prostitutes, and because the city was situated, as it were, at the crossroads of Greece. Accordingly, just as the good physician should go and offer his services where the sick are most numerous, so, he said, the man of wisdom should take up his abode where fools are found in great numbers in order to convict them of their folly and correct them.

[6] So, when the time for the Isthmian games⁴ arrived and everyone was in the Isthmus, he went down also. He did this because it was his custom at the great assemblies to make a study of the pursuits and ambitions of men, of their reasons for being abroad, and of the things on which they prided themselves. [7] He also gave his time to anyone who wished to talk with him, remarking that he was surprised by the fact that if he had claimed to be a physician for the teeth, everybody would flock to him who needed to have a tooth pulled. Yes, and by Zeus, if he had professed to treat the eyes, all who were suffering from sore eyes would present themselves. And similarly, if he had claimed to know of a medicine for diseases of the spleen or for gout or for a runny nose. [8] But when he declared that all who followed his treatment would be relieved of ignorance, wickedness, and licentiousness, not one man would listen to him or seek to be cured by him—no matter how much richer he might become thereby. It was as though they were less inconvenienced by these spiritual complaints than by the other kind. Or as

though it were worse for them to suffer from an enlarged spleen or a decayed tooth than from a soul that is foolish, ignorant, cowardly, rash, pleasure-loving, unfree, prone to anger, unkind, and wicked—in fact, utterly corrupt.

[9] That was the time, too, when one could hear crowds of miserable sophists[5] around Poseidon's temple shouting and reviling one another, and their disciples, as they were called, fighting with one another. And there were many writers reading aloud their senseless works; many poets reciting their poems, while others applauded them; many jugglers showing their tricks; many fortune-tellers interpreting fortunes; countless lawyers perverting judgment; and not a few peddlers selling whatever they happened to have.

[10] Straightaway, a crowd naturally also gathered around Diogenes. There were no Corinthians, however, for they did not think it would be at all worth their time since they were accustomed to see him every day in Corinth. The crowd that gathered was composed of strangers. And each of these, after speaking or listening for a short time, went his way, fearing his refutation of their views.

[11] Just for that reason, Diogenes said he was like the Laconian dogs.[6] There were plenty of men to pat them and play with them when they were shown at the general assemblies, but no one was willing to buy one because he did not know how to deal with them.

And when a certain man asked whether Diogenes had also come to see the contest, he responded, "No, but to take part."

Then when the man laughed and asked him who his competitors were, [12] he said with that customary glance of his, "The toughest there are and the hardest to beat—men whom no Greek can look straight in the eye. They are not competitors, however, who sprint or wrestle or jump, or those who box and throw the spear and hurl the discus, but those that correct and chasten a man."

[13] "Tell me, who are they?" the other asked.

"Hardships," he replied, "that are very severe and impossible to overcome for gluttonous and folly-stricken men who feast all day long and snore at night, but which yield to thin, spare men, whose waists are more pinched in than those of wasps. [14] Or do you think those big bellied men are good for anything?—those creatures whom sensible people ought to lead around, submit to the ceremony of purification, and then thrust beyond the borders. Or, rather, they should kill and quarter and use them as food just as people do with the flesh of large fish, you know, boiling it in brine and melting out the fat, the way our people at home in Pontus do with the lard of pigs when they want to anoint themselves. For I think these men have less soul than hogs have.

[15] "But the noble and excellent man believes that his hardships are his greatest opponents, and always wants to battle with them day and night—not to win a sprig of parsley, as so many goats might do, nor for a bit of wild olive, or of pine, but to win happiness and virtue throughout all the days of his life, and not merely when the Eleans make proclamation, or the Corinthians, or the Thessalian assembly. He is afraid of none of those opponents nor does he pray to draw another, [16] but he challenges them one after another, grappling with hunger and cold, withstanding thirst, and disclosing no weakness even though he must endure the lash or give his body to be cut or burned. Poverty, exile, loss of reputation, and the like have no terrors for him. No, he holds them as mere trifles, and while in their grip, the perfect man is often as sportive as boys with their dice and their colored balls.

[17] "Of course," he continued, "these antagonists do seem terrible and invincible to all who are bad men. But if you treat them with contempt and meet them boldly, you will find them cowardly and unable to master strong men. In this way, these opponents very much resemble dogs that pursue and bite people who run away from them, while some they seize and tear to pieces. On the other hand, they fear and slink away from men who face them and show them a fight, eventually wagging their tails when they come to know them. [18] Most people, however, are in mortal terror of these opponents, always avoiding them by flight and never looking them in the face. It is no different from skillful boxers. They are not hit at all when they anticipate their opponents; rather, they often actually end up winning the match themselves. On the contrary, if they give

ground through fear, they receive the heaviest blow. In the same way, if we accept our hardships in a spirit of contempt for them and approach them cheerfully, they avail very little against us. But if we hang back and give way, they appear altogether greater and stronger. [19] You can see that the same thing also applies to fire. If you attack it most vigorously, you put it out; but if you do so with caution and fear, you get badly burned, just as children do when in sport they sometimes try to put out a fire with their tongues. The adversaries of this class are a good deal like the all-fighters who engage in pankration, the ones who strike, choke, tear apart, and occasionally kill.

[20] "And yet there is another battle even more terrible, a struggle that is no small thing, but much greater and more dangerous than the former. I mean the fight against pleasure. Nor is it like that battle Homer speaks of when he says,

Fiercely, then, around the ships the struggle was renewed . . .
They fought with common axes and with sharp battle-axes
and with mighty swords and two-edged spear.[7]

[21] No, it is no such battle—for pleasure uses no open force but deceives and casts a spell with baneful drugs, just as Homer says Circe drugged the comrades of Odysseus, and some straightaway became swine, some wolves, and some other kinds of beasts.[8] Yes, such is this thing pleasure, which hatches no single plot but all kinds of plots, and aims to undo men through sight, sound, smell, taste, and touch, [22] with food too, and drink and sexual lust, tempting alike those awake and those asleep. It is not possible to station guards and then lie down to sleep as in ordinary warfare. No, it is just then of all times that pleasure makes her attack [23]— at one time weakening and enslaving the soul by means of sleep itself, at another sending mischievous and insidious dreams that bring her to mind.

"Now pain and hardship come by means of touch for the most part and continue in that way, [24] but pleasure assails a man through each and every sense that he has. And while he must face and grapple with pain and hardship, he should flee from pleasure as far as possible and only have unavoidable dealings with her. Here the strongest man is more or less the most excellent man, the one who is able to flee the greatest distance away from pleasure—for it is impossible to dwell with pleasure or even to linger with her for any length of time without being wholly conquered and en-slaved. Therefore, when she gains dominion and overpowers the soul by means of her charms, her enchanted drugs, the rest of Circe's sorcery at once follows. [25] With a stroke of her wand, pleasure coolly drives her victim into a sort of pigsty and pens him up. And now, from that time on, the man goes on living as a pig or a wolf.

[26] "Pleasure also brings diverse and deadly vipers into being, and other crawling things that are always with her as they stand by her doors. And though yearning for pleasure and serving her, they nevertheless suffer countless hardships and suffering all in vain. For pleasure, after overpowering and taking possession of her vic-tims, delivers them over to the most hateful and most difficult hard-ships.

[27] "This is the contest which I steadfastly maintain, and in which I risk my life against pleasure and hardship, yet not a single wretched human being turns his attention to me—but only to the jumpers and runners and dancers. Neither, however, did men re-ally look at the struggles and hardships of Heracles or have any in-terest in them. Still, perhaps even then they were admiring certain athletes such as Zetes, Kalais, Peleus[9] and other like runners and wrestlers. And some they would admire for their beauty and others for their wealth—as, for example, Jason[10] and Cinyras.[11] [28] About Pelops,[12] too, the story ran that he had an ivory shoulder, as if there were any use in a man having a golden or ivory hand or eyes of diamond or malachite. But men did not notice the kind of soul he possessed. As for Heracles, they pitied him while he toiled and struggled in hardship and called him "the one who struggles most," which is to say the most wretched and miserable of human beings. In fact, this is why they gave the name "struggles" or "contests" to his toil and hardships, as though a toilsome life were wretched. But

now that he is dead, they honor him beyond all others, name him a god, and declare Hebe[13] is his wife, and they all pray to him [29] so that they may not themselves be wretched—to him who in his hardships suffered wretchedness exceedingly great.

"They have the idea, too, that Eurystheus had him in his power and ordered him around[14]—Eurystheus, whom they considered a worthless fellow and to whom no one ever prayed or sacrificed. Heracles, however, roved all over Europe and Asia, [30] even though he did not look at all like any of these athletes. For where could he have advanced, had he carried so much flesh, or required so much meat or drink, or fell into such depths of sleep? No, he was alert and lean like a lion, with sharp eyes and sensitive ears. He didn't worry about when it was hot or cold, and he had no use for a bed, or a shawl, or a rug. He was clad in a dirty skin, with an air of hunger about him, as he helped the good and punished the bad.

[31] "And Diomede the Thracian?[15] Because he wore such fine clothing and sat on a throne drinking all day long in luxury, and treated his guests without justice as well as his own people, and kept a large stable of horses, Heracles struck him with his club and smashed him as if he had been an old wine-jar. Then there was Geryones,[16] who had many cattle and was the richest of all lords in the west, where the sun sets, and the most arrogant. Heracles killed him along with his brothers, and he drove his cattle away.

[32] "And when he found Busiris[17] very diligently training, eating all day long, and exceedingly proud of his wrestling, Heracles burst him open like an over-filled sack by dashing him to the ground. He loosened the girdle of the Amazon,[18] who flirted with him and thought to master him by means of her beauty. But after having sex with her, he made her understand that he could never be overcome by beauty and would never tarry far away from his own possessions for the sake of a woman.

[33] "And Prometheus,[19] whom I take to have been a sort of sophist, he found being destroyed by popular opinion since his liver swelled and grew whenever he was praised and shriveled up when he was censured. So Heracles took pity on him, frightened off the smoke-like eagle, and thus relieved him of his vanity

and inordinate ambition. And straightway he disappeared after making him whole.

"Now in all those exploits he was not doing a favor to Eurystheus at all. [34] As for the golden apples that he got and brought back—I mean those of the Hesperides—he gave them to him since he had no use for them himself. He explained that apples of gold are not useful to men, nor were they to the Hesperides.[20]

"Then, at the very end, when he was becoming slower and weaker, he—from fear that he would not be able to live as before, I suppose, and also because he was attacked by some disease—he made the best provision that was humanly possible for himself. He stacked a pyre of the driest wood in the courtyard and showed very little concern for the fiery heat.

[35] "But before that, to avoid creating the opinion that he did only impressive and mighty deeds, he went and cleaned out the dung in the Augean stables, that immense accumulation of many years.[21] For he thought that he should fight stubbornly and war against opinion as much as against wild beasts and wicked men."

[36] While Diogenes spoke in this manner, many stood around and listened to his words with great pleasure. Then—possibly with this thought of Heracles in his mind—he stopped speaking and, squatting on the ground, he performed an inglorious act. Seeing this, the crowd straightway scorned him and called him crazy.

And again the sophists[22] raised their din—like frogs in a pond that do not see a water-snake.

NOTES

[1] The translation that follows is a modified version of J.W. Cohoon's translation of Dio's eighth oration, *Diogenes*, or *On Virtue* (1932).
[2] Plato, the philosopher; Aristippus, the founder of the Cyrenaic school of philosophy; Aeschylus, in this case, was not the playwright, but a philosopher, a student of Socrates; Antisthenes, the Cynic philosopher; Euclides, the founder of the Megarian school of philosophy.
[3] The Craneum was a grove of cypress trees just outside Corinth, as Diogenes Laertius puts it, "at the gates."
[4] The Isthmian games were held at Corinth every two years in honor of the god Poseidon.

[5] The sophists were Presocratic philosophers and itinerant teachers from all over the Greek world who offered instruction for pay.

[6] Laconian or Spartan dogs were powerful hunting dogs.

[7] Homer, *Iliad* 15.696, 711.

[8] For Circe and Odysseus' men, see Homer, *Odyssey* 10.210 ff.

[9] Zetes, Kalais, and Peleus were Argonauts, men who took part in Jason's expedition on the Argo to find the Golden Fleece. Peleus was Achilles' father.

[10] Jason was the leader of the Argonautic expedition to find the Golden Fleece.

[11] Cinyras was traditionally identified as a son of Apollo and the first king of Cyprus.

[12] Pelops was the son of Tantalus, who cooked and served his son to the gods. When the gods restored Pelops to life, they gave him an ivory shoulder.

[13] The daughter of Zeus and Hera, the goddess Hebe is the personification of youth (*hēbē*).

[14] Eurystheus was the king of Mycenae, who assigned the twelve labors to Heracles. Dio mentions a number of the labors in what follows.

[15] Diomede the Thracian possessed four wild mares that fed on human flesh. They were captured by Heracles as one of his twelve labours.

[16] Geryones was a three-headed monster. He was a king in the far west.

[17] Busiris was a king of Egypt. According to legend, he sacrificed every stranger who visited his country.

[18] The Amazon was Hippolyta, the queen of the Amazons.

[19] For Prometheus, who attempted to trick Zeus (regarding the portions of the sacrifice) and stole fire for human beings, and whom was punished by Zeus, see Hesiod, *Theogony* 521-561, and *Works and Days* 47-89.

[20] The Hesperides were the guardians of the golden apples that Heracles had to retrieve as one of his labors.

[21] Augeas (Augias) had a herd of cattle whose stalls were left uncleaned for decades. Heracles cleaned them out in one day as one of his labors.

[22] For the sophists, see the note above.

THE LETTERS
OF DIOGENES OF SINOPE[1]

IN BRIEF: *With his typical wit and direct counsel, Diogenes alternatively criticizes and admonishes, hitting upon typical Cynic themes such as the benefit of virtue and living a simple life.*

LETTER 1 To the Sinopians: You sentenced me to exile, but I sentence you to staying![2] Accordingly, you will live in Sinope while I live in Athens—which is to say, you will live among merchants, and I with Solon and those men who have liberated Greece from the Persians. *Diogenes reminds the Sinopians of whom they have to deal with—the Heniochians and Achaeans, who are hostile to all Greeks, he says. His only fear is that Sinope's reputation might make others believe he is not a measured man. For this reason, it is actually a good thing that Sinope exiled him. Moreover,* it is far better to be disparaged by you than to be praised by you.

LETTER 2 To Antisthenes: *Diogenes recounts the time when he was walking from the Piraeus up to Athens, and he motivated a group of young men to attire themselves in proper fashion. They quietly listened to him. They had originally moved away from* "the dog," *but Diogenes had replied,* "Be courageous! This dog doesn't bite beets."

LETTER 3 To Hipparchia: I admire you for your yearning—that, even though you are a woman, you reached out for philosophy and have become a member of our school, which has terrified even men by its severity. Be earnest to bring to completion what you have begun. You will do so, I know well, if you do not let Crates, your husband, leave you behind, and if you frequently write letters to me, your benefactor in philosophy. For letters are worth a lot and are not inferior to conversation with those who are with you.

Letter 4 To Antipater: *Diogenes asks Antipater, a Macedonian ruler, to pardon him for what he said about him* ("for judging Athenians a salt preferable to your table"), *and for not coming to him when Antipater summoned him. He was not motivated by arrogance but by truth.*

Letter 5 To Perdiccas: If you are presently fighting against opinions and appearances, enemies which, I say, are stronger and harm you more than both the Thracians and Paeonians, and if you are working to subdue the human passions, then send for me. I say this because I am able to battle against these as a general does. *But if you require help battling men, Diogenes finishes, you should ask for soldiers.*

Letter 6 To Crates: *Diogenes relays the bit of wisdom he picked up by observing a servant drink at the well of Panops. He learned he could use his hands rather than a cup. He further explains that he is not ashamed to learn noble ways from a servant. Crates should do the same while he's in Thebes—he should spend time in the marketplace, observing the people there and learning wise practices from them. The goal for Cynics, says Diogenes, is to get behind opinions and appearances in order to restore the practices of nature for the salvation of human beings.* Nature is mighty. It is this that we restore as the deliverance and preservation of humankind, since nature has been tossed from life thanks to the influence of opinion and appearance.

Letter 7 To Hicetas: Do not be distressed, father, that I call myself a dog, and I clothe myself with a doubled over tattered cloak, and I carry a leather bag over my shoulders, and I have a staff in my hand. It is not fitting to be upset by such matters. Instead, be delighted that your son is content with little and that he is free from popular opinion, to which everyone, both the Greeks and barbarians, are enslaved.

Diogenes explains that he is heaven's dog . . . living according to nature, free under Zeus. *As for his clothing, it was invented by the gods, he says. He knows this thanks to Homer's account of Odysseus,* the wisest of the Greeks, *who dressed in a similar manner when returning home from Troy. Citing Homer's* Odyssey, *he relates that it was the goddess Calypso who gave Odysseus a nasty cloak to wear and a staff and a leather bag full of holes.*[3]

LETTER 8 To Eugnesius: *Diogenes describes the time he came upon Dionysius, the tyrant of Sicily, teaching school children after he had been deposed. He reveals that he criticized his teaching and told him that he should have perished in Sicily for all the evil he caused rather than escaping to Greece.*

LETTER 9 To Crates: *Diogenes commends Crates for setting himself free of his property by giving it to his homeland.* Standing amid the assembly, you proclaimed, "Crates, the son of Crates, sets Crates free." *He also thanks Crates for stopping his fellow citizens from sending for him (Diogenes) to speak with them. Finally, he advises Crates to speed back to Athens since he still has more training to undergo. He says,* It is no longer safe to spend time where no one else is like you.

LETTER 10 To Metrocles: Be confident, Metrocles!—*regarding your clothing, name, way of life, and in begging, which is not shameful. Even kings beg for things from their subjects; and the sick from doctors; and lovers from boys. The point, he explains, is to beg for the deliverance of everyone. Beg for what nature demands. Be like Heracles and give back something superior in comparison to what you received. A last point: Socrates used to argue that in begging, wise men are merely getting back what belongs to them since they are the friends of the gods, to whom everything belongs.*

LETTER 11 To Crates, Do well: Beg for your daily bread even from the statues of men set up in the marketplace. A practice such as this is good considering you'll happen upon men in your begging that are even more unfeeling than statues. *Don't be amazed that people give to eunuchs and those with filthy mouths, for these work to please the many.*

LETTER 12 To the Same, to Crates, Do well: Whenever they hear about a shortcut leading to happiness, the many throw themselves at it just as we do with philosophy. But when they reach the path and see how difficult it is, they retreat, going backwards, as if weak or sick. And rather than complaining about their own softness they find fault with our freedom from passion and suffering.

Well then, let them sleep with their pleasures as they are eager to do! For if they live this kind of life, then even greater hardship will befall them than those by which they slander us. And so they are shamefully enslaved in every circumstance.

As for you, keep training just as you began, and earnestly set yourself in equal measure against both pleasure and hardship. . . . The one carries us off to shameful deeds, while the other, through fear, takes us away from that which is noble.

LETTER 13 To Apolexis, greetings: I've emptied my leather bag of many heavy things. I've learned that a hollowed out loaf of bread is a plate and that the hands are a drinking cup. And I learned that there is no shame in the beggar's remark that, "I was yet a child." Nor should we ignore—on account of its age—a useful discovery. Instead, we should accept it.

LETTER 14 To Antipater, greetings: You find fault with my life for how hard and toilsome it is, and that no one will practice it because it is so difficult and harsh. But I have increased its difficulty on purpose so that those who imitate me might know not to enjoy fine things.

LETTER 15 To Antipater, greetings: *Diogenes explains why it is beneficial to practice simplicity in terms of practices such as wearing a tattered cloak and carrying a leather bag. These are not for show; rather, they are for the sake of one's own soul.* We should not profess and promise much and then practice what is not sufficient. Rather, we should demonstrate that our lives correspond with our words. This is what I attempt to do in my own case—what I hope to be a witness of. *And I am not only thinking of others.* I am speaking of my own soul, whose notice I cannot escape when I miss the mark.

LETTER 16 To Apolexis, greetings: I spoke with you about a place to live. Thank you for taking this on. But when I beheld a snail, I found a house that would keep off the wind—that is, the wine jar in the Mētrōon.[4] So then I release you from this service. Let us rejoice over this discovery of nature.

LETTER 17 To Antalcides, greetings: *Diogenes advises Antalcides to be virtuous rather than merely writing him letters about virtue.*

LETTER 18 To Apolexis, greetings: *Wise men require no introduction as their life and words are sufficient. Thus, there's no need to satisfy the wish of certain Megarian youths to introduce the philosopher Menodorus.*

LETTER 19 To Anaxilaus the wise, greetings: *In response to Pythagoras' claim to have been Euphorbus, the son of Panthus, Diogenes explains that he sees himself as Agamemnon.[5] His staff, tattered cloak, and leather bag match Agamemnon's scepter, mantle, and shield.*

LETTER 20 To Melesippus, greetings: *Diogenes advises Melesippus not to be upset that he, Diogenes, was beaten up by some drunken Athenian youths.* Know well that even though Diogenes' body was struck by the drunkards, his virtue was not dishonored since it is not its nature to be honored or shamed by base men. Diogenes was not insulted; rather, it was the people of Athens, some who supposed they were superior to virtue, that suffered badly. *People will only avoid destruction when they check their senselessness from the very beginning and refuse to listen to foolish individuals.*

LETTER 21 To Amynander, greetings: *No man or woman needs to thank his or her parents for being born or for how he or she is or for their choice to bring him or her into the world. All these things are due to nature, the mixing of certain elements, and those things having to do with Aphrodite, with sex, which are done for pleasure and not procreation. This may seem harsh to some, Diogenes admits, but it accords with nature rather than vanity. It is simply true.*

LETTER 22 To Agesilaus, greetings: For me life is so unreliable and uncertain that I cannot rely on lasting here until I finish writing this letter to you. Regardless, a leather bag stores enough for it. . . . I myself am only sure about one thing—that death comes after birth. Knowing this, I blow away the empty hopes that fly around the body, and I encourage you not to think too much for a human being.

LETTER 23 To Lacydes, greetings: *Diogenes declares his own personal freedom from the Macedonian king Alexander.*

LETTER 24 To Alexander, greetings: *Given Alexander's lust for Hephaestion, Diogenes doubts he wishes to be noble and good.*

LETTER 25 To Hippon: *Rather than learning about what happens after death, something controlled by nature, Diogenes affirms that* it is sufficient to live according to virtue, which is up to us. *Such knowledge doesn't help one become better philosopher.*

LETTER 26 To Crates: *Diogenes encourages Crates to keep on the path of life-long poverty. Don't let the Thebans tell you that you are unhappy. Let the resolved spirit of Heracles urge you on—your tattered cloak as his lion's skin; your staff as his club; your leather bag as the resources of land and sea.*

LETTER 27 To Anniceris, greetings: *Diogenes, who practices a simple life, explains that it is unfortunate for the Spartans that they have barred him from entering Sparta. Although they defend themselves well from external enemies by means of their courage,* the Spartans have surrendered their unprotected souls to the passions, stationing no auxiliary forces against them. While they appear terrible to those who border them, they're at war with various illnesses and afflictions within. So then, let them banish virtue by which alone the soul can be strengthened and delivered from its afflictions.

LETTER 28[6] *Diogenes laments and sharply criticizes his fellow Greeks for their life that is not lived according to nature. He wants them to become true Greeks rather than behaving like barbarians, humans rather than apes.*

Nothing, however, is sufficient for these men who love honor, are irrational, and have been incompetently brought up. They are always waging war, even during times of peace; always putting people to death by capital punishment. But should they not, Diogenes asks, educate those who are unjust as they educate the uneducated? *They're full of envy and hard to please. Compared with the poor, who are often healthy, they are sick thanks to their lack of self-control. Life is not about eating, drinking, and having sex. While they gratify their bellies and members below for a short time, they end up experiencing greater pain.*

What should they do? They should listen to wise Socrates and to Diogenes. They should learn to control their sensual desires or go hang themselves! These so-called Greeks should be more like those they call barbarians, who, rather than attacking others, are satisfied with what they have. Again, they should become real Greeks and live according to the simple demands of nature. If they don't, nature will catch up to them anyway and take vengeance on them. Even now death hangs over each of them.

LETTER 29 To Dionysius: *Diogenes recognizes that Dionysius lives in an advanced condition of moral corruption. . . .* Wretched man, *he says,* there is nothing more burdensome than the course set by your fathers, the tyrants. *Tyranny is a sickness. Still, since Diogenes recognizes that Dionysius is determined to take care of himself, he will help him by sending a man to help train him and teach him courage, which will free him from softness. He will get up earlier and eat less. This man will be no flatterer like those who usually congregate around Dionysius for his own destruction.* What you need is a man to rule you with a whip and not someone who will marvel at you and flatter you. *You need someone to chastise you as if you were a horse or cow—to recall you to your senses and correct your passions. As it is, dear man, you can neither delight in yourself nor be strong.*

LETTER 30 To Hicetas, Do well: I came, Father, to Athens, and learning that Socrates' associate[7] was teaching about happiness, I went to him.

And he happened to be speaking about the paths that lead to happiness. He declared that there are two and not many paths—

and that one is a shortcut and the other is long. *It is up to us to choose which path we follow, he said.*

When I heard this, I kept quiet. But when we went to him again the next day, I called on him to show to us the paths.

Quite readily, he stood from his chair and led us into the city, straight through it to the acropolis.[8] And when we had drawn near, he showed us two paths leading upward. The one is short, steep and troublesome; the other is long, smooth and easy.

When he brought us down, he said, "Such are the paths leading up to the acropolis. And such are the paths leading to happiness. Choose the path as you wish, and I will guide you."

While the others, who were struck with fear at the troublesome and steep nature of the one path, called on him to lead them along the long and smooth one, I, superior to the hardships, chose the steep and troublesome path—for the man speeding on to happiness must go on even if it is through fire and sword.

After choosing this path, Antisthenes equipped me with the clothing and gear I would require: a doubled over tattered cloak; a leather bag with bread, a cup and a bowl (in order to carry my house, he said); an oil flask with a scraper; and a staff. After, he explained what each was for.

LETTER 31 To Phaenylus, Do well: *Diogenes relates a conversation he had with the pancratiast Cicermus, a man who was full of vanity after winning the Olympic wreath in pankration. When asked what he prided himself on, Cicermus boasted of his victory, that he had defeated everyone. Nevertheless, in dialoguing with him, Diogenes got him to admit that he had only beat some men, and ones inferior to him at that. Where is the pride in that? he asked. Rather, Cicermus should learn to endure the blows and wounds of* poverty, a bad reputation, low birth, and exile. For when you train to look down on these things, you will live blessedly and will die in a manner that is bearable. *Otherwise,* you will live miserably, *Diogenes finished. In the end, Cicermus took off his wreath and departed.*

LETTER 32 To Aristippus[9], greetings: *Diogenes explains that he is better off leading a life of poverty, a life in imitation of Socrates, rather than im- itating Aristippus, who busies himself with the feasts of the Sicilian tyrant*

Dionysius and his comrades—despite their oftentimes wicked behavior toward others. Diogenes prefers the freedom that existed during the rule of Kronos.[10]

LETTER 33 To Phanomachus, Do well: *Diogenes relates the encounter he had with Alexander, the son of Philip.*

While Diogenes was working on gluing together a book, Alexander came and blocked the light of the sun. After joking with him, Diogenes told Alexander that he meant nothing to him since he did not battle against him for anything that belonged to him. When Alexander hinted that he could relieve Diogenes of poverty, the latter responded that his kind of poverty is nothing bad. Rather, he said, the fact that Alexander desires everything is true poverty. "Poverty," he said, "does not consist in not having money, nor is begging something bad. Instead, poverty consists in desiring everything." *By contrast, Diogenes is satisfied with what nature provides.* "We Cynics live as we were born." *Not Alexander, though! Hearing this, Alexander declared to a comrade that if he were not already himself, then he would choose to be Diogenes.*

LETTER 34 To Olympias, Do well: Do not grieve my friend, Olympias, with the fact that I wear a tattered cloak and go about begging among human beings. For this is nothing shameful, as you say, nor is it anything to look down on relative to free men. Rather it is noble and can serve as weaponry against the appearances and opinions that battle against life. It was not from Antisthenes that I first learned these lessons. No, it was from the gods and heroes and those men who turned Greece toward wisdom—men such as Homer and the tragic poets. *He cites the examples of the goddess Hera; of Telephus, the son of Heracles; and of Odysseus, the son of Laertes. And while these others lived poorly and begged on account of various motivations, Diogenes lives this way for the sake of happiness.*

LETTER 35 To Sopolis, Do well: *Diogenes reports two encounters he had while in Miletus. In the first, he asked a teacher how he could teach letters even though he himself had never learned them. In the other, he asked the superintendent of a wrestling school how, given the way things usually work, he could expect the older men not to mess around with the handsome, younger men.*

LETTER 36 To Timomachus, Do well: *Diogenes relates the counsel he gave to a man in Cyzicus who, like everyone else, had the following inscription written upon his door*: The child of Zeus, the gloriously triumphant Heracles, lives here, may no bad thing enter—*things such as sickness, poverty, death.*

If the inscription is so helpful, asked Diogenes, then why don't you have it written upon your city gates? Or what about the marketplace? Or why not upon yourselves?

When the man asked him what other inscription would be better, Diogenes suggested that it would be far better to inscribe: "Poverty lives here, may no bad thing enter."

"Say something good, man!" he said. "But this itself is something bad." . . .

"What does it do that you say it is a bad thing?" Diogenes said.

"Poverty is responsible for hunger," he said, "and cold and contempt."

Diogenes denied that poverty is responsible for these.

"Poverty is not responsible for harmful things; rather, wickedness is. And what else," he said, "would poverty accomplish if it lived with you? Would poverty not be chosen when it drove other even stronger, more violent bad things away from you?"

"What kind of bad things?" he asked.

"Jealousies, hatreds, false accusations, people breaking into other people's houses, indigestion, colic—other painful afflictions. Write, therefore, that poverty lives among you and not Heracles. For you are not afraid of the things that Heracles is able to destroy: water serpents, bulls, lions, kerberos dogs. . . . But whatever poverty drives away, these are fearful."

The man was not convinced and asked what else he could write. Diogenes answered, "Justice lives here, may no bad thing enter." *The man agreed to write justice alongside Heracles and thanked Diogenes.*

LETTER 37 To Monimus, Do well: *Diogenes tells Monimus about his visit to Rhodes and his eventual stay with Lacydes. Since he could not initially find Lacydes, he sought the hospitality of the gods.*

When he did finally catch up with Lacydes, and he went to his house, he found it far too luxurious in terms of its furniture, tableware, servants, food, and wine. Consequently, Diogenes asked his host to remove everything. Going on, he said, "But let the drinking cups from which we drink be of clay, small and cheap. And may our drink be spring water, and our food a loaf of wheat bread, and the seasoning be salt or cardamom. I learned to eat and drink these things from Antisthenes, . . . things one is quite able to find on the path leading to happiness."

Diogenes went on to describe the nature of the path—how it is straight uphill and rough. Even the one who is stripped down struggles. The one who is weighed down with trouble and chains would not make it alive. No, he said. Rather, "one must practice eating cardamom and drinking water and wearing a light, tattered cloak."

Diogenes explained how he quickly came to the path to happiness. "And coming to the place where happiness exists, I said, 'Because of you, Happiness, and the greater good, I persisted in drinking water and eating cardamom and sleeping on the ground.' Responding to me, Happiness said, 'But rather than a hardship, I will make these things sweeter to you than the goods of wealth that human beings honor before me. But they do not understand that they are nourishing a tyrant for themselves.' And from that point on, when I listened to Happiness talking about this, I no longer ate or drank these things as a matter of practice, but as a pleasure."

He continues, he explained, by means of strength and habit.

LETTER 38[11] *Diogenes relates what he did after the addressee of the letter had departed from the games at Olympia. He saw many people in the marketplace—salesmen, rhapsodes, philosophers, and diviners. Observing one man talking about the sun, he asked him if he had been up to the heavens. Seeing a diviner, he queried if he was good at his art. When the man failed to predict whether Diogenes would hit him or not with his staff (he hit him), Diogenes called him a bad diviner. Diogenes gained a following and spoke about and actually lived patient endurance. So it was that some gave him money and other things of worth. He only received gifts from those who benefited from him and were grateful, he explains. And once, when he was invited to dinner in a house that was all decorated with gold, he convinced the boy there (by spitting on him) to follow him after giving up his wealth and clothing himself like a Cynic.*

LETTER 39 To Monimus, Do well: You should also consider your migration from here. You will do so if you practice dying, that is, separating the soul from the body while you are still living. For this, it seems to me, is what the friends of Socrates call death. And the practice is very easy. *When the soul practices living apart from the body, apart from sensation, it is not dismayed when it leaves the body behind at death. Indeed, one's life is free and thus sweet, and there is a certain harmony for the whole.*

LETTER 40 Diogenes the Cynic to Alexander: *Diogenes urges Alexander (the Great) on to a better life.*

LETTER 41 To Melesippus: It doesn't seem to me that everyone is capable of living virtuously as we understand it. *This is so thanks to the teachings of some that destroy moral values—such as those teachings of Homer that declare Zeus the father of wicked offspring.* So then, the Cynic will only be able to do those things that are done according to virtue.

LETTER 42 To the wise Melesippe, greetings: *Satisfaction of things having to do with Aphrodite may be accomplished more easily than those having to do with the belly.* Cynicism, as you know, is an inspection of nature.

LETTER 43 To the Maroneans, Do well: *Diogenes lauds the citizens for changing the name of their city from Maroneia (so-called after the wine merchant[12]), to Hipparchia (after a woman, yes, but a philosopher).*

LETTER 44 To Metrocles, Do well: It is not only bread and water, and a bed of straw, and a tattered cloak that teach moderation and patient endurance. No, if I may say so, I proclaim it is also the hand of the shepherd.

Rather than having sex with women, which takes up a lot of time and distracts one on the short path to happiness, Diogenes recommends that Metrocles follow the counsel of Pan in using "the hand of the shepherd." Though the many, untrained as they are, enjoy sex with women, they are nevertheless harmed by this practice. It is better to learn from Pan to do the work yourself, he says.

And don't turn back even if, because of this life, people call you a dog or some other worse name.

LETTER 45 To Perdiccas, Do well: *Diogenes states that Perdiccas should be ashamed to threaten him with death. He warns him of possible penalties.*

LETTER 46 To Plato, the wise man, greetings: You spit on my tattered cloak and leather bag as though they were burdensome and difficult for me, and on my life as though it were useless, doing no good. *This is because you are without virtue.*

As for me, I pursued these things with virtue. What greater proof can I offer than not changing my course toward a life of pleasure and luxury, even though I could have? *Diogenes contends that his life is beneficial.* What enemy would march against one who is self-sufficient and simple? And against which king or people would those satisfied with these things carry on a war? In conformity with this, the soul has been purified of vice and has been released from empty opinion. It has cast out immoderate desires and has been taught to speak the truth and to show contempt for other false things. If you are not persuaded by this, then practice the love of pleasure and tease us for not knowing much.

LETTER 47 To Zeno, Do well: One should neither marry nor have children since our kind, humankind, is weak, and marriage and children overload human weakness with troubles. *Diogenes suggests that marriage and children promise support but deliver troubles.* But the one who is free from the passions and supposes his own property is enough for patient endurance shuns marriage and the production of offspring. *But, you may ask, what will happen to the human population? Ah, if only everyone would be so wise!*

LETTER 48 To Rhesus, greetings: Phrynichus the Larissaean, a student of mine, longs to see Argos, "where horses graze." He will not need much from you since he is a philosopher.

LETTER 49 The Cynic to Aroueca: Know yourself—for in doing this you would do well. If there is some sickness such as folly in your soul, then grab a doctor for it—*a good doctor, not merely an apparently good one. In this way you will be valuable to me and others.*

LETTER 50 To Charmides, greetings: Your acquaintance Euremus offered me many sophisms and dark sayings . . . But I don't think virtue is exalted by this sort of speech. Rather, *virtue is exalted by a simple life and simple words.* . . . Anyway, if he truly grew up with virtue, then he should have never introduced into himself a desire for money, which is the cause of every evil. Or through holy philosophy he should have rid himself of every passion. *The Athenians hope to heal others even though they cannot heal themselves.*

LETTER 51 To Epimenides, greetings: You stay at home delighting your belly and adorning your body instead of enduring by means of virtue. I hear that you profess virtue—and such an act did not seem incredible to me, for, according to Simonides, it is difficult to be good but easy to profess goodness.[13]

NOTES

[1] As mentioned in the introduction, the letters are not considered genuine, which is to say that Diogenes himself (nor Crates in the next chapter) did not actually compose them. That said, they are clearly Cynic insofar as they remain faithful to Cynic themes. Translated here are what we at The Classics Cave believe are the best parts of the letters. Italics provide a summary of the remainder of the letter, hitting on the significant points.

[2] Compare to Diogenes Laertius, *Lives* 6.49.

[3] See Homer, *Odyssey* 13.434-438. The hero Odysseus stayed with the nymph Calypso for seven years before setting off for Ithaca.

[4] The Mētrōon was the temple of the mother goddess Cybele in Athens.

[5] According to Heraclides Ponticus, Pythagoras claimed that he was the Trojan hero Euphorbus, the son of Panthus, in a previous life. During the Trojan War,

Euphorbus speared Achilles' dear friend Patroclus and was in turn killed by the Achaean hero Menelaus. See Homer, *Iliad* 16.801-854 and 17.8-89. For the account of Heraclides Ponticus, see Diogenes Laertius, *Lives* 8.4-5. Diogenes playfully claims to be Agamemnon, the leader of the Achaeans during the Trojan War.

[6] No addressee is given. That said, the letter opens with, "Diogenes the dog to the so-called Greeks."

[7] The reference is to Antisthenes.

[8] The acropolis was the highest point in any Greek city.

[9] Of the same generation as Socrates, and his companion, Aristippus of Cyrene (c. 435-356 BC) was the founder of Cyrenaicism (called such after his home city), a philosophy that promotes pleasure as the chief goal of life.

[10] Many ancient Greeks believed that the time when Kronos ruled was a happy time. See Hesiod, *Works and Days* 109-120 and an interpolation that begins after line 173; Plato, *Laws* 4.713a-e; Plato, *Statesman* 269b, 271c-272b; Plotinus, *Enneads* 5.1.4. See *Happiness: What the Ancient Greeks Thought and Said about Happiness* (Sugar Land: The Classics Cave, 2021), 70-72.

[11] No addressee is given.

[12] Maro (Maron) was the priest of Apollo who gave Odysseus the gift of very fine wine for not harming him or his family when Odysseus and his men were sacking the Cicones. It is the wine that Odysseus uses to intoxicate the Cyclops. For Maro and the wine, see Homer, *Odyssey* 9.196-211.

[13] Simonides was a sixth and fifth century BC poet from the Greek island of Ceos. In one poem he says that "excellence dwells upon rocky peaks that are hard to climb. . . . She guards a holy place. She may not be seen by the eyes of all mortals. Only the one who experiences heart-vexing sweat from within may see her, the one who reaches the peak of manliness."

THE LETTERS
OF CRATES OF THEBES[1]

IN BRIEF: *In accord with his reputation as the "Door-opener," as one who entered into the lives of others in order to encourage them along the way of a better life, Crates urges on those he writes, offering sage Cynic counsel.*

LETTER 1 To Hipparchia: *Crates admonishes his wife Hipparchia to come back quickly in order to see Diogenes before he dies so that she may* come to know what philosophy may do in the most fearful circumstances.

LETTER 2 To His Students: *Crates gives advice on begging—that Cynics should only beg from those* who have been initiated into philosophy. *For, he says,* it is not right that virtue is supported by vice. *Begging is really a matter of* asking for what belongs to you.

LETTER 3 To the Same, His Students: Take care of your soul—but your body only so far as what is necessary, and externals not even that much. I say this because happiness is not a pleasure that requires external things, nor does perfect virtue require these.

LETTER 4 To Hermaiscus: Whether you want to work hard or you want to avoid working hard, work hard. This way you won't be working hard. Why? Because when you slack off you're not actually avoiding hard work; rather, you're making things harder.

LETTER 5 To His Students: Law is a fine thing, but it is not better than philosophy. I say this because law forces a man to do no wrong, whereas philosophy instructs him. *Crates explains that philosophy is*

better than law insofar as acting willingly is better than acting under com-
pulsion. It is better to know the means by which humans are instructed to do right and act honestly than to know the means by which they are forced to do no wrong.

LETTER 6 To the Same, His Students: Do philosophy more often than you breathe. I say this because living well, which philosophy produces, is more choiceworthy than simply living, which breathing produces. Don't do philosophy as others have done it, but as Antisthenes first practiced it, that which Diogenes brought to fulfillment. But if doing philosophy in this manner is troublesome or difficult, at least it is short. One must go for happiness, as Diogenes used to say, even if the going is through fire.

LETTER 7 To the Wealthy: Hang yourselves! I say this for this reason: although you possess lupine beans and dried figs and water and Megarian tunics, you nevertheless sail the sea to trade, and you farm a great deal of land, and you commit treachery and behave as a tyrant and murder, and you do other such things as these. You should be still and keep quiet! By contrast we Cynics are completely at peace—free from every bad thing thanks to Diogenes of Sinope. Although we have nothing, we have everything. But you who possess everything have nothing thanks to your love of strife and jealousy and fear and vanity.

LETTER 8 To Diogenes: We are in fact already liberated from riches. Still, we have not yet been set free from our enslavement to reputation—though, by Heracles, we are doing everything to be set free from her. *Crates announces his plans to visit and give himself to Diogenes in Athens.* It is your word that delivered us.

LETTER 9 To Mnasos: Do not abstain from the most beautiful adornment, but adorn yourself each day so that you may be different from others. The most beautiful adornment is the one that adorns you most beautifully. But the one that adorns you most beautifully is the one that produces a well-ordered, regular, moderate life. It is this adornment that produces this well-ordered life. It seems to me that both Penelope and Alcestis adorned themselves in this manner.[2] Even now they are hymned and honored for their virtue. So that you might be a match for their kind, then, try to cling to this advice.

LETTER 10 To Lysis: *Crates exhorts the athlete Lysis, who has been drinking too much and too often, to* learn to drink wine in a useful manner. *He says,* Learn to drink it with self-control together with self-controlled men. *The goal is to honor the god's gift of wine and to enjoy its pleasures for their benefit without regrets and toward the ultimate end of speaking and behaving justly in all things.* They say that men become three times happy as three goods multiply in their lives. How could those who have a self-controlled soul, a healthy body, and independence relative to possessions not be three times happy?

LETTER 11 To His Students: Train yourselves to need very little—for this is closest to god, while the opposite is farthest. It is possible for you to become like the superior kind of being rather than the inferior since you are midway between the gods and irrational animals.

LETTER 12 To Orion: *Living in the city or on a farm is not what makes a child good or bad. Rather, Crates argues that it is* time spent with good and bad men *that makes one good or bad. So it is that Orion should send his sons to spend time with a philosopher, a lover of wisdom.* Virtue enters the soul by means of training—not automatically as happens with vice.

LETTER 13 To Eumolpus: *While a Cynic may not have the luxury of the Carthaginians or Persians, or the easy life of Sardanapalus,*[3] *their life is nevertheless freer, healthier, and more secure. And since these latter goods are better than the others, Diogenes' philosophy, which is* the short path to happiness, *is better than other ways of life.*

LETTER 14 To Young Ones: Get used to eating barley cakes and drinking water. Don't even give a taste to fish or wine. I say this because the latter two, like the drugs of Circe, turn old men into animals and young males into females.

LETTER 15 To His Students: Flee not only from the worst of the vices, injustice and a lack of self-control, but also what produces them, pleasure and enjoyment. . . . Pursue not only the best of goods, self-control and endurance, but also what produces them, hard work and toil. *In doing the latter you will exchange what is inferior for what is superior, as you would bronze for gold. Consequently, you will exchange* hard work and toil for virtue.

LETTER 16 To His Students: *Crates advises those who are upset at being accused of* living like a dog *and being called* dogs *to let go of their distress. Just as a good man is not upset when he is called bad, so too should those who practice Cynicism—the* doggish philosophy *and* the shortcut in doing *philosophy—not be upset when they are called* dogs. *The latter is merely opinion.*

LETTER 17 To the Same, to His Students: *Just as it is not dishonorable to ask a doctor for medicine in order to treat indigestion, so too it is not shameful to beg others for bread to treat hunger, which is, according to Diogenes, another stomach condition.* Indigestion is caused by gluttony and vice, whereas hunger is caused by a lack of resources.

LETTER 18 To Young Ones: Get used to washing in cold water, drinking water, eating nothing that has not come to you by means of toil and sweat, wearing a tattered cloak, and spending your time on the ground. *That way, Crates continues, you will never be without warm baths, wine and meat, clothes died purple, and a bed.*

LETTER 19 To Patrocles: *Do not call Odysseus the father of Cynicism simply because he put on the clothing of the Cynic.* The clothing does not produce a Cynic; rather, the Cynic the clothing. *Although Odysseus put on the typical outfit of the Cynic, his behavior was often not that of a Cynic since he honored pleasure above all else. Instead, we should call Diogenes the father of Cynicism and imitate him since he behaved like a Cynic throughout his life, conquering* both toil and pleasure, *and* freeing many from evil to virtue. *He was* courageous in his practice of virtue.

Letter 20 To Metrocles: *Crates advises the Cynic Metrocles to exercise and run where there are young men in order to teach them how to be healthy. The reason:* deeds teach endurance more quickly than words. *Crates relates his own experience of exercising before young men. At first they laughed at me for running. But soon, seeing my determination, they too began to run and exercise rather than merely rubbing themselves down with oil. Soon, he says,* they thanked me for being the cause of their health. *And they followed me around, listening to me and imitating me.*

Letter 21 To Metrocles the Cynic: *The Cynic way is not a way of words alone. On the contrary, it is a practice, a regimen, a doing rather than merely a saying.* Long is the path that leads to happiness through words alone. But the path that leads to happiness through the practice of daily deeds is short.[4]

Letter 22 To Metrocles: *Metrocles should beg from* the worthy. *Moreover, he should accept less from those who are sensible and moderate (since they will be in the position to give again) and more from the profligate (since they will spend all their money before the next time comes around).*

Letter 23 To Ganymedes: For as long as you fear the tattered cloak and the leather bag and the staff and the long hair *of the Cynic,* and as long as you are fond of clothing died with purple and luxury, you will not stop leading on your lovers, just as Penelope led on her suitors. *That said, when you realize how troublesome they are to you,* put on the armor and carry the weapons of Diogenes. *With these you will be able to drive away every lover.*

Letter 24 To the Thessalians: Humans did not come into being as a boon for horses, but horses as a boon for humans. *The Thessalians, who are famous for their horses, should take care of themselves more than their horses so that they will be worth more than their horses.*

LETTER 25 To the Athenians: *The Athenians should do what it takes to satisfy their needs rather than merely satisfying them with a vote. If they need money, then they should sell their horses. On the other hand, if they need horses (something they may not need as much), then they may resort to a vote—in this case they can vote that their asses are horses.*

LETTER 26 To the Same, to the Athenians: *Understand that when Diogenes demands from you what is owed him, he does so as a wise man, who is friends with god. You have no problem when a god demands anything from you. Neither, therefore, should you be bothered by Diogenes' claim. The reason? Since all things belong to god, and friends hold all things in common, it follows that the wise man, who is friends with god, is owed all things.*

LETTER 27 To the Same, to the Athenians: *Crates once again makes the argument—following Diogenes—that all things belong to the wise man thanks to his friendship with god.*

LETTER 28 To Hipparchia: Women are not by nature worse than men. *Consider the deeds of the Amazons, who are not inferior to men in anything. Therefore, do not forsake the Cynic way of life you have taken up with me, your husband.* It would be shameful . . . now to change your mind and turn back when you are halfway down the path.

LETTER 29 To the Same, to Hipparchia: *We are called Cynics not because we are* indifferent *to things but* because we doggedly stick with things that are unbearable to others on account of softness and mere opinions. . . . Stand your ground, therefore, and practice Cynicism with me (since you are not by nature worse than we male Cynics are, since female dogs are not inferior to male dogs). Do this so that you may be liberated from nature insofar as all slaves are enslaved either through the law or by means of vice.

LETTER 30 To the Same, to Hipparchia: *Returning a fine tunic that she has made for him to Hipparchia, his wife, Crates explains that their life is not about appearances. Consequently, there is no need to appear to the many to care for him, her husband, by means of such a gift. Rather, she should embrace the Cynic philosophy* for which you yourself have yearned. *In this way, he finishes, she will* be of greater benefit to human life.

LETTER 31 To the Same, to Hipparchia: Reason is commander of the soul, a noble thing, the greatest good for human beings. So then, seek how to acquire this good for yourself, for then you will cling to a happy life along with this possession. And seek wise men, even if you have to go to the ends of the earth.

LETTER 32 To the Same, to Hipparchia: *Once again, Crates calls on his wife to give up weaving and giving him tunics for the sake of pride. She should do this in order to practice philosophy—the whole reason she married him.* Leave the wool-spinning, which profits little, to other women, to those who have not yearned for the things you do.

LETTER 33 To the Same, to Hipparchia: I hear that you have given birth without any trouble. . . . I'm grateful to god and to you.

You are persuaded that working hard is the reason why one does not have to work hard. I say this because you would not have given birth without any trouble if you had not, while pregnant, continued to work hard and toil as athletes do. *This approach is contrary to most women who are debilitated when pregnant and give birth to unhealthy babies.*

Anyway, Crates goes on, now you should take care of our baby with due concern. Bathe him in cold water; dress him in a tattered cloak; give him a moderate amount of milk; let him sleep in a tortoise shell. And when he is older, offer him the usual staff, tattered cloak, and leather bag—all these are far better than a sword.

LETTER 34 To Metrocles: *Crates conveys his relief upon hearing the story about how Diogenes handled himself when he was taken by pirates.*

First—said the man who told the story, one who had been captured with Diogenes but had escaped—Diogenes pointed out the contradiction in the pirates' behavior. When they sell hogs for the use of their bodies, he said, they first fatten them up. But when they sell humans, who are also wanted for their bodies and not their souls, they give them nothing at all.

Hearing this point, the pirate slavers gave their captives bread to eat. But many refused to take it because they were so upset about their impending enslavement. Laughing, Diogenes pointed out that they had not been free to begin with but were dominated by even worse masters. He went on to suggest the possible good of being enslaved. "Now, perhaps, you may be allotted moderate masters, ones who will eliminate the luxury in your lives by which you are ruined. Rather, they will produce endurance and self-control, the most honored goods."

Hearing Diogenes speak, the buyers were amazed at his freedom from emotion. *When queried about his skills, he claimed he was skilled at ruling human beings. So, he said, if anyone needs a master, let him come forward. They laughed at this, asking him what free man would require a master.* Diogenes replied, "All base men who honor pleasure and dishonor hard work and toil, the greatest incitements to vice."

Because of these remarks, Diogenes was highly valued. Rather than selling him, the pirates took him home to learn more. Hence, finishes Crates, we should not provide a ransom for him, but we should instead rejoice at his victory.

LETTER 35 To Aper, Do well: To the point and suitable in every circumstance, my honored man, is the oracle of the ancients that says, "Do not flee from those things that are necessary." I say this because the one who flees from what is necessary is inevitably unhappy. *This may seem pedantic, admits Crates. Fine.* Still, hold fast to the ancients. I have concluded from my own life that we human beings are distressed whenever we wish to live a problem-free life. But this is impossible! For by necessity we live with the body, and by necessity we also live with human beings. The truth is that most problems arise from the folly of those who live together and — again — from the body.

So then, if a man with knowledge conducts himself by these points, then he is free from pain and disturbance, a blessed man. But if he is ignorant about them, then he will never stop being taken by empty hopes and warped by yearning.

Accordingly, says Crates, either give yourself over to the counselors of the many, the tragic poets, or, if you wish for a different kind of life, then imitate men like Socrates and Diogenes.

LETTER 36 To Dinomachus: *Crates counsels Dinomachus* to beg from the good and excellent man alone, for we say that this man and none of the others is called happy.

NOTES

[1] As mentioned in the introduction, the letters are not considered genuine, which is to say that Crates himself did not actually compose them. That said, they are clearly Cynic insofar as they remain faithful to Cynic themes. Translated here are what we at The Classics Cave believe are the best parts of the letters. Italics provide a summary of the remainder of the letter, hitting on the significant points. For a complete translation of each, see "The Epistles of Crates" in *The Cynic Epistles: A Study Edition*, ed. Abraham J. Malherbe, trans. Ronald F. Hock (Atlanta: The Society of Biblical Literature, 1977).

[2] In Homer's *Odyssey*, Penelope is the faithful wife of Odysseus. About her, king Agamemnon exclaims, "Happy son of Laertes, much-able Odysseus! You acquired for yourself an excellent wife, one of great worth. How good was the heart in blameless Penelope, the daughter of Icarius! How faithful in mind to Odysseus, her wedded husband! The glory of her virtue will never fade, but the immortals will make among men on earth a graceful song for thoughtful Penelope" (24.191-198). In Greek mythology, and particularly in Euripides' tragedy the *Alcestis*, the wife of Admetus, Alcestis, agrees to die in Admetus' place when no other of his loved ones will do so. To the Chorus she "appears noble beyond all women." Like Penelope, she is a most faithful and virtuous wife.

[3] In the ancient world, the Carthaginians and Persians, as well as the Assyrian king Sardanapalus, had the reputation for fabulously luxurious lifestyles.

[4] Crates also advises Metrocles not to fear being called a Cynic—that he should not be afraid of words.

EPICTETUS THE STOIC ON CYNICISM
THE TRUE NATURE OF THE CYNIC WAY OF LIFE

IN BRIEF: *The Stoic philosopher Epictetus expounds the true nature of the Cynic way of life—the Cynic's business and what kind of person he should be. One must be a Cynic only if God wishes it. To live as a Cynic is not what it seems. He must not blame circumstances, God or man. He must rid himself of every desire and passion. The Cynic lives in the open and does not hide anything. He is a free man not afraid of any external thing. His work is as a messenger of Zeus to reveal what is good and what is bad. He's a spy for Zeus. Accordingly, the governing part of his soul must be pure. Like Socrates, he must steer people to the true road, that of happiness, which is not found in the body or in possessions or in power. Rather, it is in that which is naturally free. The Cynic shows that the man who has nothing may live a life that flows well. His body is strong, his mind sharp. Most Cynics should not marry and have children. Rather, a Cynic is the father of all men, caring for all. He makes rounds like a physician.*

W HEN ONE OF his acquaintances—one who appeared to be inclined to Cynicism—asked Epictetus what kind of person a Cynic should be, and what was the general notion of a Cynic's business and activity, Epictetus said, "Let's inquire at leisure. [2] But I have so much to say to you. The man who attempts so great a thing without God is hateful to God and has no other purpose than to act indecently in public. [3] For in any well-managed house no man comes forward and says to himself, 'I should be manager of the house.' If he does, the master turns around, and seeing him insolently giving orders, he drags him out and flogs him.

[4] "So it is also in this great city (the cosmos). Here, also, there is a master of the house who orders everything. [5] He says, '*You*

are the sun. By going around, you can produce the year and the seasons, and make the fruits of the earth grow and nourish them, and stir the winds and calm them, and warm the bodies of men properly. Go, travel around and so administer things from the greatest to the least. [6] *You* are a calf. When a lion appears, do your proper business and run away. If you do not, you will suffer. *You* are a bull. Advance and fight since this is your business and suits you, and you can do it. [7] *You* can lead the army against Ilium—be Agamemnon. *You* can fight in single combat against Hector—[8] be Achilles.' But if Thersites came forward and claimed the command, he would either not have obtained it, or, if he did obtain it, he would have disgraced himself before many witnesses.

[9] "You should also think about the matter carefully. To live as a Cynic is not what it seems. [10] You say, 'I wear a cloak now and I will wear it then. I sleep on a hard surface now and I will sleep on a hard one then. I will take in addition a little bag now and a staff, and I will go around and begin to beg and to abuse those whom I meet. And if I see any man plucking the hair out of his body, I will rebuke him—or if he has dressed his hair in some fancy manner, or if he struts around in purple.' [11] If you imagine that being a Cynic is something like this, then stay far away from it. Do not come near to it—it is not at all for you. [12] But if you imagine it to be what it is, and you do not think yourself unfit for it, consider what a great thing it is that you undertake.

[13] "In the first place, in the things that relate to you, you must not in any way be what you are like now. You must not blame God or man. You must take away desire altogether. And you must avoid only the things that are within the power of the will. You must not feel anger or resentment or envy or pity. A girl must not appear pretty to you. And you mustn't love a little reputation. And you mustn't be pleased with a boy or a cake.

[14] "You should know that other men build walls around themselves, and houses, and they snuff out the lights so that all is darkness when they do any of the things I've just mentioned. They have many means of concealment. A man shuts the door and assigns someone to guard the room. If a person comes, he orders the man

to say that he's out—that he's unavailable. [15] But instead of all these things, the Cynic must use the respect that he has built up and gained for himself as his protection. If he does not, he will be indecent in his nakedness and under the open sky. This self-respect is his house, his door; *this* is the slave before his bedchamber; *this* is his darkness. [16] For the Cynic should not wish to hide anything that he does. And if he does, he is gone—he has lost the character of a Cynic, of a man who lives under the open sky, of a free man. He has begun to fear some external thing. He has begun to require concealment.

"But he cannot simply get concealment whenever he wants. For where will he hide himself, or how? [17] And if by chance this public instructor, *the would-be Cynic,* is detected, this pedagogue, what kind of things will he be compelled to suffer? [18] When a man fears these things, is it possible for him to be bold with his whole soul in order to manage men? No—it is impossible.

[19] "In the first place, then, you must make the governing part of your soul pure. And you must make the following the plan of your life: [20] 'From now on, as wood is to the carpenter and animal hides are to the shoemaker, my mind and thoughts will be the material with which I work. My business is the right use of appearances, *the way things present themselves to me.* [21] But the body is nothing to me. Its parts are nothing to me. And death? Let it come when it chooses— either death of the whole or some part. [22] And exile? To where? Does any man have the power to throw me out of the cosmos? No, he can't. Wherever I go, there is the sun, there is the moon, there are the stars, dreams, omens, and communion with the gods.'

[23] "Then, if he is prepared in this manner, the true Cynic cannot be satisfied with this. Rather, he must know that he is Zeus' messenger sent to human beings regarding good and bad things, to show them that they have wandered and are seeking the substance of what is good and what is bad where it is not. (But where it is, they never think about all too seriously.) He must also know that he is a spy, [24] as Diogenes was carried off to Philip after the battle of Chaeronea as a spy, a scout.[1] For in fact a Cynic reconnoiters the things that are good for men and those that are bad. [25] It is his duty to examine

carefully, and to come and report truly, and not to be struck with terror so as to point out as enemies those who are not enemies, nor in any other way to be perturbed or confused by appearances.

[26] "It is his responsibility, then, to be able with a loud voice, if the occasion arises, and appearing on the tragic stage, to say like Socrates: 'Where are you hurrying? What are you doing, you miserable men? Like blind people you are wandering up and down. You are going by another road and have left the true road. You search for prosperity and happiness where they are not. And if another shows you where they are, you do not believe him.'2

[27] "Why do you seek it outside yourself? In the body? It is not there. If you doubt it, look at Myro. Look at Ophellius.3 It is not in possessions. But if you do not believe me, look at Croesus.4 Look at those who are now rich—with what lamentations their life is filled. It is not in power. If so, those must be happy who have been two and three times consuls. But they are not. [28] Whom shall we believe in these matters? You who from without see their affairs and are dazzled by an appearance, or the men themselves? And what do they say? [29] Hear them when they groan, when they grieve, when because of these very consulships and glory and splendor they think that they are more wretched and in greater danger. [30] It is not in royal power. If it were, Nero would have been happy, and Sardanapalus.5 But neither was Agamemnon happy, even though he was a better man than Sardanapalus and Nero. And while the others are snoring, what is he doing? 'He tore out his hair by the handfuls.' And what is he saying to himself? 'I'm perplexed and disturbed. I'm tossed back and forth, and my heart is leaping out from my chest.'6 [31] Wretched man, what is so wrong? Is it your possessions? No. Your body? No—you are rich in gold and copper. What, then, is the matter with you?

"That part of you, whatever it is, has been neglected by you and is corrupted—the part by which we desire and avoid, move toward and turn away from things. [32] How has it been neglected? He does not know the essence of the good for which he is made by nature and the essence of the bad. Nor does he know what is his own and what belongs to another.

"And when anything that belongs to something or someone else goes badly, he says, 'Woe to me—the Greeks are in danger!' [33] The governing part of his soul is in poor shape, miserable. It alone is neglected and uncared for. And, 'The Greeks are going to die, destroyed by the Trojans!' And if the Trojans do not kill them, will they not die? 'Yes,' he says, 'but not all at once.' What difference does it make? For if death is an evil, whether they die all at once or one at a time, it is equally an evil. Is anything else going to happen other than the separation of the soul and the body? [34] 'Nothing.' And if the Greeks perish, is the door closed for you? Is it not in your power to die? 'It is.' Why, then, do you lament? 'Woe is me!—a king who possesses the scepter of Zeus!' An unhappy king does not exist anymore than an unhappy god exists. [35] What, then, are you? Truly you are a shepherd since you weep as shepherds do when a wolf has carried off one of their sheep, and these who are governed by you are sheep. [36] And why did you come this way? Was your desire in any danger? Or your aversion? Or your moving toward or turning away from things? He replies, 'No. But the wife of my brother was carried off.' [37] Was it not then a great gain to be deprived of an adulterous wife? And will we, therefore, be despised by the Trojans? What kind of people are the Trojans, wise or foolish? If they are wise, why do you fight with them? If they are fools, why do you care about them?

[38] "In what, then, is the good, since it is not in these things? Tell us, you who are lord, messenger, and spy. It is where you neither think it is nor choose to seek it. For if you chose to seek it, you would have found it to be in yourself. Neither would you be wandering out of the way nor seeking what belongs to others as if it were your own.

[39] "Turn your thoughts within yourself. Observe the preconceptions you have—*the general idea of things you have.* What kind of a thing do you imagine the good to be? 'That which flows easily, that which is happy, that which is not impeded.' And do you not naturally imagine it to be great? And valuable? [40] And free from harm? And where or in what, then, should you seek for that which flows with ease and is not impeded?—in that which is enslaved or in that which is free? 'In that which is free.' Do you possess a free body, then,

or one that is enslaved? 'I do not know.' Do you not know that it is the slave of fever, gout, ophthalmia, and dysentery, of the tyrant *who rules over you absolutely*, of fire, iron, and of everything that is stronger? 'Yes, it is a slave.' [41] How, then, is it possible that anything that belongs to the body can be free from hindrance? And how is a thing great or valuable that is naturally dead, earth, or mud?

"Well then, do you possess *nothing* that is free? [42] 'Perhaps nothing.' And who is able to compel you to assent to that which appears false? 'No man.' And who is able to compel you *not* to assent to that which appears true? 'No man.' By this, then, you see that there is something in you that is naturally free. [43] But to desire or to be averse from, or to move toward or away from an object, or to prepare yourself or to propose to do anything—which of you can do any of these things unless he has received an impression of that which is profitable or that which is the fitting thing to do? 'No man.' You also have in these things, then, something that is unhindered and free. [44] Wretched men, work this out, take care of this, seek for good here.

[45] "And how is it possible that a man who has nothing—who is naked, houseless, and without a hearth, who is squalid, without a slave or a city—how can such a man live a life that flows well? [46] Behold, God has sent you a man to show you that it is possible: [47] 'Look at me,' he says, 'I who am without a city, without a house, without possessions, without a slave. I sleep on the ground. I have no wife, no children, no praetorium; rather, I have only the earth and the heavens, and one poor cloak. And what do I want? [48] Am I not without pain and sorrow? Without fear? Am I not free? When did any of you see me failing in the object of my desire? Or ever falling into what I would rather avoid? Did I ever blame God or man? Did I ever accuse anyone? Did any of you ever see me with a sad face? [49] And how do I meet with those whom you are afraid of and admire? Do I not treat them like slaves? Who, when he sees me, does not think that he sees his king and master?'

[50] "This is the language of the Cynics—this their character, their purpose. 'No,' you say. 'What makes for a Cynic is the little leather bag, and staff, and great jaws. It is the devouring of all that

you give them, or storing it up, or the random abuse of everyone they meet, or the display of their bare shoulder as a fine thing.'

[51] "Don't you see how you are going to undertake so great a business? First, take a mirror. Look at your shoulders. Observe your loins, your thighs. You are going to be enrolled, my man, as a combatant in the Olympic games—no heartless and miserable contest. [52] In the Olympic games a man is not allowed to lose and leave with no other incident. No, he must first be disgraced in the sight of all the world—not only in the sight of the Athenians or Spartans or Nicopolitans. Next he must also be whipped if he has entered into the contests rashly. And before being whipped, he must suffer thirst and heat and swallow much dust.

[53] "Reflect more carefully, know yourself, consult the divinity. And without God, attempt nothing—for he will advise you *to do this or anything*. And be assured that he intends you to become great or to receive many blows. [54] For this very amusing quality is tied to a Cynic: he must be flogged like a donkey, and when he is flogged, he must love those who flog him as if he were the father and the brother of all. [55] 'No,' you say, 'if a man flogs you, you can stand in the public place and call out for Caesar, asking why it is you suffer under his protection? You can demand they bring you before the proconsul.' [56] But what is Caesar to a Cynic, or what is a proconsul, or what is any other, except the one who sent the Cynic down here, the one he serves—namely Zeus? Does he call upon any other one than Zeus? Is he not convinced that whatever he suffers, it is Zeus who is exercising him? [57] When Heracles was exercised by Eurystheus, he did not think that he was wretched, but without hesitation he attempted to execute all that he had in hand. And is he who is trained for the contest and exercised by Zeus going to call out and to be vexed—he who is worthy to bear the scepter of Diogenes?

[58] "Listen to what Diogenes says to the passersby when he had a fever. 'Miserable wretches—will you not stay? But are you going on so long a journey to Olympia to see the destruction or the fight of athletes? And will you not choose to see the battle between a fever and a man?'

[59] "Would such a man accuse God who sent him down as if

God were treating him unworthily—a man who gloried in his circumstances and claimed to be an example to those who were passing by? For what would he accuse God of? That he maintains a decency of behavior? That he displays his virtue more conspicuously? [60] Well, and what does he say about poverty, death, and pain? How did he compare his own happiness with that of the Great King?[7] He didn't. Rather, he thought that there was no comparison between them. [61] For where there are perturbations and griefs and fears and unsatisfied desires and unavoidable aversions for things and envies and jealousies, how is there a road to happiness? But wherever there are bad or unsound judgments, all these things must necessarily exist in that place."

[62] When the young man asked Epictetus whether a Cynic should accept an invitation from a friend when he has fallen sick and a friend has asked him to come to his house so that he might take care of him in his sickness, he replied, [63] "And where will you find, I ask, a Cynic's friend? For the man who invites him should be as the Cynic is so that he may be worthy of being counted as the Cynic's friend. He should be a partner in the Cynic's scepter[8] and his royalty, and a worthy minister, if he intends to be considered worthy of a Cynic's friendship—even as Diogenes was a friend of Antisthenes, and Crates was a friend of Diogenes. [64] Do you think that if a man comes to a Cynic and salutes him, that he is the Cynic's friend, and that the Cynic will think him worthy of receiving a Cynic into his house? [65] So, if you wish, reflect on this also: rather look around for some convenient dunghill on which you will endure your fever and which will shelter you from the north wind so that you will not be chilled. [66] But you seem to me to wish to go into some man's house to be well fed there for a time. Why, then, do you think about attempting something as great as the Cynic life?"

[67] "But," the young man said, "should marriage and the procreation of children as a chief duty be undertaken by the Cynic?"

"If you grant me a community of wise men," Epictetus replied, "perhaps no man will readily apply himself to the Cynic practice. For in that case, on whose account should he undertake this manner of life? [68] Nevertheless, if we suppose that he does, nothing will prevent him from marrying and begetting children since his wife will be another like himself, and his father-in-law another like himself, and his children will be brought up like himself.

[69] "But in the present state of things, which is like that of an army placed in battle order, is it not fitting that the Cynic should serve God without any distraction, able to go about among men, not tied down to the common duties of mankind or entangled in the ordinary relations of life, which, if he neglects them, he will not maintain the character of an honorable and good man? And if he observes them, he will lose the character of the messenger, the spy and herald of God. [70] For consider that it is his duty to do something for his father-in-law and the other relations of his wife, and something for his wife also. He is also excluded by being a Cynic from looking after the sickness of his own family, and from providing for their support. That's to say nothing of the rest. [71] For instance, he must have a vessel for heating water in order to wash the child in the bath, and wool for his wife when she gives birth, and oil, a bed, and a cup. Consequently, the furniture of the house is increased. [72] I say nothing of his other occupations and distractions.

"Where now is that king, the one who devotes himself to the public interests, 'the people's guardian so full of cares,'⁹ whose duty it is to look after others, the married and those who have children? He must see which man uses his wife well or badly. He must observe who quarrels, and what family is well administered or not. He's the one who makes his rounds like a physician and feels pulses. [73] He says to one, 'You have a fever,' to another, 'You have a headache, or the gout.' And, 'Abstain from food.' He orders another to eat or not to use the bath. He explains to another that he requires the knife or the cautery.

[74] "How can he have time for this—the man who is tied to the duties of common life? Is it not such a man's duty to supply clothing to his children and to send them to the schoolmaster with writing tablets and writing utensils? Besides must he not supply them with beds? I say this because his children cannot be genuine Cynics as soon as they are born. If he does not do this, it would be better to expose the children as soon as they are born than to kill them in this

way. [75] Consider, then, what we are bringing the Cynic down to—how we are taking his royalty from him. [76] 'Yes,' you say, 'but Crates took a wife.' You are speaking of a circumstance that arose from love and of a woman who was another Crates. But we are inquiring about ordinary marriages and those that are free from distractions. And making this inquiry, we do not find the affair of marriage in this state of the world a thing that is especially suited to the Cynic.

[77] "'How then,' you ask, 'will a man maintain the existence of society?' In the name of God, are those men greater benefactors to society who introduce into the world two or three grunting children who will occupy their own places, or those who superintend as far as they can all mankind, observing what they do, how they live, what they attend to, and what they neglect contrary to their duty? [78] Did they who left little children to the Thebans do them more good than Epaminondas who died childless? And did Priam, who begat fifty worthless sons, or Danaus, or Aeolus contribute more to the community than Homer?[10]

[79] "What, then? Should the duty of a general or the business of a writer exclude a man from marriage or the begetting of children, leaving him not judged as one who accepted the condition of childlessness for nothing? If so, then should not the kingship of a Cynic be counted as making up for his lack of children? [80] Do we not perceive his grandeur? And do we not justly contemplate the character of Diogenes? Or what? Do we instead turn to look at the Cynics living today, the ones who are merely dogs waiting at tables, and in no way imitate the older Cynics apart from their flatulence, but in nothing else? [81] Otherwise such matters would have never disturbed us, nor would we have wondered if a Cynic should not marry or beget children.

"Man, the Cynic is the father of all men—men are his sons and women are his daughters. So it is that he carefully visits everyone, so well does he care for all. [82] Do you think that it is from idle impertinence that he admonishes those whom he meets? He does it as a father, as a brother, and as the minister of the father of all, the minister of Zeus.

[83] "If you will, ask me as well if a Cynic will engage in the administration of the state. [84] You knob! Are you searching for a greater form of administration than that in which he is engaged? Are you asking whether he will appear among the Athenians and say something about the revenues and the supplies, the one who must talk with all men alike, with Athenians, Corinthians, and Romans—yet not about supplies or revenues or peace or war but about happiness and unhappiness, about good fortune and bad fortune, about slavery and freedom? [85] . . .

[86] "It is also necessary for the Cynic to have a certain habit of body. If he appears to be consumptive, thin and pale, his testimony will not have the same weight. [87] For he must not only, by showing the qualities of the soul, prove to the average person that it is in his power, independent of the things they admire, to be a good man, but he must also show by his body that his simple and frugal way of living in the open air does not injure even the body. [88] 'See,' he says, 'I am a proof of this, and my own body also is.' It is what Diogenes used to do. He used to go about looking fresh and bright, and he attracted the notice of the many by the appearance of his body. [89] But if a Cynic is the object of pity, he seems to be a beggar. And so people turn away from him, offended by him. He should not appear dirty so that he will not in this way drive men away. Instead, his squalor should be clean and attractive.

[90] "There should also belong to the Cynic much natural grace and mental sharpness—if this is not so, he is a stupid fellow and nothing else. He must have these qualities so that he may readily and appropriately match every circumstance that may arise. [91] Diogenes replied in such a manner to one who asked him if he was the Diogenes who did not believe that there are gods. He said, 'How can this be when I think that you are odious to the gods?' [92] Or another time, when Alexander stood over him as he was sleeping and said, 'The man who is a counselor should not sleep all night,' he responded, still half asleep, 'The people's guardian so full of cares must be watchful.'[11]

[93] "But before all, the governing part of the Cynic's soul must be purer than the sun. And if it is not, he must necessarily be a cunning

knave and a fellow of no principle since, while he himself is entangled in some vice, he admonishes others. [94] Let's see how the matter stands. To the kings and tyrants of this world their guards and arms give the power of reproving some persons, and of being able even to punish those who do wrong though they are themselves bad. But to a Cynic, instead of arms and guards, it is conscience that gives this power.

[95] "When he knows that he has watched and labored for mankind, and that he has slept in purity, and sleep has left him still purer, and that he has thought whatever he has thought as a friend of the gods, as a minister, as a participant in the power of Zeus, and that on all occasions he is ready to say, 'Lead me, O Zeus, and you, Destiny,' and also, 'If this pleases the gods, so be it,'[12] [96] then why should he not have the confidence to speak freely to his own brothers, to his children, in a word, to his kinsmen?

[97] "For this reason he is neither over curious nor a busybody when he is in this state of mind. For he is not a meddler with the affairs of others when he is superintending human affairs; rather, he is looking after his own affairs. If that is not so, you may also say that the general is a busybody when he inspects his soldiers and examines them and watches them and punishes the disorderly.

[98] "But if while you have a cake under your arm, you rebuke others, I will say to you, 'Will you not rather go away into a corner and eat that which you have stolen? [99] What do you have to do with the affairs of others? Who are you?—the bull of the herd or the queen of the bees? Show me the tokens of your supremacy, such as they have from nature. But if you are a drone claiming the sovereignty over the bees, do you not suppose that your fellow citizens will put you down as the bees do the drones?'

[100] "The Cynic should have such power of endurance that he seems insensible to the common sort, like a stone. No man reviles him, no man strikes him, no man insults him—but he gives his body up so that any man who chooses may do with it whatever he likes. . . .

[104] "Is the Cynic's assent ever hasty, his movement toward an object rash? Does his desire ever fail in obtaining its object? Does that which he wishes to avoid ever happen to him? Is his purpose

unaccomplished? Does he ever find fault? Is he ever humiliated? Is he ever envious? [105] To these points he directs all his attention and energy. As for anything else, he snores supine. All is peace. There is no robber or tyrant who takes away his will. [106] But one that snatches his body? Sure. And his possessions? Yes. But he doesn't care about ruling offices and honors. When anyone, therefore, attempts to frighten him by mentioning them, he says, 'Be off! Look for children. Masks are scary to them, but I know that they are made of clay and have nothing inside them.'

[107] "It is about such a business and activity as this that you are deliberating. Therefore, if you will, I urge you in God's name to defer the matter, and first consider your preparation for it. [108] Recall what Hector says to Andromache. 'Go,' he says, 'into the house and weave. War is the work of men—and mine above all.' [109] So it was that he was conscious of his own qualification and also of her inability."

NOTES

1 Philip II of Macedon defeated the Greeks, led by Thebes and Athens, at the battle of Chaeronea in 338 BC. For more on the Cynic as a "spy" and "scout," see sections 38 and 69 of Epictetus' *Discourse* 3.22, and Diogenes Laertius, *Lives* 6.43.
2 See (pseudo) Plato, *Cleitophon* 407a-b.
3 Myro (Myron) and Ophellius were likely famous athletes or gladiators—but nothing is known about them.
4 The Lydian ruler Croesus was fabulously wealthy—so much so that he supposed he was the happiest man in the world. See Herodotus, *Histories* 1.30.
5 Sardanapalus was an Assyrian king who, according to legend, lived a phenomenally luxurious life.
6 For Agamemnon, see Homer, *Iliad* 10.15, 91, 94-95.
7 The king of Persia, a vast empire, was called the Great King.
8 The Greek word *skēptron* also means staff, and is thus a reference to the Cynic staff, though the typical word for the Cynic staff is *baktron*.
9 See Homer, *Iliad* 2.25.
10 Priam, Danaus, and Aeolus were mythical kings who sired many sons and daughters.
11 Both Alexander and Diogenes were quoting Homer. See *Iliad* 2.24-25.
12 See Epictetus, *Handbook (Enchiridion)* 53, *Discourse* 2.23, and Plato, *Crito* 43d.

FIFTEEN

ON THE VIRTUE OF CRATES
FROM APULEIUS' *FLORIDA*

IN BRIEF: *Apuleius explores various aspects of Crates of Thebes' life as a Cynic philosopher. He gave advice to families and served as a mediator. Similar to Hercules, he conquered the monstrous passions of the soul. He gave up wealth in order to seek something more stable.*

CRATES, THE WELL-KNOWN disciple of Diogenes, was honored at Athens by the men of his own day as though he had been a household god. No house was ever closed to him, no head of a family ever had so close a secret as to regard Crates as an inconvenient intruder. He was always welcome. There was never a quarrel, never a grievance between family members, that he was not accepted as the mediator and his word as law.

The poets tell that Hercules[1] of old by his valor subdued all the wild monsters of legend, beast or man, and purged all the world of them. Even so our philosopher Crates was truly a Hercules in the conquest of anger, envy, avarice, lust, and all the other monstrous and shameful things that plague the human soul. He expelled all these pests from their minds, purged households, and tamed vice. Not only that, but he too went half-naked and was distinguished by the club he carried. And he sprang from that same Thebes where men say that Hercules was born.

Even before he became Crates pure and simple, he was accounted one of the chief men in Thebes. His family was noble, his establishment numerous, his house had a fair and ample porch. His lands were rich and his clothing sumptuous.

But later, when he understood that the wealth that had been given to him came with no safeguard on which he might lean as on a staff in the course of his life, he realized that all was fragile and transitory—that all the wealth in all the world was no help in living well, in living virtuously.

NOTES

[1] Hercules rather than Heracles because Apuleius (second century AD) wrote in Latin, and the Latin version of Heracles is Hercules.

SIXTEEN

THE CYNIC, A DIALOGUE[1]
FROM LUCIAN OF SAMOSATA

IN BRIEF: *In Lucian's dialogue, a man called Lycinus discusses Cynicism with a Cynic philosopher. Lycinus demands that the Cynic "give an account of [him]self." Why does he do what he does? Why does he appear as he does? The Cynic's simple answer is, "It meets my needs." Thus, he is self-sufficient in terms of housing, clothing, nourishment, and other necessities. He avoids the vexation and worry that many experience in chasing after other non-necessary things. Rather than being like a beast, he is more like the gods, who have no needs. He offers Heracles and Theseus as examples of a well-lived life.*

LYCINUS. GIVE AN account of yourself, my man. You wear a beard and let your hair grow. You eschew shirts, exhibit your skin, and your feet are bare. You choose a wandering, outcast, beastly life. Unlike other people, you make your own body the object of your severities. You go from place to place sleeping on the hard ground where chance finds you, with the result that your old cloak, neither light nor soft nor anything to look at to begin with, is loaded down with filth. Why?

Cynic. It meets my needs. It was easy to come by, and it gives its owner no trouble. It is sufficient for me. [2] Tell me, do you not call extravagance a vice?

Ly. Oh, yes.

Cy. And frugality a virtue?

Ly. Yes, again.

Cy. Then, if you find me living frugally, and others extravagantly, why blame me instead of them?

Ly. I do not call your life more frugal than other people's. I call it more destitute—destitution and want, that is what it is. You are no better than the poor who beg for their daily bread.

Cy. [3] That brings us to a few questions. What is want or lacking? And what is sufficiency? Shall we try to find the answers?

Ly. If you like, yes.

Cy. A man's sufficiency is that which meets his needs or is sufficient for what he requires—will that do?

Ly. I'll accept that.

Cy. And want or lacking occurs when the supply falls short of need and does not satisfy what is needful.

Ly. Yes.

Cy. Very well, then, I am lacking nothing—I am not in want. Everything I have is lined up with what I require.

Ly. [4] How do you draw that conclusion?

Cy. Well, consider the purpose of anything we require. The purpose of a house is protection, right?

Ly. Yes.

Cy. Clothing—what is that for? Protection too, I think.

Ly. Yes.

Cy. But now, tell me, what in turn is the purpose of the protection? It is the better condition of the protected, I presume.

Ly. I agree.

Cy. Then do you think my feet are in a worse condition than yours?

Ly. I cannot say.

Cy. Oh, yes you can. Look at it this way: what do feet do? What is their function or work?

Ly. It is to walk—they walk.

Cy. And do you think my feet walk worse than yours, or worse than the average man's?

Ly. I doubt it.

Cy. Then they are not in a worse condition—if, that is, they perform their function as well.

Ly. That may be so.

Cy. So it appears that, as far as feet go, I am in no worse condition than other people.

Ly. No, I do not think you are.

Cy. Well, what about the rest of my body, then? If it is in worse condition, it must be weaker, strength being the virtue of the body. Is mine weaker?

Ly. Not that I see.

Cy. Consequently, neither my feet nor the rest of my body need protection, it seems. If they did, they would be in a bad condition since want is always an evil and worsens the thing concerned. But again, there is no sign, either, of my body's being nourished any worse even though its nourishment is of a common sort.

Ly. None at all.

Cy. It would not be healthy, if it were badly nourished, since bad food injures the body.

Ly. That's true.

Cy. [5] If it is true, then it is up to you to explain why you castigate me and denigrate my life and call it miserable.

Ly. That's easy to explain. Nature, which you honor, and the gods have given us the earth and have brought all sorts of good things out of it, providing us with abundance—not merely for our necessities but for our pleasures. Nevertheless, you abstain from all or nearly all of it, and utilize these good things no more than the beasts. Your drink is water, just like theirs. Like a dog, you eat what you pick up. And the dog's bed is as good as yours—straw is enough for either of you. Then your clothes are no more presentable than a beggar's. Now, if this sort of contentment is to pass for wisdom, God must have been all wrong in making sheep woolly, filling grapes with wine, and providing all our infinite variety of oil, honey, and the rest, that we might have food of every sort, pleasant drink, money, soft beds, fine houses—all the wonderful paraphernalia of civilization, in fact, since the productions of art are God's gifts to us too. To live without all these would be miserable enough even if one could not help it, as prisoners cannot, for instance. It is far more so if the abstention is forced on a man by himself. Then it is sheer madness.

Cy. [6] You may be right. But consider this. A rich man, indulging hospitable and kindly instincts, entertains at a feast all sorts and conditions of men. Some of them are sick. Others are healthy. And the dishes provided are as diverse as the guests. Sitting there is one man to whom nothing comes contrary to his wish. He has his finger in every dish—not only the ones within easy reach but those at a distance that were intended for the sick guests—and this even though he is in good health and has no more than one stomach and requires little to nourish him and is likely to be upset by the excess. What is your opinion of this man? Is he wise—a sensible man?

Ly. Not to me.

Cy. Is he moderate?

Ly. Not that either.

Cy. [7] And what about this? There is another guest at the same table. He seems not to care about all the variety of foods. Rather, selecting some dish close by that is sufficient for his need, he eats of it as a decent, well-behaved man would, restricting himself to it without a glance at the rest. Do you not believe he is a more moderate and better man than the other?

Ly. I do.

Cy. Do you get it, or must I explain?

Ly. What?

Cy. That the good and noble host is god, who provides this variety of all kinds so that each man may have something to suit him. This dish is for the healthy, that one for the sick. This dish is for the strong, that one for the weak. It is not all for each one of us. Each man is to take what is within reach, and of that only what he most needs.

[8] Now you others are like the greedy, unrestrained person who grabs everything. Local productions will not do for you—the world must be your storehouse. Your homeland and its seas are

insufficient, so you purchase your pleasures from the ends of the earth, preferring the exotic to that which is home grown, the costly to the cheap, the rare to the common. In fact, you would rather have troubles and complications than avoid them.

Most of the precious instruments of happiness that you so pride yourselves on are won only with unhappiness and hardships. Give a moment's thought, if you will, to the gold you all pray for, to the silver, the costly houses, the elaborate clothing. And do not forget all the trouble and toil and danger they cost—the blood and death and ruin. Not only do large numbers of men perish at sea on their account, but many endure miseries in producing them. Moreover, they're very likely to be fought for—the desire for them makes friends plot against friends, children against parents, wives against husbands.

[9] How pointless it all is! Embroidered clothes have no more warmth in them than others. Gilded houses do not do better in keeping out the rain. A drink is no sweeter out of a silver cup—or a gold one for that matter. An ivory bed makes sleep no softer; on the contrary, your fortunate man on his ivory bed between his delicate sheets constantly finds himself calling on sleep in vain. And as to the elaborate preparation of food, I hardly need to say that instead of aiding nutrition it injures the body and produces diseases in it.

[10] And what is to be said about sex—about the many activities men do and suffer thanks to those things belonging to Aphrodite? This longing is easy to take care of unless a kind of licentious indulgence is the goal. And yet in this business, frenzied passion and moral corruption do not seem to be enough for these men. But these days, men pervert the use of everything they have, using it for unnatural purposes. Take the man who, rather than using a carriage, chooses to use a bed as though it were a carriage.

Ly. Is there such a person?

Cy. Yes—he is you. You for whom men are beasts of burden—you who make them shoulder your bed-carriages, slouching up there in luxury, driving your men along like so many mules, calling on them to turn this way and not that. This is one of the outward and visible signs of your blessed happiness.

[11] Again, when people use edible things not for food but to get dye out of them. Take the murex-dyers, those who deal in purple, for instance. Are they not making use of the arrangements and devices of god in a way that is contrary to nature?

Ly. Certainly not. The flesh of the murex can provide a pigment as well as food.

Cy. But it wasn't made—it didn't come into being—for that. You can force a bowl made for mixing water with wine into use as a pitcher, but that is not what it exists for.

Even so, it is impossible to detail the whole of the unhappiness of these people. It is big, though. And because I will not join them, you reproach me. My life is that of the decent, well-behaved man I described. I enjoy what comes to hand, use what is cheap, and have no desire for the elaborate and exotic.

[12] Moreover, if you think I live the life of an animal just because I need and use only a few things, that argument leads you to the conclusion that the gods are even lower than the beasts since the gods have no needs at all. But to clear your ideas on the comparative merits of great and small needs, you have only to reflect that children have more needs than adults, women more than men, the sick more than the well, and, generally, the inferior more than the superior. Accordingly, the gods have no needs, and those men who have the fewest needs are nearest the gods.

[13] Take Heracles, the best man that ever lived, a divine man, and rightly considered a god. Was it unhappiness that made him go around in nothing but a lion's skin, insensible to all the needs you feel? No, he was not unhappy, the man who relieved the misfortunes of others. He was not poor, he who ruled land and sea. Wherever he went, he was master. He never met his superior or his equal as long as he lived. Do you suppose, then, that he could not get coverings or clothes or shoes, and that's why he went around as he did? We cannot draw this conclusion. Rather, he possessed self-

control and was able to endure. His will was to be powerful, strong; his wish wasn't for luxury.

And his disciple Theseus, who was king of all the Athenians, son of Poseidon, as people say, and the best of his generation—[14] he too chose to go without shoes and to be naked. He was content to let his hair and beard grow. He was not the only one; rather, all those of old who lived when he lived were satisfied in this way. They were better men than you and would no more have let you shave them than a lion would. Soft, smooth flesh was fine for women, they thought. As for them, however, they were men, and they wanted to look like men. They acknowledged the beard was man's adornment—like the horse's or the lion's mane, to whom god had added a certain grace of splendor and adornment just as he added the beard to men. So it is that I admire the men of old and want to imitate them. As for today's men, I do not admire them for their "amazing" happiness caught up in eating and clothing and smooth bodies—every part!—the hair forbidden to grow wherever nature meant it to grow.

[15] I pray that my feet might be hoofs, like Chiron's in the story.² And that I might need bedding no more than the lion, and costly food no more than the dog. Let my sufficient bed be the whole earth, my house this cosmos, and my chosen food the easiest to get. May I have no need—I nor any that I call friend—for gold and silver. For every human misfortune is generated by a longing for these—civil strife and wars, conspiracies and slaughters. The fountain of them all is a longing for more. That's not me. May I bear with less rather than desiring more and more.

[16] Such are our aspirations—they are considerably different from other people's. It is no wonder that our outfit is different since the peculiarity of our underlying principle is so different. I cannot understand why you allow a harpist his proper attire, as well as the fluteplayer and tragic actor, but you will not be consistent and recognize an outfit or uniform for a good man. The good man must be like everyone else, of course, regardless of the fact that everyone else is all wrong. Well, if good men are to have a uniform of their own, there can be none better than that which a licentious man will consider most improper and will decisively reject for himself.

[17] Now my uniform consists of a rough hairy skin, a thread-bare cloak, long hair, and bare feet, whereas yours is that of a cata-mite. There is not much difference between you—the colors, the soft texture, the number of garments you are swathed in, the shoes, the slick hair, your smell. For the happier you are, the more you smell of perfume. What value can one give to a man who smells like a catamite? Accordingly, you can tolerate no more toil or hardship than they can, and you are just as much a slave to pleasure as they are. You feed like them, sleep like them, walk like them—rather, you do not wish to walk any more than they do, but are carried like luggage, some by human beings, some by herds of animals.

As for me, my feet take me anywhere I want to go. I can put up with cold and heat and I am not displeased with the works of the gods—such a miserable wretch am I. By contrast, thanks to your happiness, you all are displeased with everything that happens and grumble without ceasing. What is, is intolerable. What is not, you pine for. In winter you want summer; in summer, winter. In heat you pine for cold; in cold, for heat. You're as fastidious and peevish as invalids are—only their reason is to be found in their illness, whereas yours is in your way of life.

[18] And then, because we occasionally make mistakes in prac-tice, you advise us to change our plan and correct our principles, when in fact you behave randomly in your own affairs, never acting as a result of deliberation or reason, but always thanks to habit and longing.

You are no better than people washed around by a flood. They drift with the current, and you with your longings. There is a story of a man on a vicious horse that describes your situation. The horse ran away with him, and at the pace it was going, he could not get off. A man in the way asked him where he was off to. "Wherever this animal takes me," he said. So if one asked you where you were going, if you cared to tell the truth, you would say, generally speaking, wherever your longings decide to go. Or, more specifically, you would say, wherever your pleasure decides to go. Or at times greed. Or anger. Or fear. Or at other times some other thing appears to carry you off. You're not just on one horse. No, you're mounted on many that carry you. And they're all mad with passion! They carry you toward pits and cliffs, but you do not realize that you are bound for a fall until the fall itself comes.

[19] The tattered cloak, the shaggy hair, the whole outfit that you ridicule has the effect that it enables me to live a quiet life, doing what I want and keeping the company I wish to keep. No ignorant, uneducated person will have anything to say to one dressed like this. And the ones who live softly turn the other way as soon as I come into view. But refined and reasonable men approach me, those who long for virtue. These are attached to me most of all since I delight in these kinds of men. I don't hang out at the doors of the so-called happy men. Rather, I judge their gold crowns and purple vanity and laugh at these men.

[20] There's something else to know about my outfit. It is not only fitting for good men but for the gods—even though it is ludicrous to you. You'll learn this if you take a look at the statues of the gods to see whether they look like you or me. And not only Greek statues, but inspect those found in non-Greek temples too. See whether they let their hair grow long and grow a beard or their sculptors and painters shave them. And, to be sure, you will see that they are just like me insofar as they have no *extra* tunic. So then how do you still dare to say that my outfit is pathetic when it seems like it is fitting enough for the gods?

NOTES

[1] The translation that follows is a modified version of H.W. Fowler and F.G. Fowler's version from *The Works of Lucian of Samosata* (1905).

[2] The son of Kronos (in the form of a horse) and Philyra, Chiron (or Cheiron) was a centaur (part human and part horse), who dwelled in a cave on Mount Pelion. Among others, Chiron brought up and educated the heroes Jason and Achilles, and the god Asclepius.

SEVENTEEN

TWO ORATIONS
FROM JULIAN THE EMPEROR

IN BRIEF: *In Oration 6, Julian presents what he knows about philosophy (various definitions and philosophy's origin), with a focus on Cynicism. He does so for those considering life as a Cynic. He claims that Cynicism is a universal philosophy, one that follows nature and requires no special study. He asserts that the god Apollo founded it. Its chief practitioners were Antisthenes, Diogenes, and Crates. The goal of Cynicism is happiness. Diogenes was a truly happy man. One may be happy by listening to the voice of the mind and by quieting the voice of pleasure and passion. Living virtuously is key. Cynics should seek truth by knowing themselves. They should also develop freedom, self-sufficiency, justice, moderation, piety, gratitude, and a rational approach to acting. Finally, given man's social and political nature, Cynics should care for their fellow human beings by preaching. In Oration 7, Julian explains what the true shortcut of Cynicism is, "to know oneself and to become like the gods" by means of the proper judgment of what is valuable, and a simple, ascetic life.*

ORATION 6: TO THE UNEDUCATED CYNICS[1]

BEHOLD THE RIVERS are flowing backward!—as the saying goes.[2] Here is a Cynic who declares that Diogenes[3] was conceited, and who refuses to take cold baths for fear they may injure him. This even though his body is exceedingly healthy, and [181] he is vigorous and in the prime of life, and though the Sun-god is now nearing the summer solstice.

[181] *And he refuses to eat raw octopus, and he believes that death is an evil (as if he knew), and when sick, he uses his illness as an excuse to live luxuriously.*

[181] Come now, let me set down for the benefit of the public what I learned from my teachers about the Cynics, so that all who are entering on this mode of life may consider it. And if they are convinced by what I say, [182] those who are now aiming to be Cynics will, I am sure, be none the worse for it. And if they are unconvinced but cherish aims that are brilliant and noble, and set themselves above my argument not in words only but in deeds, then my discourse will at any rate put no hindrance in their way.

[182-187] *As for others, those who are "enslaved by greed or self-indulgence" or "by the pleasures of the body," we won't concern ourselves with them. Rather, let us pursue the argument in due order, beginning with some words about philosophy itself since Cynicism is a particular kind of philosophy.*

The gods gave the gift of reason and mind—fire from the sun—to mankind. Philosophy may be given three related definitions: one, the highest kind of art and knowledge; two, an effort to become like god; and, three, the journey to "Know Yourself" as commanded by the Pythian Oracle.[4] Regardless, since truth is one, "so too is philosophy one"—though we may take various roads to truth, even as we may go by different ways to Athens.

When we know ourselves, we come to know all things—the divine through the divine within us, including universals; our souls and their powers; and our bodies, along with whatever things and arts that support them, such as medicine and agriculture. This self-knowledge takes the lead in every kind of art and knowledge. Moreover, when we know ourselves, we are like god, in that the gods know all things and particularly themselves. Other philosophers have called on their followers to know themselves—Heraclitus, Pythagoras, Aristotle, and the Stoics, the followers of Zeno of Citium.[5]

As for the Cynics, we must not mistake their playful writings for their earnest thoughts. To do so would be to mistake the inessential and even vicious outer parts of a city for the parts within its walls, including the priests and sacred precincts.

[187] I will borrow those famous phrases of Alcibiades in his praise of Socrates. I declare that the Cynic philosophy is like those statues of

Silenus that sit in the statue shops, the ones that the craftsmen make with pipes or flutes in their hands, but when you open them, you see that inside they contain statues of the gods.⁶ . . . *Similarly,* Cynicism itself is something very different, as I will presently try to prove. Let us consider it in due course from its works and actual practice, and pursue it like hounds that track down wild beasts in the chase.

Now the founder of this philosophy to whom we are to attribute it, in the first instance, is not easy to discover, even though some think that the title belongs to Antisthenes and Diogenes. At least the saying of Oenomaus seems to be not without good grounds: "The Cynic philosophy is neither Antisthenism nor Diogenism."⁷ Moreover, the better sort of Cynics assert that in addition to the other good things bestowed on us by mighty Heracles, it was he who gave to mankind the greatest example of this way of life.

But for my part, while I wish to speak with due reverence for the gods and for those who have attained to the divinity, I still believe that, even before Heracles, not only among the Greeks but among the non-Greeks also, there were men who practiced this philosophy. For it seems to be in some ways a common or universal philosophy, and the most natural, and to demand no special study whatsoever. But it is enough simply to choose the excellent by longing for virtue and fleeing from vice. And so there is no need to turn over countless books. For, as the saying goes, "Much learning does not teach understanding."⁸ Nor is it necessary to subject oneself to any part of such a discipline as they must undergo who enter other schools of philosophy.

[188] No—it is enough merely to listen to the Pythian god when he counsels these two precepts, "Know Yourself," and "Alter the currency."⁹ So then it is clear to us that the founder of this philosophy is the one who, I believe, is the cause of all the fine and noble things established by the Greeks, the universal leader of Greece, and law-giver and king, I mean the god of Delphi, *Apollo*. And since it is not right to attribute ignorance of anything to a god, we know the fitness of Diogenes did not escape the god's notice. And he urged him on not by exhortations spoken in verse, as he does for other men, but he instructed him symbolically with two sayings.

The one was, "Alter the currency." The other, "Know Yourself," he addressed not only to Diogenes, but to other men also, and he still does, as the saying stands there engraved in front of his shrine.

And so we have finally discovered the founder of this philosophy, even as the divine Iamblichus[10] also declares. And we have discovered its chief men as well, namely Antisthenes and Diogenes and Crates. The aim and end of their lives was, I think, to know themselves, to be aware of empty opinions, and to lay hold of truth with their whole understanding. This is so because truth—both for gods and men—is the beginning of every good thing.

[188-189] *The truth is what Plato, Pythagoras, Socrates, the Peripatetic philosophers (those who came after Aristotle), and Zeno of Citium struggled for, wishing to know themselves rather than the empty views of the many. They are one in this aim and in their zeal for virtue, whether they strive for the goal more through words, as Plato did, or through deeds, as Diogenes of Sinope did.*

[189] Why then should we not study the character of the Cynic philosophy using the acts and practices of Diogenes?

[189] *In somewhat of an aside, Julian suggests that we should value things like our eyes and ears over things like our hair and nails because it is through our sense organs that we understand what is around us and have knowledge. But, he says, this has little to do with the overall point.*

[190] So we must bring to mind the parts of the philosophy of the Cynics. It seems they held that there were two parts of philosophy, as did Aristotle and Plato, namely the theoretical and the practical. The Cynics held this evidently because they had observed and understood that man is by nature suited both to action and to the pursuit of knowledge. And though they avoided the study of natural philosophy, that does not affect the argument. I say this because Socrates and many others also, as we know, devoted themselves to speculation or contemplation even though it was solely for practical ends. For they thought that even self-knowledge meant learning

precisely what must be assigned to the soul, and what to the body. And to the soul they naturally assigned the leading role, and to the body the role of those who are led and serve. This seems to be the reason why they practiced virtue, self-control, non-vanity, and freedom, and why they shunned all forms of envy, cowardice, and superstition. But this, you will say, is not the view that we hold about them. Rather, we are to think that they were not in earnest, and that they hazarded what is most precious in thus despising the body—this as Socrates did when he declared, and rightly, that philosophy is the practice and preparation for death.[11]

[190] *Why did he endure hardships anyway? Why eat raw meat? Surely not for applause!*

[190] At any rate, when you imitate one of those Cynics by carrying a staff and wearing your hair long, as it is shown in their pictures, do you think that you thereby gain a reputation with the crowd, though you do not yourself think those habits worthy of admiration?

[190-191] *Very few applauded Diogenes (in his lifestyle and when he ate raw meat). Most were simply shocked by him even though the gods did not judge him ignoble.*

[191] For just as Socrates said of himself that he embraced the life of cross-examining[12] because he believed that he could perform his service to the god only by examining in all its bearings the meaning of the oracle that had been uttered concerning him, so I think Diogenes also, because he was convinced that philosophy was ordained by the Pythian oracle, believed that he ought to test everything by facts and not be influenced by the opinions of others—views that may happen to be true or false. Accordingly, Diogenes did not think that every statement of Pythagoras, or any man like Pythagoras, was necessarily true. For he held that the god and no human being is the founder of philosophy.

[191-193] *What does this have to do with eating raw meat (raw octopus)?* *For Diogenes, eating raw meat was a way to settle a dispute with strong* *views and many books on either side—one asserting that eating meat is* *natural for human beings, the other denying its suitability. His idea was* *that if meat causes no harm and is easy to prepare, then it is natural or* *follows nature; if not, then it is not.*

First, though, says Julian, "I must describe more clearly the end and *aim of that philosophy. The Cynics regard freedom from emotion as the* *goal—and this is equivalent to becoming a god."*

Back to the point: aside from custom, there is no reason why we only *eat cooked meat and not raw meat. Cooking meat doesn't make it any less* *disgusting (if it is) than it is by nature. Nor does passing it through fire* *somehow make meat pure or holy. But here you are criticizing Diogenes* *for eating raw octopus when you, an Egyptian, eat everything. Not only* *that, but people who live near the sea eat many raw things—sea urchins,* *oysters, and the like, with no addition of fire. How is an octopus different* *from those things? Both are bloodless. Both are animate and feel pleasure* *and pain (and here we must not consider Plato's teaching that plants are* *also animated). Regardless, the difference between Diogenes and you is* *that Diogenes judged he should eat things in their natural state whereas* *you do violence to a thing's nature in all your preparations. Anyway,* *enough of this topic.*

[193] Now the aim and end of the Cynic philosophy, as with every philosophy, is to be happy—but to be happy in a life lived according to nature and not according to the opinions of the many.[13] Plants also do well, and indeed all animals also, whenever each one, without hindrance, reaches the goal that follows from and is in accord with nature. But even among the gods, this is the definition of happiness—that their state should be according to their nature, and that they should be independent.

[194] And so too in the case of human beings we must not be busy about happiness as if it were hidden away outside ourselves. Neither the eagle nor the plane tree nor anything else that has life, whether plant or animal, vainly troubles itself about wings or leaves of gold or that its shoots may be of silver or its stings and spurs of iron, or,

rather, of adamant. Instead, where nature in the beginning has adorned them with such things, they consider that they themselves are doing well and flourishing—if only they are strong and serviceable for speed or defense. So then, is it not laughable when a man tries to find happiness somewhere outside himself, and thinks that wealth and birth and the influence of friends, and, generally speaking, everything of that sort is of the utmost importance?

If, however, nature had bestowed on us only what she has bestowed on other animals—I mean the possession of bodies and souls like theirs—so that we need concern ourselves with nothing beyond, then it would be enough for us, as for all other animals, to be satisfied with the advantages of the body, and to pursue happiness within this field. But in us has been implanted a soul that in no way resembles that of other animals. And whether this soul is different in being or essence, or it is not different in being or essence but is superior in its activity or function alone—just as, I suppose, pure gold is superior to gold alloyed with sand (for some people hold this theory to be true of the soul)—either way, we surely know that we are more intelligent than other animals. For according to the myth in the *Protagoras*,[14] nature dealt with them very generously and bountifully, like a mother. But to compensate for all this, mind was given to us by Zeus. Therefore, we must say that happiness resides in our minds, in the best and most excellent part of us.

Now consider whether Diogenes did not profess this belief since he freely submitted his body to toil and hardships so that he might make it stronger than it was by nature. [195] He allowed himself to act only as the light of reason shows us that we ought to act. And the disturbances and confusions that attack the soul and are derived from the body—to which this envelope of ours often constrains us for its sake to pay too much attention—he did not take into account at all. Consequently, by means of this training the man made his body stronger, I believe, than that of any who have contended for the prize of a crown in the games. And his soul was so disposed that he was happy. And in this happiness he was a king no less—if not even more!—than the Great King, as the Greeks used to call him in those days, by which they meant the king of Persia.

Does he then seem to you of no importance, this man who was "without a city, homeless, a man without a country, owning not even a coin, neither an obol nor a drachma, and not a single slave," —no, not even a barley-cake (and yet Epicurus declares that if has enough bread, then he is not inferior to the gods regarding happiness[15]). This is not to say that Diogenes tried to compete with the gods. Still, he lived more happily than one who is counted the happiest of men. And he actually used to assert that he lived more happily than such a man. But if you do not believe me, try his way of life not by talking about it but by doing it. Then you'll get it.

[195-196] *If we look at the matter rationally, we'll see that freedom is the greatest good. Even things such as property, money, birth, strength, and beauty are only blessings if we are free. But what is freedom? Or what is slavery? Are we slaves only when we fear the punishment, the stick, of a master? No. Instead, there are many kinds of slavery.*

[196] So then, never believe, my friend, that you are free as long as the belly rules you, and the parts below the belly, since you will then have masters who can either provide you with pleasure or deprive you. And even if you become better than these, as long as you are slave to the opinions of the many, you have not yet approached freedom or tasted its nectar. . . . I do not mean by this that we should be shameless before all men and do what should not be done. Rather, in all that we abstain from and all that we do, let us not abstain from or do anything merely because it seems to the many somehow excellent or base but because it is forbidden by reason and the god within us, that is, the mind.

[196-198] *It's fine for the many to follow common opinions as these views actually often follow nature. In doing so the many will avoid being shameless. But not so the man who lives according to the light of the mind. Regardless, we should not pay attention to the views of the many until we have disciplined the raucous part of our souls and persuaded it to listen to and obey the divine part—mind and intelligence. Contrary to what many followers of Diogenes think today, and to how they behave, this discipline*

is most important. Let me tell a story about Diogenes to make the point. Even though he saw nothing inherently shameful in farting in public, he once chastised a young follower of his for doing so before he had done the harder work of training his soul to quiet the voice of pleasure and passion. In other words, it is easy to disregard public opinion; it is hard to practice hardship.

People lure the young away from practicing philosophy by slandering the genuine philosophers among us—the true followers of Pythagoras, Plato, and Aristotle. Or they pity them. Such they do with truly serious Cynics. I experienced this myself when my tutor pitied my classmate Iphicles for taking on the outfit of the Cynics. He pitied him and his parents. So do most people pity genuine Cynics. That's not so bad. The problem, rather, is this—

[198] Do you see that people persuade the young to love wealth, to hate poverty, to take care of the belly, to endure any toil for the body's sake, to fatten that prison of the soul, to keep up an expensive table, never to sleep alone at night,[16] provided only that they do all this in the dark and are not discovered? Is not this worse than Tartarus? Is it not better to sink beneath Charybdis and Cocytus[17] or countless fathoms beneath the earth than to fall into a life like this, enslaved to your genitals and your belly? . . .

How much better it is to abstain from all of this! And if this is not easy, then the rules of Diogenes and Crates on these matters are not to be despised: "Hunger releases you from desire. And if this doesn't work, a noose."[18]

Do you not know that those great men lived as they did to introduce among men the way of simple or frugal living? "For," says Diogenes, [199] "it is not among men who eat barley-bread that you will find tyrants but among those who feast lavishly." Moreover, Crates wrote a hymn to Thrift: "Greetings, goddess queen, the delight of wise men, Thrift, the child of glorious Moderation."[19]

[199-200] *The Cynic should be reverent toward sacred things as was Diogenes, who obeyed the Pythian oracle and worshipped the gods with the whole of his soul. Led on by reason, the Cynic should train hard to subdue*

the passionate part of his soul. We see in Crates' hymn to the Muses that his one wish was to "possess justice and to collect riches that are easily carried, easily acquired, and valued for virtue." You may discover more about his character in Plutarch's Life of Crates.[20]

[200] But let me go back to what I said before, that he who is beginning to be a Cynic should first censure himself severely and cross-examine himself, and without any self-flattery ask himself the following questions in precise terms: whether he enjoys lavish and expensive food; whether he cannot do without a soft bed; whether he is the slave of honor and reputation; whether it is his ambition to get people to look at and admire him; and, even though it is empty, he still judges it an honor.

Nevertheless, he must not let himself drift with the current of the crowd or touch luxury even with the tip of his finger, as the saying goes, until he has succeeded in trampling on it. Only then, and not before, may he permit himself to dip into that sort of thing if it happens to come his way. For instance, I am told that bulls that are weaker than the rest separate themselves from the herd, and they pasture alone while they store up their strength in every part of their bodies by degrees. Only then do they rejoin the herd in good condition. And then they challenge its leaders to contend with them, in confidence that they are more fit to take the lead.

Therefore, let the man who wishes to be a Cynic philosopher not adopt merely their tattered cloak [201] or leather bag or staff or their way of wearing the hair, as though he were like a man walking unshaved and illiterate in a village that lacked barbers' shops and schools, but let him consider that reason rather than a staff, and a certain plan of life rather than a leather bag are the marks of the Cynic philosophy. And he must not employ frank speech until he has first demonstrated how much he is worth—as I believe was the case with Crates and Diogenes.

For they were so far from bearing with a bad grace any threat of fortune, whether one call such threats caprice or wanton insult, that once, when he had been captured by pirates, Diogenes joked with them. As for Crates, he gave his property to the state, and being physically deformed he made fun of his own disabled leg and curved shoulders. But when his friends gave a feast, he used to go, whether invited or not, and would reconcile his nearest friends if he learned that they had quarreled. He used to reprove them not harshly but with a charming manner, and not so as to seem to persecute those whom he wished to correct but as if he wished to be of use both to them and to those listening.

Yet even this was not the main goal of those Cynics. Rather, as I said, their chief aim was how they themselves might be happy. They concerned themselves with other men only insofar as they understood that man is by nature a social and political animal. And so they benefited their fellow citizens, not only by serving as an example but by their conversation as well.

Then let him who wishes to be a Cynic, to be an excellent man, first take himself in hand like Diogenes and Crates, and expel the passions from his own soul and from every part of it. And let him entrust all his affairs to reason and intelligence and steer his course by them—for this was the central point, I suppose, of Diogenes' philosophy.

[201-202] *In short, before he does anything that is commonly judged with reproach, such as visiting a prostitute—if Diogenes ever actually did this—the man who wants to be a Cynic should develop "freedom, self-sufficiency, justice, moderation, piety, gratitude, and the same care not to act randomly or purposelessly or irrationally since these are also characteristic of Diogenes' philosophy." And may there be no vanity. Rather they should call out those who wrongly rob others in the marketplace and make unjust accusations in the assembly—the very same ones who take great care to do their body's natural business in the dark as if it is something unnatural. To counter this sort of vanity, Diogenes farted and did his other business in public.*

[202] In our own day, however, the imitators of Diogenes have chosen only what is easiest and least burdensome and have failed to see his better, nobler side.

[202-203] *As for you, you have strayed far from Diogenes' plan of life. He's no object of pity but was a man much admired by the generation of Plato and Aristotle. And his student Crates was Zeno of Citium's teacher. Surely they were not all deceived! More likely, you are mistaken and should have made a closer study of his character. Every Greek was amazed by his powers to endure, to sleep in a wine jar, to eat crusts of bread, to bathe in cold water, and to dry himself with the air alone. Even Alexander of Macedon admired him—as you would know if you were in the habit of reading. But you're not. You'd rather imitate wretched women! Regardless, you may be improved some by my words. If not, I do not regret speaking well of a great man.*

ORATION 7: TO THE CYNIC HERACLEIOS

The majority of Oration 7 has to do with the proper—or improper—use of myths. Regarding Cynicism, the oration addresses the question of whether or not it is better for the Cynic to write discourses or myths. Julian criticizes Heracleios' use of myth and suggests that he would have been better off—if, indeed, he had to resort to using myth at all—writing a myth on the model of Prodicus of Ceos, who famously wrote about Heracles' encounter with Virtue and Vice.[21] Otherwise, as in what follows, he offers advice regarding what true Cynicism is.

[225] Shall I tell you how you all have made it easy to despise philosophy? It is because the rhetoricians who are most oblivious—those whose tongues King Hermes himself could not purify, nor could Athena herself make them wise with Hermes' help—these, having picked up their skill from running around public places (for they do not know the truth of the current proverb, "Grape ripens near grape"), all then rush into Cynicism. They adopt the staff, the tattered cloak, the long hair, the ignorance that goes with these, the rashness, the effrontery, and, in a word, everything of the sort.

They say that they are travelling the short and severe road to virtue. If only you were going by the longer one! For you would more easily arrive by that road than by the one you're on. Are you not aware that shortcuts usually involve one in great difficulties?

For just as is the case with the public roads, a traveler who is able to take a shortcut will more easily than other men go all the way around, whereas it does not at all follow that he who went around could always go the shortcut, so too in philosophy the end and the beginning are one, namely, to know oneself and to become like the gods. That is to say, the first principle is self-knowledge, and the goal of conduct is be like those who are better, the higher powers.

So then, he who desires to be a Cynic despises all human customs and opinions and first turns his mind to himself and the god. For him gold is not gold and sand is not sand, if he looks into their value with a view to exchanging them. And leave it to him to rate them at their proper worth—[226] for he knows that both of them are but earth. And the fact that one is scarcer and the other easier to obtain he thinks is merely the result of the vanity and ignorance of mankind. He will judge of the shamefulness or nobility of an action not by the applause or blame of men but by its intrinsic nature.

He avoids excessive or extravagant food. He turns away from sex, from those things that belong to Aphrodite. When overpowered by the needs of the body, he does not cling to reputation, nor does he wait around for a cook and sauces and a savory smell, nor does he ever look around for *the prostitutes* Phryne or Lais or for So-and-so's wife or young daughter or serving-maid. But as far as possible, he satisfies his body's needs with whatever he happens to find. And by thrusting aside the body's troubles, he looks down from above, from the peaks of Olympus, at other men who are "wandering in darkness in the meadows of Bewilderment"[22]— those who are, for the sake of a few wholly trifling enjoyments, undergoing torments greater than any by the Cocytus or Acheron,[23] those such as the most ingenious of the poets are always telling us about.

This way is the shortest way. A man must stand apart from himself and come to know himself, that he is divine, belonging to god. He must not only keep his mind untiringly and steadfastly fixed on divine and undefiled and pure thoughts, but he must also neglect the needs of the body and consider it, according to Heraclitus, "more worthless than dirt."[24] And he must care for the body in the easiest way possible, so long as the god commands him to use it as a tool for doing things.

NOTES

[1] The translation that follows is a modified version of W.C. Wright's translations of "To the Uneducated Cynics" and "To the Cynic Heracleios" (1913).

[2] Euripides, *Medea* 410.

[3] Diogenes of Sinope, the Cynic.

[4] The Oracle of Delphi, that of Apollo.

[5] Heraclitus of Ephesus was a sixth and fifth century BC Presocratic philosopher known for his view that all of reality is in flux, in constant motion; nevertheless, he posited an underlying structure to reality, the *logos*, which is an unchanging law that rules and directs all of reality. Pythagoras was a sixth century BC Presocratic philosopher known for his mystical philosophy centered upon numbers and mathematics. Aristotle (c. 384-322 BC) studied with Plato for twenty years. He later opened his own school, the Lyceum. Aristotle is known for his wide-ranging interests and work in the fields of natural science, literature, rhetoric, politics, economics, and philosophy—including epistemology, logic, metaphysics, and ethics. Zeno of Citium (c. 334-262 BC) initially practiced philosophy, or a life of radical virtue, with the Cynic Crates of Thebes. He went on to found his own school named after a covered colonnade (*stoa*) in Athens (thus *Stoicism* and the *Stoics*). Zeno taught that all of reality consists of matter and mind, or divine reason, which makes, orders, and governs that which is natural. To live well is to live naturally, which is to say rationally or virtuously.

[6] Alcibiades was a fifth century BC Athenian student of Socrates, as well as a significant politician and leader during the Peloponnesian War. For his remark regarding Socrates, see Plato, *Symposium* 215a-b.

[7] Oenomaus of Gadara was a Cynic philosopher, who, according to W.C. Wright, likely flourished during the second century AD.

[8] See Heraclitus, fragment 40.

[9] The Pythian god is Apollo. The precepts come from Apollo's oracle at Delphi.

[10] Iamblichus was a second and third century AD Neoplatonist philosopher.

[11] See Plato, *Phaedo* 81a.

[12] For Socrates' account of his turn to a life of cross-examining others, see Plato, *Apology* 20e-22e.

[13] For happiness as the aim and end or goal of philosophy, see *Happiness: What the Ancient Greeks Thought and Said about Happiness* (Sugar Land: The Classics Cave, 2021).

[14] See Plato, *Protagoras* 321a-b.

[15] See Diogenes Laertius, *Lives* 10.11.

[16] Julian has Plato's seventh letter in mind (see Plato, *Letter* 7.326b).

[17] Tartarus is a region deep beneath the earth where Zeus imprisoned the Titans. Charybdis is a sea monster that three times daily sucks down gargantuan quantities of water (see Homer, *Odyssey* 12.103-106). Cocytus is a river in Hades.

[18] See Diogenes Laertius, *Lives* 6.59 and 6.86 for a similar saying.

[19] Thrift or Simple Living or Cheapness (*Euteleia*).

[20] Plutarch's *Life of Crates* is no longer extant.

[21] For Prodicus' myth, see Xenophon, *Memorabilia* 2.1-34.

[22] Empedocles, fragment 121. "Bewilderment" or "Blindness" (*Atē*).

[23] Rivers in Hades, the Underworld.

[24] Heraclitus, fragment 96.

POINTS OF WISDOM
& WAYS OF PRACTICE
FROM THE CYNICS

- Plan of Life Following the Cynics

- Points of Wisdom from the Cynics

- Ways of Practice Following the Cynics

PLAN OF LIFE
FOLLOWING THE CYNICS

AS WITH ANY other plan, a plan of life is made to accomplish many goals or possibly just one significant goal. In the case of the "Plan of Life Following the Cynics," the goal is bare survival on the one side and happiness and thriving on the other—for we do not merely wish to live but to live well (as a later Greek philosopher would say). The following plan consists of the most significant Cynic goals and practices from ancient Cynic philosophy.

1. **Live according to virtue, according to nature.** Turn down the noise of convention, of human customs. Hear instead the hum of nature alone. Observe how animals behave, how they are content. Nature directs us to what is *actually* virtuous rather than merely *apparently* virtuous. Accordingly, we may discover what is good, bad, and indifferent; and so, we are able to "alter the currency," to shift our conception of what is truly valuable and what is not.

2. **Cultivate shamelessness.** Be a dog. Imitate the behavior and attitude of dogs. Do what needs to be done, what *you* need to do, without worrying about what others will think or say. Practice shamelessness. Do something usually judged embarrassing today.

3. **Exercise frankness.** Don't hide your thoughts; don't let your words imprison you. Don't be fake, wearing a sham speech-mask that is not you. Speak freely to be free and to aid others in the same.

4. **Build soul wealth.** Understand that happiness is a matter of internal goods such as contentment and inner strength rather than external things like fine clothing, gourmet food, a "good" reputation, political power, piles of money, and other possessions. Soul wealth is built by fostering soul health—by engaging in specific practices related to following the Cynic plan of life.

5. **Keep freedom in mind.** Know that everything we do has the potential to liberate or enslave us. Ask yourself: will *having* something release or restrict me? Will *doing* something liberate or bind me? Will *feeling* or *thinking* something free or fetter me? Will *saying* something help or hinder me? The Cynic always moves toward freedom and flees enslavement — for himself and for others (like Crates of Thebes or Heracles).

6. **Practice endurance.** Embrace toil, hardship, and suffering. When necessary, stand your ground against the allure of pleasure. Practice in the manner of Diogenes, who walked barefoot in the snow, rolled in the hot sand, bravely battled a fever, and begged alms from a statue to practice rejection.

7. **Reduce your desires.** Know that desire always leaves us desiring more. As such, desire indicates dissatisfaction. By reducing desires, we are able to reduce dissatisfaction. Said another way, desire reduction increases satisfaction. Reduce your desires, therefore, to expand your overall sense of contentment and satisfaction.

8. **Develop self-control.** Desire reduction is essential for the Cynic development of self-control. The reason is simple: self-control increases as desire decreases. Thus, as you practice reducing your desires, know you are simultaneously establishing self-control.

9. **Strive for self-sufficiency.** Be independent — of life conditions, of others, of desires or wants that are hard to satisfy. Focus on what is necessary. Practice contentment with what is near to hand and easy to get. What are you? What do you have? What are you doing? What do you feel? May these be sufficient. Say, "I am satisfied with—."

10. **Live simply.** Wear simple clothes. Reduce your possessions. Eat basic fare. Drink water. Living in this way, simply or frugally, follows upon the practices of desire reduction and self-sufficiency. Imitate Socrates who rejoiced in all the things he could go without.

POINTS OF WISDOM
FROM THE CYNICS

The following points of wisdom come from the Cynics. Each begins in italics with a single word or more indicating the point's topic. For more points of wisdom from the Cynics organized by topic, read The Classics Cave's The Wisdom & Way of the Cynics.

Seek the goal of life—happiness The main goal of the Cynics . . . was how they themselves might be happy.—*Julian*

Go for happiness One must go for happiness, as Diogenes used to say, even if the going is through fire.—*Crates of Thebes*

Look for happiness in the right place by listening to Socrates say, "Where are you hurrying? What are you doing, you miserable men? Like blind people you are wandering up and down. You are going by another road and have left the true road. You search for prosperity and happiness where they are not. And if another shows you where they are, you do not believe him."—*Epictetus (citing Socrates)*

Do happiness (rather than talking or thinking about it) Long is the path that leads to happiness through words alone. But the path that leads to happiness through the practice of daily deeds is short.
—*Crates of Thebes*

Choosing and doing happiness versus reading books I still believe that even before Heracles, not only among the Greeks but among the barbarians also, there were men who practiced this *Cynic* philosophy. For it seems to be in some ways a universal philosophy, and the most natural, and to demand no special study whatsoever. But it is enough simply to choose the honorable by desiring virtue and avoiding evil. And so there is no need to turn over countless books. For as the saying goes, "Much learning does not teach men to have understanding."—*Julian*

Do philosophy like a Cynic Do philosophy more often than you breathe. I say this because living well, which philosophy produces, is more choiceworthy than simply living, which breathing produces. Don't do philosophy as others have done it, but as Antisthenes first practiced it, that which Diogenes brought to fulfillment.

—*Crates of Thebes*

Live according to nature I am heaven's dog . . . living according to nature.—*Diogenes of Sinope*

Practice following nature Rather than unprofitable, toilsome exercises, men should prefer those which follow nature in order to live happily.

—*Diogenes of Sinope*

Follow nature by altering the currency Diogenes granted nothing at all . . . to human custom and law; rather, he followed nature. In this way he practiced "altering the currency," which is to say he reevaluated human customs.—*Diogenes Laertius*

How to follow nature It was by watching a mouse—how it didn't long for a marriage bed, and how it didn't care about the dark, and how it didn't long for things that have a reputation for causing pleasure—that Diogenes discovered the means of adapting himself to circumstances.—*Theophrastus of Eresos (about Diogenes of Sinope)*

Do virtue; practice Virtue is something you do—it's a matter of deeds. It doesn't require a stockpile of arguments or much learning. . . . Virtue is sufficient for happiness. . . . Virtue is a weapon that cannot be taken away.—*Antisthenes*

The goal is virtue, which strengthens and heals The Cynics hold that the goal of life is to live according to virtue. . . . Virtue alone is that by which the soul can be strengthened and delivered from its afflictions.

—*Diogenes of Sinope*

Imitate Diogenes' example Diogenes was courageous in his practice of virtue. . . . Put on his armor and carry his weapons. —*Crates of Thebes*

Strive to be a good and noble man Men strive in punching and kicking to outdo one another, but no one strives to become a noble and good man. —*Diogenes of Sinope*

Know yourself When he was asked what result he obtained from philosophy, Diogenes said, "The ability to be in my own company and to be acquainted with myself."
                          —*Diogenes Laertius (citing Diogenes of Sinope)*

Soul care Take care of your soul—but your body only so far as what is necessary, and externals not even that much. I say this because happiness is not a pleasure that requires external things, nor does perfect virtue require these. —*Crates of Thebes*

Cultivate yourself We must look into the good and bad done in our own households. —*Diogenes of Sinope*

Harmonize yourself Observing a foolish man tuning a harp, he said, "Are you not ashamed to give this piece of wood harmonious sounds while you fail to harmonize your soul with your life?"
                          —*Diogenes of Sinope*

Obey the commander of your soul Reason is commander of the soul, a noble thing, the greatest good for human beings. —*Crates of Thebes*

Steer your life with reason Let a person entrust all his affairs to reason and intelligence and steer his course by them—for this was the central point, I suppose, of Diogenes' philosophy. —*Julian*

Seek freedom The Cynic Diogenes declared that his manner of life was the same as that of Heracles. He preferred freedom more than everything else. —*Diogenes Laertius*

Freedom from others So long as you are a slave to the opinions of the many you have not yet approached freedom or tasted its nectar."

—*Julian*

Be free of what others think Do not be distressed, father, . . . Instead, be delighted that your son is . . . free from popular opinion, to which everyone, both the Greeks and barbarians, are enslaved.

—*Diogenes of Sinope*

Train; practice; do Absolutely nothing in life is successful without training, which has the power to conquer anything.—*Diogenes of Sinope*

Two kinds of training Diogenes declared that there are two kinds of exercise—training of the soul and training of the body. And that the latter exercise gives rise to perceptions that facilitate virtuous deeds. Each practice is incomplete and ineffectual without the other.

—*Diogenes Laertius*

The need to train Virtue enters the soul by means of training—not automatically as happens with vice.—*Crates of Thebes*

Exercise using pleasure and hardship Keep training just as you began and earnestly set yourself in equal measure against both pleasure and hardship—*Diogenes of Sinope*

Practice self-control and endurance Flee not only from the worst of the vices, injustice and a lack of self-control, but also what produces them, pleasure and enjoyment. . . . Pursue not only the best of goods, self-control and endurance, but also what produces them, hard work and toil. In doing so, you will exchange hard work and toil for virtue.—*Crates of Thebes*

Practice endurance Making his home in the Piraeus, Antisthenes used to walk about five miles to Athens every day in order to hear Socrates. He learned the art of endurance from him, imitating his indifference to suffering. So it was that he began the Cynic philosophy and the Cynic way of life.—*Diogenes Laertius*

Come up with specific ways to train In summertime, Diogenes used to roll in his wine-jar house over hot sand. And in wintertime, he used to hug statues of men covered with snow. He practiced endurance in every way. —Diogenes Laertius

Need or desire reduction Train yourselves to need very little—for this is closest to god, while the opposite is farthest. —*Crates of Thebes*

Look down on unnecessary things When you train to look down on poverty, a bad reputation, low birth, and exile, you will live blessedly. . . . Otherwise, you will live miserably. —*Diogenes of Sinope*

Train while eating and drinking Get used to eating barley cakes and drinking water. —*Crates of Thebes*

Be content with simple things; practice self-sufficiency Diogenes used to teach the boys in his care to supply their own needs, and to be content with simple food and water to drink. —*Diogenes Laertius*

Cultivate contentment with little Do not be distressed, father, that I call myself a dog, and I clothe myself with a doubled over tattered cloak, and I carry a leather bag over my shoulders, and I have a staff in my hand. It is not fitting to be upset by such matters. Instead, be delighted that your son is content with little. —*Diogenes of Sinope*

Practice rejection Diogenes once begged alms from a statue. When asked why he did this, he said, "To practice being rejected."
—*Diogenes Laertius*

Go your own way (not with the crowd) Diogenes was going into a theater while everyone else was going out in the opposite direction. When someone asked him why, he said, "This is what I practice doing every day of my life." —*Diogenes Laertius*

Stand apart from what people say When Antisthenes was applauded by bad men, he said, "I'm afraid that I have done something wrong." One man said to him, "The many praise you." In response, he said, "Why? What wrong have I done?" — *Diogenes Laertius*

Reputation A bad reputation is a good thing. — *Antisthenes*

Reinterpretation When someone reminded Diogenes that the citizens of Sinope had sentenced him to exile, he said, "And I sentenced them to stay there." — *Diogenes Laertius*

A real human being Diogenes lit a lamp in the middle of the day and walked around saying, "I'm searching for a human being."

— *Diogenes Laertius*

Wealth and evil Wealth is the origin of all evils. — *Diogenes of Sinope*

Where blame belongs We blame everything else more than we do our own irritability and unhappiness. . . . We blame old age, poverty, chance encounters, the day, the season, the place. . . . Many mad men lay the blame on circumstances rather than on themselves.

— *Teles the Cynic*

A trouble-free life is impossible I have concluded from my own life that we human beings are distressed whenever we wish to live a problem-free life. But this is impossible! For by necessity we live with the body, and by necessity we also live with human beings.

— *Crates of Thebes*

Meet circumstances as they are One should not attempt to change circumstances; rather, one should get ready for them as they are. Do this as sailors do. They don't try to change the winds and the sea. Instead, they ready themselves so that they are able to respond to these things. — *Teles the Cynic*

Jealousy As iron is devoured by rust, so are jealous people consumed by their own jealousy. — *Antisthenes*

WAYS OF PRACTICE
FOLLOWING THE CYNICS

The following ways of practice, inspired by the Cynics, are offered with the goal of practice in mind, the application of ancient wisdom and ways to our contemporary lives. We hope they will serve, in some small measure, as a source of inspiration and motivation. Use them to contemplate your life—where you are now, where you are going, and how you can better get there. For these exercises and practices and other similar ones, pick up The Classics Cave's The Cynics Workbook & Journal. *One last note. You will likely find that the space given for responses is not enough. If so, jot your thoughts and practices down in a separate place.*

PRACTICE 1: GOING FOR HAPPINESS

"The main goal of the Cynics . . . was how they themselves might be happy." —Julian

"It is the Cynic's responsibility . . . to say like Socrates, 'Where are you hurrying? What are you doing, you miserable men? Like blind people you are wandering up and down. You are going by another road and have left the true road. You search for prosperity and happiness where they are not.' . . . The philosopher should be able to show everyone the battle in which they whirl around, giving mind to everything except for that which they truly want. They want those things that will bear them along to happiness, but they search for them in the wrong place." —Epictetus

Q • We've all searched for happiness in various things and places, experiences and people, feelings, thoughts, and activities. Looking at my past, where have I searched for happiness (whether rightly or wrongly, healthily or not)? List your top two or three.

_____

_____

_____

Q • To go for happiness, to make it our goal, we should have some clear idea of *what* it is. How do I understand happiness? What feelings does it involve? Thoughts? Acts or activities? Experiences? People? Circumstances? What else?

_____

_____

_____

_____

"One must go for happiness, as Diogenes of Sinope used to say, even if the going is through fire." —*Crates of Thebes*

(Circle) your answer • True   or   False

No matter the obstacle (say, "fire"), I doggedly pursue happiness.

My Obstacles • What are the top three obstacles to my happiness? How do I "go through" them (as it were)—or around, or over, or under them? How can I practice this "go through"? Be specific.

Obstacle 1: _____

My go through for 1: _____

Practice 1: _____

_____

Obstacle 2: _____

My go through for 2: _____

Practice 2: _____

_____

Obstacle 3: _____

My go through for 3: _____

Practice 3: _____

PRACTICE 2: DESIRE REDUCTION

"Diogenes used to say that it was characteristic of the gods to need nothing, and that, consequently, when a man desires very little or nothing at all, he is like the gods." —Diogenes Laertius

The earliest Greeks held that happiness amounted to the satisfaction of desire. For them, the gods were entirely happy (or blessed) because they could and did satisfy their every desire. In fact, the satisfaction of their great and god-sized desire resulted in off-the-charts happiness. By contrast, the Cynics believed the gods, being gods, needed nothing at all—which is to say they lacked or wanted nothing. Because of this, because they desired (or were lacking) nothing, they had everything and were thus entirely satisfied or happy. It followed that humans could be godlike and happy if and only if they reduced their own desires to "very little or nothing at all." As desire vanishes so does satisfaction appear. That is the Cynic formula for happiness. They still held that happiness equaled the satisfaction of desire. But the trick, they believed, was to set the "desire" part of the equation as close as possible to zero in order to raise the satisfaction part to godlike numbers.

Q • What do you think about the traditional Greek formulation of happiness, that $H = SD$ (happiness equals the satisfaction of desire)? Have you ever experienced this sort of happiness? When? Where? With whom or what?

Q • What do you think about the Cynic reformulation of the traditional Greek formulation, that happiness equals the greater satisfaction that results from the reduction of desire? Have you ever experienced this sort of happiness? How so?

_____

_____

"Bad men obey their desires as house slaves obey their masters."
—Diogenes of Sinope

"You behave randomly in your own affairs, never acting as a result of deliberation or reason, but always thanks to habit and longing. You are no better than people washed around by a flood. They drift with the current, and you with your longings."—the Cynic

✓ *Check the box before the line that best describes you.*

☐ I am fully in control of my desires. The thought of my desires being out of control is strange.

☐ I am mostly in control of my desires—though some are out of control sometimes.

☐ My desires are out of control. I obey my desires more than they obey me.

DESIRE REDUCTION

Identify two desires you can reduce or get rid of all together in order to experience greater satisfaction or happiness.

Desire 1: _____

Desire 2: _____

Practice • How can you practice the reduction of each desire? Try to be specific and concrete in your practice. For instance, if you wish to reduce your desire for food, do it a few bites at a time and increase each day or week. Then review: how is your practice going?

Practice 1: _____

_____

_____

Practice 2: _____

_____

_____

PRACTICE 3: EMBRACING TOIL, HARDSHIP & SUFFERING

"Antisthenes argued that hard work, with all its toil and suffering, is something good." —Diogenes Laertius

Why would anyone declare toil and suffering to be "something good"? The Cynic logic was something along these lines: if the ability to endure is something positive, and hard work and its consequent suffering as well as other hardships are the means by which one develops the ability to endure, then hard work, suffering, and hardship is in fact something positive.

"Pursue not only the best of goods, self-control and endurance, but also what produces them, hard work and toil." —Crates of Thebes

Circle one . . .

TRUE   or   FALSE   •   I typically embrace hard work.

TRUE   or   FALSE   •   I typically accept suffering.

Q • In the past, what hard work have I made harder by putting it off or doing it reluctantly?

_____

_____

_____

_____

Q ▪ In the past, what suffering have I brought on myself by embracing suffering's opposite (that is, comfort or ease or pleasure or some such thing)? Or by refusing to accept the suffering (that is, mentally straining against the suffering)?

_____

_____

_____

_____

EMBRACING TOIL, PRACTICING SUFFERING

Identify one way you can embrace toil and one way you can practice suffering over the next few weeks. ▪ Ideas for embracing toil include enthusiastically doing household chores or something your work (whether school or a job) requires. As for practicing suffering, you could eat a healthy food you don't usually care for. Or take a lukewarm or cold shower when you want a hot one. Or ride with your windows down on a hot or cold day. Or mindfully listen to someone blather on about something you could care less about. Or take the day off from your phone. As you go along, note how your embrace of hard work and practice of suffering change how you feel about each. If the Cynics are right, you'll experience positive results.

Embracing Toil Way 1: _____

_____

_____

Practicing Suffering Way 2: _____

_____

_____

OTHER MATTERS OF INTEREST
RELATED TO THE CYNICS

THE CAST OF SIGNIFICANT CYNICS
A QUICK REFERENCE & CHRONOLOGY

CYNICISM: a philosophy and way of life that seeks freedom from desire and wants through a virtuous, self-sufficient life of radical simplicity and poverty. Cynicism may be defined as the art of endurance that produces true happiness. It is a path that follows the lead of nature rather than human convention. As such, Cynics prize the naturalness and shamelessness of dogs and other animals (thus the name "dog" from the Greek *kyōn* or *kuōn*). Central to Cynicism is training or exercise, the active embrace of hardship and suffering. Cynicism was developed in the late fifth into the fourth century BC.

THE EARLY CYNICS—late fifth into the third century BC

ANTISTHENES: the son of Antisthenes (an Athenian citizen) and a Thracian woman; born in Athens c. 445 BC. Antisthenes began as a rhetorician listening to the lectures of the sophist Gorgias, among others, but turned to philosophy under the influence of Socrates, from whom he learned the art of endurance. He may have been the first to be called "Dog" and the first to reduce his clothing and possessions to the Cynic uniform—a tattered cloak, a leather bag, and a staff. He reportedly wrote many works, but only fragments remain. Antisthenes believed in the positive value of hardship and suffering. Among other points, he taught that the wise man is self-sufficient and that virtue is enough for happiness. The "strength of Socrates," or endurance, amounts to virtue. Antisthenes died c. 365 BC.

DIOGENES OF SINOPE: the son of Hicesias, who was a banker and money-changer; born in Sinope (a city on a peninsula in northern Turkey that juts out into the Black Sea) c. 410 BC (dates vary). Diogenes was exiled from Sinope, apparently for debasing the coinage. He subsequently made his way to Athens, where he reportedly encountered Antisthenes and turned to philosophy and particularly to Cynicism or the Cynic way of life. Diogenes was nicknamed

"Dog" (from the Greek *kyōn* or *kuōn*, the source of "Cynic") since he lived a radically simple life of poverty, rejected human customs by "altering the currency," and practiced shamelessness, doing like a dog in public what was usually done in private. Plato called Diogenes "a Socrates gone mad" because he took Socrates' "art of endurance" to an extreme—living as a homeless beggar, embracing every manner of hardship and suffering, practicing pain, and shunning pleasure. Diogenes advocated ongoing training to develop the ability to endure. Frankness or freedom of speech was essential to Diogenes' mission as a Cynic, in which he preached and called on passersby to embrace a simpler, freer life. He famously carried a lamp in broad daylight declaring, "I'm searching for a human being." Although he wrote several works, only fragments remain. He died c. 323 BC.

CRATES OF THEBES: the son of Ascondas; born in Thebes (central Greece) c. 365 bc. Crates is known for his radical conversion to Cynicism. He was Diogenes of Sinope's student and eventually his successor. Though originally a wealthy man, one account states that he converted all his property into wealth and gave it away to follow the Cynic way of life. As one who made his way into people's houses in order to admonish and advise them, he was known as the "Door-opener." Among his other teachings, he declared that "wealth is prey to vanity." Contrary to most Cynics who did not marry, Crates married Hipparchia of Maroneia, a young woman who wished to pursue the Cynic way of life with him. Zeno of Citium, the founder of Stoicism, was originally the student of Crates. Although Crates wrote several works, including tragedies "characterized by a very lofty philosophy," only fragments remain. He died c. 285 BC.

MONIMUS OF SYRACUSE: a household slave who feigned madness in order to be dismissed and have the liberty to learn from and follow Diogenes of Sinope. He also followed Crates of Thebes. Monimus is known for the saying, quoted by Marcus Aurelius, among others, that "all opinion is vanity." Nothing of his two significant writings survive. He lived and died during the fourth century BC.

ONESICRITUS: born on the Greek island of Astypalaea, though possibly Aegina (an island near Athens), c. 360 BC; the student of Diogenes of Sinope. Onesicritus reportedly accompanied Alexander the Great on his campaign east that ended in India. There Onesicritus observed what the ancient Greeks called "gymnosophists," naked philosophers. He reported that these philosophers were similar to the Cynics in their ideas and way of life. Although none of it remains, Onesicritus wrote a work about how Alexander the Great was educated. He died c. 290 BC.

METROCLES OF MARONEIA: born in Maroneia in Thrace (northern Greece); the brother of Hipparchia of Maroneia. Originally the student of Theophrastus, the Peripatetic philosopher who was the successor of Aristotle, Metrocles eventually converted to Cynicism following the lead of Crates of Thebes, who helped him overcome an embarrassing incident and practice shamelessness. Metrocles' sister Hipparchia married Crates. Metrocles lived and died during the fourth century BC.

HIPPARCHIA OF MARONEIA: born in Maroneia in Thrace (northern Greece); the sister of Metrocles of Maroneia. Hipparchia is known for her practice of the Cynic philosophy and way of life and for her husband, Crates of Thebes. Although Crates was unattractive and lived the life of a homeless beggar, Hipparchia fell in love with him for his teachings and practice, and eventually married him after dramatically convincing her parents to give her permission. They subsequently pursued the Cynic path together, living a simple life. She lived and died during the latter half of the fourth and early part of the third century BC.

BION OF BORYSTHENES: born in Borysthenes, also called Olbia (Ukraine, near the mouth of the Dnieper River) c. 325 BC. Although Bion was early on a slave, he was eventually liberated and travelled to Athens where he studied philosophy in the Academy and Lyceum. He was also influenced by the hedonist Theodorus, called "the Atheist," and by Crates of Thebes. Bion is credited with developing the diatribe, a literary genre that frankly "treats of ordinary human problems in a common-sense spirit." He died c. 250 BC.

OTHER CYNICS: The following are Cynics briefly mentioned by Diogenes Laertius in his *Lives*. Students of Diogenes of Sinope were Menander, Hegesias of Sinope, and Philiscus of Aegina. Menippus the Phoenician and Menedemus were students of Crates of Thebes.

TELES OF MEGARA: aside from the detail that Teles was a teacher in Megara (a city near Athens) in the third century BC, little is known about him. The much later Joannes Stobaeus (fifth century AD) preserved seven lengthy extracts from Teles. Among other topics, they address self-sufficiency, exile, poverty and wealth, pleasure (that it is not the goal of life), and how one might be free from the passions, emotion, and various feelings.

LATER CYNICS—first century into the sixth century AD

DEMETRIUS: from Corinth, a Cynic who lived in Rome during the first century AD through the reigns of the emperors Caligula, Nero, and Vespasian. Demetrius is celebrated for refusing Caligula's offer to change his way of life for a very large sum of money. He is also recognized for his opposition to the emperors, particularly to Vespasian. Along with other philosophers, he was expelled from Rome in 71 AD. Though a typical Cynic in his teachings and practice, Demetrius promoted total resignation to the will of God (likely in a Stoic sense) in contrast to the usual Cynic resignation to Fate.

DIO CHRYSOSTOM: born in Prusa (Brusa, Turkey) c. 40 AD, Dio Chrysostom ("the Golden-Mouthed") originally practiced rhetoric in Rome until he was banished in 82 for his opposition to the emperor Domitian. Thereafter, Dio lived and taught as a Cynic, wandering throughout the Roman Empire and even beyond. When his exile was lifted, he focused once again on writing and speech making. We possess some eighty orations composed by Dio, a number of them with Cynic themes centering on Diogenes of Sinope. One,

Oration 6, demonstrates the blessings of a Cynic way of life compared to the suffering brought on by the usual pursuit of ease and pleasure. Another, *Oration* 8, explores Diogenes of Sinope's turn to Cynicism under the tutelage of Antisthenes, and offers a speech by Diogenes given at the Corinthian games explaining his own ongoing contest with hardship and pleasure. Dio Chrysostom was friends with the emperor Nerva, and the emperor Trajan favored him. He died c. 112 AD.

DEMONAX: born in Cyprus, Demonax was well educated. Turning to philosophy, he learned from the Stoics and Cynics. Though he professed eclecticism, he lived and dressed as a Cynic. He eventually made his way to Athens and lived there as a citizen for the remainder of his life, even taking part in its political life (something unusual for a Cynic). Demonax devoted himself to exhorting others, recalling the ephemeral nature of fortune, and consoling friends in the midst of personal suffering. While his dates are uncertain, scholars place him in the second century AD.

PEREGRINUS: born in Parium (Turkey) c. 95 AD, Peregrinus began his philosophical career as a Christian in Palestine, spending some time in prison for his role in leading the Christian community. After being released, he renounced his property and began to dress as a Cynic, though he was still supported by various Christians. When he was finally expelled from the Christian community, he spent time in Egypt with Agathoboulos, a particularly stringent Cynic, and in Italy speaking critically against the emperor. Peregrinus dramatically ended his life by self-immolation at the Olympic festival in 167 AD.

SALLUSTIUS OF EMESA: born c. 430 AD, Sallustius of Emesa (Homs, Turkey) likely lived into the early years of the sixth century. Beginning his life by studying law and practicing as a rhetorician, he eventually travelled to Athens and Alexandria, turning at some point to philosophy and finally to the Cynic way of life. Sallustius is the last known Cynic (mentioned by the Neoplatonist Damascius in his *Life of Isidore*).

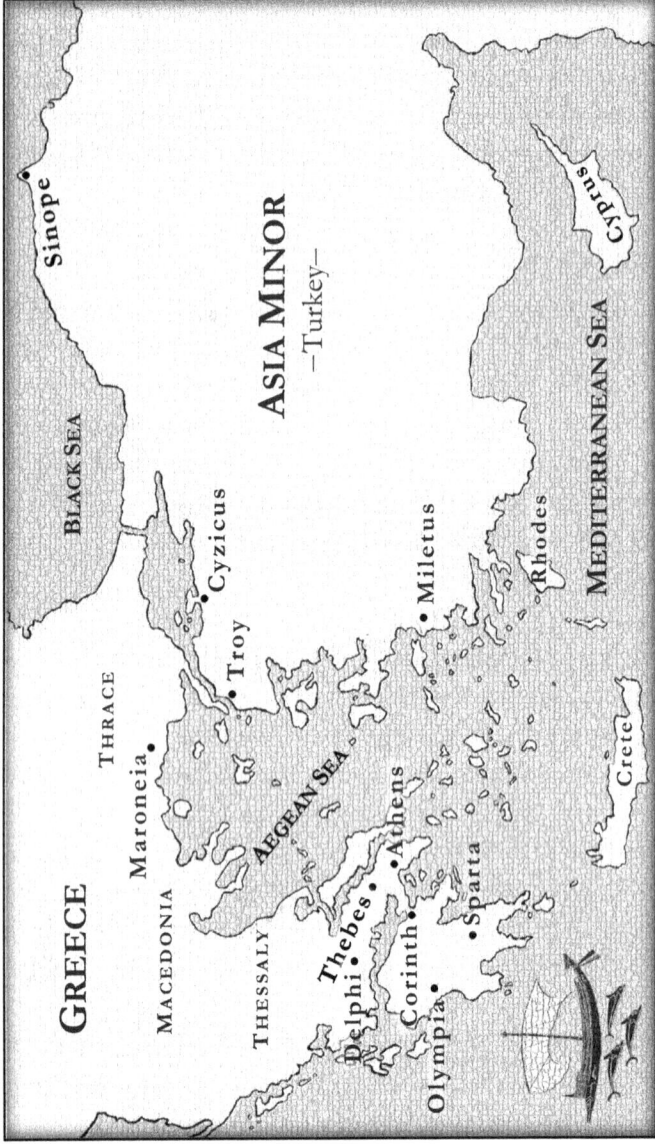

Greece and Asia Minor (Map 1)

Antisthenes was from Athens, Diogenes from Sinope, and Crates from Thebes.

GLOSSARY
OF ENGLISH WORDS AND GREEK EQUIVALENTS
THAT APPEAR IN THE CYNICS

According to nature, following nature: *kata phusin* or *physin* (κατά φύσιν).

To **admonish**, put in mind, advise: *noutheteō* (νουθετέω).

To **alter the currency**, debase the currency; restamp or revalue the currency; used metaphorically in reference to the Cynic project to revalue or reevaluate common values or customs or commonly valued things: *paracharattein* (or *paracharassō*) *to nomisma* (παραχαράττειν [or παραχαράσσω] τό νόμισμα). *Nomisma* is anything sanctioned by usage, custom, an institution; thus, the sanctioned coinage or currency.

Anecdote, saying; an anecdote with a pithy saying; a maxim frequently illustrated by an anecdote: *chreia* (χρεία).

Bad, worthless; cowardly; a bad man or thing; evil: *kakos* (κακός). Also *ponēros* (πονηρός)—bad, worthless, knavish, base.

Barley bread; barley-cake: *maza* (μᾶζα).

Beard: *pōgōn* (πώγων).

Beauty: *kallos* (κάλλος) or *kalos* (κάλος).

To **beg**: *aiteō* (αἰτέω).

To **blame**, censure: *phegō* (ψέγω).

Blameless, without fault: *anamartētos* (ἀναμάρτητος).

Blessed, happy: *makarios* (μακάριος). Related to *makar* (μάκαρ).

Character; a way of life, habit, custom: *tropos* (τρόπος).

Citizen of the world: *kosmopolitēs* (κοσμοπολίτης).

Common, mean, bad: *phaulos* (φαῦλος).

Conscience or consciousness: *sunoida* (σύνοιδα).

Courage, manliness: *andreia* (ἀνδρεία). Courage; boldness: *tharsos* (θάρσος).

Courageous; stout of heart: *eupsuchos* or *eupsychos* (εὔψυχος).

Cynic, dog-like: *kunikos* (κυνικός).

Cynicism; Cynic philosophy or conduct: (κυνισμός).

Cynosarges, the "White Dog" gymnasium; a gymnasium outside Athens for those who were not fully Athenian; the place where Antisthenes reportedly lectured: *Kunosarges* or *Kynosarges* (Κυνόσαργες).

Desire, love: *erōs* (ἔρως) or eros (ἔρος). **Longing**, yearning, desire: *epithumia* (ἐπιθυμία).

Difficult; hard to bear, painful, grievous: *chalepos* (χαλεπός).

To **do well**: *eu prattein* (εὖ πράττειν).

Dog; what a Cynic was called (see Cynic); a word of reproach denoting shamelessness: *kuōn* or *kyōn* (κύων).

Drinking party, symposium: *sumposion* or *symposion* (συμπόσιον).

Drunkenness; strong drink: *methē* (μέθη).

Education; training: *paideia* (παιδεία).

Endurance, patience; patient endurance; the art of endurance; the ability to endure: *karteria* (καρτερία).

Endure, hold out: *epiteinō* (ἐπιτείνω).

Enjoyment: *hēdupathēma* (ἡδυπάθημα).

Ethics; that which pertains to the ethical: *ēthikos* (ἠθικός).

Excellent (man); good (man); serious (man): *spoudaios* (σπουδαῖος).

Exercise, practice, training: *askēsis* (ἄσκησις). To **exercise**, practice, train: *askeō* (ἀσκέω).

Exile: *phugē* (φυγή).

Extravagance; great expense: *poluteleia* (πολυτέλεια).

Fault, failure; sin: *hamartēma* (ἁμάρτημα).

Without **fear**, fearless: *aphobos* (ἄφοβος).

Flawless, faultless; unerring; infallible: *adiaptōtos* (ἀδιάπτωτος).

Flesh, the body: *sarx* (σάρξ).

To **fold over**, double over: *diploō* (διπλόω).

Fortune, chance, luck: *tuchē* or *tychē* (τύχη).

Frankness, outspokenness; freedom of speech: *parrhēsia* (παρρησία).

Freedom, liberty: *eleutheria* (ἐλευθερία).

Freedom from emotion or the passions; insensibility: *apatheia* (ἀπάθεια).

Goal, end: *telos* (τέλος).

Good; the good, serviceable: *agathos* (ἀγαθός).

Good habit; good habit of body, good health: *euexia* (εὐεξία).

Harmful: *blaberos* (βλαβερός).

Happiness; prosperity: *eudaimonia* (εὐδαιμονία). **Happy,** fortunate, blest: *eudaimōn* (εὐδαίμων). **Happy,** prosperous, fortunate, lucky: *eutuchēs* or *eutychēs* (εὐτυχής).

To **be healthy, sound:** *hugiainō* or *hygiainō* (ὑγιαίνω).

Herbs, vegetables: *botanē* (βοτάνη).

Hunger: *limos* (λιμός).

Indifferent; things neither good nor bad: *adiaphoros* (ἀδιάφορος).

Indifference to suffering; freedom from suffering or emotion; unaffected: *apathēs* (ἀπαθής).

Insatiate desire, greediness: *aplēstia* (ἀπληστία).

Justice, righteousness: (δικαιοσύνη). **Just:** *dikaios* (δίκαιος).

Leather bag or pouch; knapsack: *pēra* (πήρα).

Lentil: *phakos* (φακός). **Lentil soup;** a dish of lentils: *phakē* (φακῆ).

To **live in luxury,** luxuriously, softly; to be extravagant: *truphaō* (τρυφάω). **Softness,** luxuriousness, daintiness: *truphē* (τρυφή).

To **live well:** *eu bioō* (εὖ βιόω). Also: *eu zaō* (εὖ ζάω).

Logic; relating to the logical, dialectical, argumentative: *logikos* (λογικός).

Longing, yearning, desire: *epithumia* (ἐπιθυμία).

Love of money, what Diogenes terms "the origin of all evil": *philarguria* (φιλαργυρία).

Lupin bean; a lupine: *thermos* (θέρμος).

Manly, like a man: *andrōdēs* (ἀνδρώδης).

Moderate; sober, self-controlled; sensible: *sōphrōn* (σώφρων).

Moderation; soundness of mind: *sōphrosunē* (σωφροσύνη).

Nature: *phusis* or *physis* (φύσις). Opposed, by Cynics, to **convention,** custom; law: *nomos* (νόμος). **Natural;** of or in the order of nature: *phusikos* or *physikos* (φυσικός). **According to nature,** following nature: *kata phusin* or *physin* (κατά φύσιν).

Necessity: *anankē* (ἀνάγκη).

Need; requirement: *chreia* (χρεία). **Want;** lacking: *endeēs* (ἐνδεής). For the Cynic in Lucian of Samosata's dialogue, want occurs when one's needs or requirements remain unfulfilled.

Noble birth; high descent, nobility of birth: *eugeneia* (εὐγένεια).

Noble and good: *kalos kagathos* (καλὸς κάγαθὸς), from *kalos kai agathos* (also *kalokagathos* [καλοκάγαθός], often given as noble and good; a perfect gentleman).

Passion, emotion: *pathos* (πάθος).

Philosophy, love of wisdom: *philosophia* (φιλοσοφία). To do philosophy, pursue wisdom: *philosopheō* (φιλοσοφέω).

Pious, religious: *eusebēs* (εὐσεβής). Related to **piety**; reverence toward the gods: *eusebeia* (εὐσέβεια).

Pleasure; delight, enjoyment: *hēdonē* (ἡδονή).

To **poor scorn on**, regard haughtily: *katasobareuomai* (κατασοβαρεύομαι).

Poverty, need: *penia* (πενία).

Practical wisdom, prudence: *phronēsis* (φρόνησις).

Practice, training, exercise: *askēsis* (ἄσκησις). To **practice**, train, exercise: *askeō* (ἀσκέω).

To **praise**; approve, applaud, comment: *epaineō* (ἐπαινέω).

Procreation of children: *paidopoiia* (παιδοποιία).

Reason: *logos* (λόγος). For the Cynics, reason is opposed to and able to control feeling, passion, emotion: *pathos* (πάθος).

Reputation, the opinion that others have of one; outward appearance: *doxa* (δόξα). Bad reputation; disgrace; obscurity: *adoxia* (ἀδοξία).

Role, mask; face: *prosōpon* (πρόσωπον).

To be **satisfied with**; to be content; to be enough; to ward off; to be strong enough: *arkeō* (ἀρκέω).

Saying(s): *chreia* (χρεία)—see anecdote.

Scout, spy; one who reconnoiters: *kataskopos* (κατάσκοπος).

Self-control, self-restraint, continence; mastery over: *enkrateia* (ἐγκράτεια). Lack of self-control, incontinence: *akrateia* (ἀκράτεια).

Self-sufficiency, self-supporting, self-reliant; having enough; independent (of others): *autarkēs* (αὐτάρκης).

Serious or earnest (man); excellent (man); good (man): *spoudaios* (σπουδαῖος).

Shameless: *anaidēs* (ἀναιδής). **Shamelessness**: *anaideia* (ἀναίδεια).

Shortcut; cut short, abridged: *suntomos* or *syntomos* (σύντομος).

Slavery, bondage: *douleia* (δουλεία). **Slave**: *doulos* (δοῦλος).

Simple, frugal, thrifty; easily paid for: *euteles* (εὐτελής).

Simplicity, frugality, thrift: *euteleia* (εὐτέλεια).

Simply, frugally: *litōs* (λιτῶς).

Soul; mind: *psuche* or *psyche* (ψυχή).

Staff; stick: *baktron* (βάκτρον).

To be **strong**: *ischuō* (ἰσχύω).

Sufficient, enough, adequate: *hikanos* (ἱκανός).

Tattered cloak, worn garment; threadbare cloak; the typical single piece of clothing worn by Cynics: *tribōn* (τρίβων).

Toil, hard work; hardship, suffering: *ponos* (πόνος).

Training, exercise, practice: *askēsis* (ἄσκησις). To **train**, exercise, practice: *askeō* (ἀσκέω).

Traveling supplies: *ephodion* (ἐφόδιον).

Truth, reality: *alētheia* (ἀλήθεια).

Unhappy, miserable: *kakodaimōn* (κακοδαίμων).

Unnatural, strange, odd; out of place: *atopos* (ἄτοπος).

Vain, empty, frivolous; thoughtless: *mataios* (μάταιος).

Vanity, conceit; delusion; smoke, vapor: *tuphos* (τῦφος).

Vice; badness: *kakia* (κακία).

Virtue; goodness, excellence: *aretē* (ἀρετή). **Virtuous**: *enaretos* (ἐνάρετος).

Want; lacking: *endeēs* (ἐνδεής). **Need**; requirement: *chreia* (χρεία). For the Cynic in Lucian of Samosata's dialogue, want occurs when one's needs or requirements remain unfulfilled.

Way, path, road; way or path of life: *hodos* (ὁδός).

Way of living, mode of life: *diaita* (δίαιτα).

Wealth, riches: *ploutos* (πλοῦτος).

Wine: *oinos* (οἶνος).

Wine-jar of the largest kind: *pithos* (πίθος).

Wise man: *sophos* (σοφός).

Word, saying, statement; account; reason: *logos* (λόγος).

Wretched, miserable; pitiable: *athlios* (ἄθλιος).

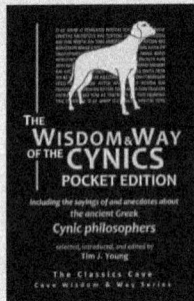

SOURCES & FURTHER READING

The Classics Cave's rendition of Diogenes Laertius' writing about the earliest Cynics (Part 1) was made using the Greek text found in R.D. Hicks' translation of Diogenes Laertius' *Lives and Opinions of Eminent Philosophers* (1925), as well as the Greek texts and other immensely helpful tools found online at the Perseus Digital Library (www.perseus.tufts.edu). Otherwise, the Cave checked its own version against the translations of C.D. Yonge (1853) and R.D. Hicks (1925), as well as the more recent ones of Robin Hard (2012) and Robert Dobbin (2012). For Part 2, the Cave utilized the same at the Perseus Digital Library, as well as other readily and publicly available resources. The Cave's translation and summaries of Teles' *Discourses* were made using the Greek text of Otto Hense (2nd ed., 1909), with an eye on Edward O'Neil's translation (1977). As for Diogenes' and Crates' *Letters*, our translation and summaries were made using the Greek text of R. Hercher (1873), with an eye on Benjamin Fiore's (Diogenes) and Ronald F. Hock's (Crates) translations (1977). Where public domain translations were suitable, the Cave occasionally made use of them with little to no alteration.

SUGGESTIONS FOR FURTHER READING

Branham, B. and M. Goulet-Cazé, eds. *The Cynics: The Cynic Movement in Antiquity and Its Legacy*. Berkeley: University of California Press, 1996.

Copleston, Frederick. *Greece and Rome: From the Pre-Socratics to Plotinus*. Vol. 1 of *A History of Philosophy*. Westminster: Newman Press, 1946.

Cutler, Ian. *Cynicism from Diogenes to Dilbert*. Jefferson: McFarland & Co., 2005.

Desmond, William D. *Cynics*. Book 3 in *Ancient Philosophies*. Berkeley: University of California Press, 2008.

———. *The Praise of Poverty: Origins of Ancient Cynicism*. Notre Dame: University of Notre Dame Press, 2006.

Diogenes Laertius. *Lives and Opinions of Eminent Philosophers.* Translated by R.D. Hicks. Cambridge: Harvard University Press, 1925.

Downing, F. Gerald. *Cynics and Christian Origins.* Edinburgh: T&T Clark, 1992.

Dudley, Donald R. *A History of Cynicism—From Diogenes to the 6ᵗʰ Century A.D.* Strand: Methuen & Co. Ltd, 1937.

Hadot, Pierre. *What Is Ancient Philosophy?* Translated by Michael Chase. Cambridge: The Belknap Press of Harvard University Press, 2002.

Frischer, Bernard. *The Sculpted Word: Epicureanism and Philosophical Recruitment in Ancient Greece.* Berkeley: University of California Press, 1982.

Gottlieb, Anthony. *The Dream of Reason: A History of Western Philosophy from the Greeks to the Renaissance.* New York: W.W. Norton & Company, 2016.

Grafton, Anthony, Glenn W. Most, and Salvatore Settis, eds. *The Classical Tradition.* Cambridge: The Belknap Press, 2010.

Kenny, Anthony. *Ancient Philosophy.* Vol. 1 of *A New History of Western Philosophy.* Oxford: Oxford University Press, 2004.

Laursen, John Christian. "Cynicism Then and Now." *Iris. European Journal of Philosophy and Public Debate.* 1, no. 2 (2009): 469-482.

Malherbe, Abraham J., ed. *The Cynic Epistles: A Study Edition.* Translated by Benjamin Fiore, S.J., Ronald F. Hock, Anne M. McGuire, Stanley K. Stowers, David R. Worley. Atlanta: The Society of Biblical Literature, 2006.

Mazella, David. *The Making of Modern Cynicism.* Charlottesville: University of Virginia Press, 2007.

Meyer, Susan Sauvé. *Ancient Ethics: A Critical Introduction.* Abingdon: Routledge, 2008.

Navia, Luis. *Diogenes the Cynic.* Amherst: Humanity Books, 2005.

Teles (The Cynic Teacher). Translated and edited by Edward O'Neil. Atlanta: The Society of Biblical Literature, 1977.

Sayre, Farrand. *Greek Cynics.* Baltimore: J.H. Furst Company, 1948.

Shea, Louisa. *The Cynic Enlightenment: Diogenes in the Salon.* Baltimore: The Johns Hopkins University Press, 2010.

Will you help the Cave? Here's how . . .

- **Buy** a book. **Join** a club. **Sponsor** the Cave. **Give** a donation.
  - **Talk** to friends and family about Cave books and the free online Cave content at the Cave (www.theclassicscave.com).
- Leave a **positive review** online—if possible, **five stars** with a **brief remark** about what you liked. This truly helps!
  - **Write us** at contact@theclassicscave.com to let us know how you've benefited from our work. This inspires us to do more!

THE CLASSICS CAVE is a small, shoestring operation, on fire to spread the wisdom and ways of ancient Greek literature. We **rely on you**, the friend of the Cave, to let people know how you liked and benefited from what we're doing. We also **depend on you** to **improve our books**. Did you see something that requires editing? Something we got wrong? Something we need to add? Despite our great effort and care to get everything right, it happens. So please **let us know** by emailing us at contact@theclassicscave.com. Otherwise, **visit** the Cave to benefit from our ever-growing collection of free online content at www.theclassicscave.com. And don't forget to **support our mission** to spread the wisdom and ways of ancient Greek literature by **buying** and **reading** Cave Books, **enjoying** Cave Gear, **joining** The BAGL Club or AAGS, or by **sponsoring** or **giving** to the Cave. **Thanks!**

Read and enjoy more from **the Cave!**

If you benefited from reading *The Best of the Cynics*, you may wish to pick up another Cave book presenting the ancient Greeks. There are many now available or in the works.

Visit the Cave at . . .
www.theclassicscave.com

www.theclassicscave.com

Looking for the **best books** ever?
And new ways to read and benefit from them?

Hunting for **wisdom** and **ways** that
are time-tested and people-approved?

READ A CAVE BOOK

VISIT THE CAVE ONLINE
www.theclassicscave.com

When you read a Cave book, an ancient classic,
you'll have a better idea about where you're
going in life and how to get there.

You'll feel smarter. Be wiser.
And if you practice what you've encountered,
you'll live a better life. Be a little happier.

Enjoy the Cave's **free online content**. Or **choose a book** from one
of **our series**. The Cave Best of Series. The Cave Wisdom & Way
Series. The Cave Workbook & Journal Series. And more!
You'll be glad you did!

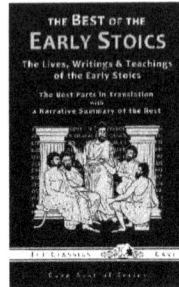

THE CLASSICS CAVE
THE EARLIEST LIGHT FOR A BRIGHTER LIFE
www.theclassicscave.com

Pick up a **CAVE** book . . .

from HOMER . . .

THE BEST OF
HOMER's ILIAD
The Best Parts in Translation
with
a Narrative Summary of the Rest
THE CLASSICS CAVE
Cave Best of Series

THE
WISDOM & WAY
OF HOMER
POCKET EDITION
Including the human, heroic & divine sayings of
the Iliad & Odyssey of
Homer
selected, introduced, and edited by
Tim J. Young
The Classics Cave
Cave Wisdom & Way Series

THE BEST OF
HOMER's ODYSSEY
The Best Parts in Translation
with
a Narrative Summary of the Rest
THE CLASSICS CAVE
Cave Best of Series

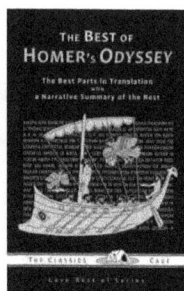

from the CYNICS . . .

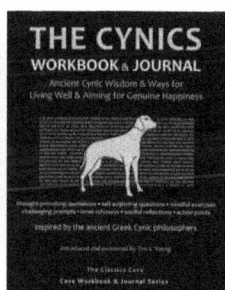

THE BEST OF
THE CYNICS
The Lives, Writings & Teachings
of the Ancient Cynics
The Best Parts in Translation
with
a Narrative Summary of the Rest
THE CLASSICS CAVE
Cave Best of Series

THE
WISDOM & WAY
OF THE CYNICS
POCKET EDITION
including the sayings of and anecdotes about
the ancient Greek
Cynic philosophers
selected, introduced, and edited by
Tim J. Young
The Classics Cave
Cave Wisdom & Way Series

THE CYNICS
WORKBOOK & JOURNAL
Ancient Cynic Wisdom & Ways for
Living Well & Aiming for Genuine Happiness
introduced and produced by Tim J. Young
The Classics Cave
Cave Workbook & Journal Series

From EPICURUS . . .

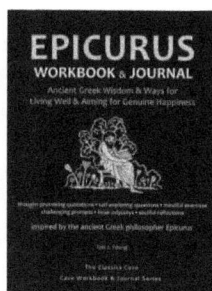

THE BEST OF
EPICURUS
The Life, Writings & Teachings
of Epicurus the Greek Philosopher
The Best Parts in Translation
with
a Narrative Summary of the Rest
THE CLASSICS CAVE
Cave Best of Series

THE
WISDOM & WAY
OF EPICURUS
POCKET EDITION
including the ideas, teachings & sayings of
the ancient Greek philosopher
Epicurus
selected, introduced, and edited by
Tim J. Young
The Classics Cave
Cave Wisdom & Way Series

EPICURUS
WORKBOOK & JOURNAL
Ancient Greek Wisdom & Ways for
Living Well & Aiming for Genuine Happiness
inspired by the ancient Greek philosopher Epicurus
Tim J. Young
The Classics Cave
Cave Workbook & Journal Series

www.theclassicscave.com

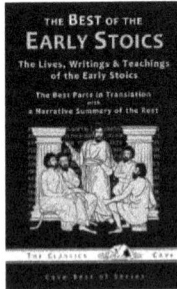

www.ingramcontent.com/pod-product-compliance
Lightning Source LLC
Chambersburg PA
CBHW031832090426
42741CB00005B/218